D1393646

THE WORKING MEN'S
COLLEGE
AUSPICIUM
MELIORIS
ÆVI.
MDCCCLIV.
1913

Testaments of Radicalism: Memoirs of Working Class Politicians 1790-1885

Testaments of Radicalism

Memoirs of Working Class Politicians 1790-1885

Edited and introduced by
David Vincent

London
Europa Publications Limited

Europa Publications Limited
18 Bedford Square, London, WC1B 3JN

ISBN: 0 905118 01 4

Printed and bound in England by
STAPLES PRINTERS LIMITED
at The Stanhope Press, Rochester, Kent.

Contents

Preface

The five memoirs included in this volume, the first in a series of republications of nineteenth-century working men's autobiographies, are presented in their entirety. For reasons outlined in the introduction, which discusses the context within which the memoirs were produced and some of the implications of their content, much of the value of such works is lost if they are in any way cut or condensed. Each work is preceded by its own brief introduction, giving details of the circumstances of composition and publication together with biographical notes on those portions of the author's career not covered by his memoir. Where necessary, footnotes have been added to the texts to clarify the career and comments of the author; for those unfamiliar with the background of the various events mentioned in the accounts, brief bibliographies are provided. In the interest of authenticity, the texts of the autobiographies have been reprinted with the original spelling and punctuation, although obvious printer's errors have been removed. The footnotes are the editor's, except for the unnumbered notes to Hardy's *Memoir*, which are the author's. I should like to thank John Briggs, W. H. Chaloner, Robert Fyson, Iorwerth Prothero, Edward Royle, James Walvin and my wife for their help in the preparation of this volume, and Nicola Pike for typing the manuscript.

DAVID VINCENT
University of Keele

Introduction
Working Men and their History

The first political event recorded in these autobiographies is the crisis over the American colonies which led to the outbreak of war in 1775. Thomas Hardy, a shoemaker newly arrived in the capital from Scotland, plunged into the debate and became converted to the cause of the colonial rebels. The concluding event takes place just over a century later in the summer of 1885 when Benjamin Wilson, a sometime farm labourer, weaver, navvy, quarryman and gardener, summons the surviving Halifax Chartists to a "Social Evening at Maude's Temperance Hotel" to celebrate the passing of the Third Reform Bill. Hardy stands at the watershed between the eighteenth century tradition of dissent and the emergence of the world's first working class movement. Wilson ends his narrative as the working class is on the verge of discovering both Marxism and the path towards institutional security through the formation of the modern Labour Party and trades union movement. Their lives, which overlap by eight years, encompass the whole of the movement for political emancipation, and taken together, the five autobiographies presented here cover the major movements of the period, commencing with the formation of the London Corresponding Society in 1792 and proceeding through Peterloo, the struggle of the unstamped press, infidelism and freethough, the 1830–32 Reform Bill crisis, Owenism and Owenite trade unionism, Chartism, the campaign for democracy in local government, temperance, co-operation, the Second Reform Bill, and working class Liberalism.

As a form of source material, working men's autobiographies are of value to the historian at a number of different levels. Most obviously they possess the quality of personal testimony. They are the words of the working men themselves, not those of outside observers. Furthermore, in the sense that they are autobiographies and not merely eye-witness accounts of single events, they offer unique insights into the continuity and coherence of the individual's life. The historian is able to explore the relationship between the various parts of the working man's life: the way in which his political activity connects with his previous social and economic experience, and how his political activity develops over a long period of time. The significance of Thomas Hardy's view of the formation of the London Corresponding Society, of which he was the first secretary, was quickly appreciated by the man who set out to write the first history of the organization, Francis Place. He commissioned a narrative from Hardy and incorporated it into his draft history of the movement, and although this was never published, the memoir which Hardy rewrote from his original commission is still the single most important source for the early years of the prototype of all subsequent working class organizations. James Watson's autobiographical speech presents a cameo self-portrait of one of the leading members of the most intransigent wing of working class radicalism of the period. Thomas Dunning's memoir is the only extant personal record of the short-lived but immensely important explosion of Owenite trade unionism in 1834, and provides a particularly interesting insight into the relationship between local and national class conflict. In its moving portrayal of the private economic and social sufferings which lead up to a political commitment, John Bezer's extraordinary serialized autobiography explains, as no other single document, what it meant to be a Chartist. Finally, Benjamin Wilson's record of radicalism in Halifax from Peterloo to the Third Reform Bill provides a detailed and thought-provoking description of change and continuity in working class protest.

At the same time these writings possess a more general relevance for the study of class relations. An autobiography is not just a reconstruction of the past but an interpretation. From the point at which the autobiography is written, in every case here except Bezer's, towards the end of the author's life, the events, the activities, the thoughts, are subject to an overall analysis, each aspect accorded a certain symbolic value in the formation of the working man's personality, of the development of his consciousness of his identity in society. That identity is to some extent shared, by definition of the fact that all these autobiographers are consciously writing as working men, seeing themselves as part of a single evolving working class movement, and here we come face to face with the crucial issue in the formation of class consciousness: how it is that individual working men, in all the diversity of their separate personalities, can arrive at a common interpretation of the meaning of their world through their participation in a set of social and economic relations. The form of the autobiography imposes upon the author an attempt to comprehend the coherence of the relationship between the self and the outside world; thus, to understand how the working man understood himself is to take up a position at the very centre of the formation of his class consciousness.

This, then, is the challenge of reading these autobiographies. They must be read as individual works, their contents controlled by the circumstances of publication, the personality and situation of the author, the nature of the movements in which he participated, their relevance directed towards specific areas of activity at specific points in time. But they must also be read as fragments of the single mosaic of the developing working class as it made itself and its own history in its struggles for economic and political freedom.

It was not common for a working man to write his autobiography during the nineteenth century. About sixty are known to have survived of men whose lives cover some part of the period up to 1850, ranging in length from abbreviated memoirs in radical journals and brief autobiographical introductions to volumes of poetry, to full length life histories such as those of Samuel Bamford and Thomas Cooper which have rightly taken their place as minor classics of Victorian literature.[1] Yet this handful of working men's autobiographies is evidence of a major change in the way in which working men viewed their lives. Thomas Hardy must be seen as a literary as well as a political innovator for no working man had ever set out to write the sort of autobiography that he began to compose sometime during 1798.

Hardy's major literary inheritance was the tradition of puritan autobiography which stretched back into the early seventeenth century.[2] The puritan autobiographies were founded on a number of assumptions about the nature of human existence which necessarily underpin the working class autobiographies. Their narratives were rooted in a sense of passing time; the life of the soul was understood as being essentially a matter of movement and change. The interpretation of the personality rested on the conviction that only in man's experience of external reality could the true state of his soul be recognized. And perhaps most important of all, each of the 181 extant works published during the most prolific period up to 1725 was a statement of the right of every individual to work out his own salvation. The puritan doctrine that the only intermediary between man and God was the Bible not only sustained a tradition of free speech but also provided justification and encouragement for the most humble and non-literate of individuals to analyse and set down their own experiences. But if we find among these spiritual autobiographies a number written by labouring men, there is a crucial difference between the puritan genre and that which commences with Hardy and his London Corresponding Society comrade, John Thelwall, and with a related group of ex-servicemen's memoirs which appeared in the 1820s and 1830s.[3] As may be gauged from its title, the events described in the

[1] The standard reference work, William Matthews's *British Autobiographies* (California, 1955), lists only a quarter of those autobiographies which are now known to have survived. John Burnett includes extracts from 27 works covering the period from the 1820s to the 1920s in his *Useful Toil* (London, 1974). Recent reprints of separate volumes include the autobiographies of Alexander Somerville (London, 1951), Joseph Arch (London, 1966), Samuel Bamford (London, 1967), William Lovett (London, 1967), Charles Smith (London, 1967), William Dodd (London, 1968), Charles Shaw (London, 1969), Joseph Gutteridge (London, 1969) and Thomas Cooper (Leicester, 1971).

[2] See Owen C. Watkins, *The Puritan Experience* (London, 1972), *passim*; Paul Delaney, *British Autobiography in the Seventeenth Century* (London, 1969), pp. 6–104; John C. Morris, *Versions of the Self* (New York, 1966), chaps. II and III.

[3] See John Thelwall, "Prefatory Memoir" in *Poems chiefly written in Retirement* (Hereford, 1801); Robert Butler, *Narrative of the Life and Travels of Sergeant B* (Edinburgh, 1823); Anon, *Recollections of an eventful life chiefly passed in the army. By a soldier* (2nd ed. Glasgow, 1825); John Harris, *Recollections of Rifleman Harris* (London, 1848); "G.B.", *Narrative of a Private Soldier, Written by Himself* (Glasgow, 1829); Anon, *Life on Board a Man-of-War, by a British Seaman* (Glasgow, 1829); John Green, *Vicissitudes of a Soldier's Life* (London, 1827).

Wonderfull prophesies revealed to Nicholas Smith shoe-maker, living at Tillington near Petworth in Sussex. . . . Manifested unto me Nicholas Smith on Matthias Day last, by a Spirit from God; and am now come up to London to doe the work I am commanded, and lie at the signe of the Flying Horse in Thomas Street, where I will by the Grace of God be ready to attest the truth hereof with my life . . . (1652) had a significance only in the sense in which they illustrated some aspect of the inner spiritual life of the individual. Whereas the equally devout shoemaker Thomas Hardy characterizes his life in quite different terms, the title page offering the "Memoir of Thomas Hardy, Founder of, and Secretary to, the London Corresponding Society . . . From its Establishment, in Jan. 1792, until his arrest, on a False Charge of High Treason, On the 12th of May, 1794". The meaning of Hardy's life is to be understood in relation to a secular external event at a specific point in time. The same approach is conveyed by the title page of the last of the memoirs included in this volume, that of Benjamin Wilson, who describes himself not, like Bunyan in the most widely read of all the puritan autobiographies, as the "Chief of Sinners", or even as "a sinner", but as "an Old Chartist", the meaning of whose life is to be found in its relationship to a number of particular historical movements and events which are listed beneath the heading. There is now a new understanding of the significance of the actions, ideas and experiences which made up the working man's life. The spiritual autobiographies lack any recognition that the external events which they depict have a significant existence independent of the apprehension of the autobiographer. In this sense they are essentially subjective in their treatment of time and place where the working class autobiographies are fundamentally objective. Such a change in attitude was an essential precondition for the emergence of a class identity founded on an understanding of the historical actuality of the working men's society and their place in it.[4]

The working class autobiographies were written by men who shared a wide range of occupations and preoccupations. All were literate men, concerned in one way or another with the experience of the self-educated working man in an industrializing society, but the freedom of selection and organization enjoyed by the autobiographers produced considerable diversity in the content of the narratives. Some saw themselves primarily as poets and set out to explain the development of their artistic persona. Others were anxious to portray the details of their work experience, and a number may be seen as the earliest social historians. And there is a group which may be considered "political" in that their authors spent some part of their adult lives engaged in political and related activities, and organized the narrative structure of their works around their political career and experiences. About half the autobiographers held some official or unofficial posts of leadership in the succession of movements in the century which followed the founding of

[4] The only detailed study of the changing attitudes to the past among working men, and of the significance of the growth of an objective sense of history, is to be found in Christopher Hill, "The Norman Yoke" in John Saville (ed.), *Democracy and the Labour Movement* (London, 1954).

the London Corresponding Society. For some, like the Kettering weaver-poet J. A. Leatherland, the experience was peripheral to their life's work, but there are over a dozen whose autobiographies are dominated by their political activity.

It is no coincidence that the founder of the prototype working men's association should have been the prototype autobiographer. The London Corresponding Society represented a demand by working men to participate in the history of the nation, and in turn the fortunes of the Society constituted the prologue to the working class's own history. As soon as the Society had been finally crushed by the arrest of its entire General Committee on 19 April 1798, Francis Place, the Charing Cross tailor who was himself a leading member of the society in the period following Hardy's arrest and trial, was urging Hardy to make a record of his experience, and Hardy was only too anxious to do so. As is clear from the preface and the opening lines of the *Memoir* itself, Hardy was acutely conscious that the radicals who had just fought for the First Reform Bill were inheriting a historical tradition founded by the London Corresponding Society, and that he himself was a historical figure with a "right" and a "duty" to "leave to posterity a true record of the real motives that influenced his conduct".[5] In turn each of the autobiographers in this volume, for all the diversity in their outlook, were motivated by a twin desire to make and record their own history.

As political historians, the working class autobiographers were attempting to fill an historiographical vacuum. Since the publication of E. P. Thompson's enormously influential study, *The Making of the English Working Class* in 1963, the London Corresponding Society has taken its place as a major event in the body of formal history. With the work of Edward Royle and Patricia Hollis in particular, the world of infidelism and underground newspapers inhabited by James Watson has become visible to the modern reader.[6] Chartism became a historical event with a series of studies published during and just after the First World War, and after a period of relative neglect has now become a major research industry. Yet if we look back from say, 1906, when the modern Labour Party was founded, down the years to the 1790s, the political history of the working class scarcely exists. It was in 1906 that G. S. Veitch began to collect material for the first study to look at the politics of the last decades of the eighteenth century from below. His book was published in 1913, and was quickly followed by no less than five histories of aspects of Chartism.[7] Until then the total output by

[5] See p. 37.

[6] Edward Royle, *Victorian Infidels* (Manchester, 1974); Patricia Hollis, *The Pauper Press* (Oxford, 1970).

[7] G. S. Veitch, *The Genesis of Parliamentary Reform* (London, 1913, 1965); H. U. Faulkner, *Chartism and the Churches*, Frank F. Rosenblatt, *The Chartist Movement in its Social and Economic Aspects*, P. W. Slosson, *The Decline of the Chartist Movement* (all Columbia, 1916); Mark Hovell, *The Chartist Movement* (Manchester, 1918); Julius West, *A History of the Chartist Movement* (London, 1920).

British historians on Chartism amounted to just one article, twenty pages on the "Early History of Chartism" in the *English Historical Review* of 1889 by the economic historian E. C. K. Gonner. More was written in Germany on Chartism in this period than in England.[8] References in the general histories of the period are both slight and slighting, the movement and in particular its leaders being treated with derision and consigned to the scrap heap of failed and irrelevant historical events.[9] In school history textbooks, which were becoming an increasingly important medium of transmitting knowledge about the past as the elementary school system developed after 1870, the few authors who mentioned the movement stressed only the violent and deluded nature of the Chartists.[10] A certain amount of work was carried out by local historians towards the end of the period, but the only attempt at a general history was made by one of the later Chartist leaders, R. G. Gammage, who between 1853 and 1854 produced a book which stood half way between being a history and an intervention in the continuing debate over personalities and tactics. The book was almost completely ignored when it first appeared, and despite its republication in 1894, never reached a wide audience. Benjamin Wilson, for instance, seems to have been unaware of its existence. As a historical event Chartism, like the movements before it, had been almost obliterated. In 1905 one of the last remaining Chartists, G. J. Holyoake, summarized the movement's fate: "The Chartists have made as much noise in the world as they know how—yet to the generation of today they are ambiguous. They have had no historian."[11]

The significance of the existence and nature of the formal history was as clear to Hardy as it was to Holyoake. Any radical movement is heavily dependent on the knowledge of its past in the formulation of its current ideology and programme, and as the nineteenth century progressed knowledge became increasingly that which was printed. The very presence of the working men's autobiographies may be seen as one aspect of the invasion of a pre-industrial oral culture by the written word. The working class became increasingly reliant on literature, as both producers and consumers, to discover and transmit a knowledge of their identity in society, and in turn the governing class became more and more proficient at using literature as a weapon of social and political control. The quite unprecedented circulation of Paine's *Rights of Man* in the 1790s, which stimulated and was in turn promoted by the London Corresponding Society, provoked a response in

[8] See John Tildesley, *Die Enstehung und die ökonomischen Grundsätze der Chartistenbewegung* (Jena, 1898); L. Brentano, "Die Englische Chartistenbewegung", *Preussiche Jahrbücher*, vol. 33 (Berlin, 1874); Gotthilf Dierhamm, *Die Flugschriftenliteratur der Chartistenbewegung* (Naumberg, 1909).

[9] For a discussion of the treatment of Chartism by nineteenth-century historians, see J. Saville, "R. G. Gammage and the Chartist Movement", introduction to 1969 reprint of R. G. Gammage, *The History of the Chartist Movement* (1894).

[10] Valerie Chancellor, *History for their Masters* (Bath, 1970), pp. 35–6, 61–2.

[11] G. J. Holyoake, *Bygones Worth Remembering* (London, 1905), vol. 1, p. 84.

kind from the political and religious establishment. The Cheap Repository Tract Society was set up and in the twelve months from March 1795 to March 1796 the Society distributed an estimated 2,000,000 copies of moral tales and ballads, in an attempt to counter the influence of the radical propaganda.[12] Thereafter access to and use of the means of publication became a central component of class struggle, and in this struggle what was transmitted about the past became as important as what was transmitted about the present.

At one level it was simply a case of trying to prevent one generation of working men being cut off from the rest by the combined effect of the passage of time and the poverty of the formal record. Speaking of the 1790s in a letter written in 1826, Hardy noted anxiously that "a new generation have arisen who know but little of that period".[13] At the other end of the century we find the Staffordshire potter Charles Shaw complaining bitterly that "This generation might be as far from the time of my youth as the age of the Sphinx. It seems to know as little, too, of the Forties in England as of the condition of Egypt in the time of the early Pharaohs."[14] There were at least three ways in which the working men could attempt to prevent this situation arising.

The first task was to try to preserve the ever-increasing volume of documents—tracts, addresses, newspapers, correspondence and minutes—which the increasingly sophisticated organizations produced, before they decayed or were dispersed. For almost half a century the chief archivist of the working class movement, or at least the London section of it, was Francis Place. he began to collect material as soon as the first phase of the radical movement had ended, and after his early retirement from business in 1815 he devoted himself in earnest to the task. He turned his home in the Charing Cross Road into what was in effect a semi-public library and assiduously accumulated material from every available source on every aspect of the working class movement.[15] As Hardy says in his Preface, he had a fixed intention of writing the official history of the London Corresponding Society, and by 1837 he had acquired all of Hardy's papers, all the journals and papers published by the London Corresponding Society and a mass of manuscripts. Hardy deferred to Place in the composition of the history which Place never managed to finish, but even in his personal *Memoir* found it necessary to include the full texts of all the major addresses issued by the society during the period in which he was actively associated with it. So much of the identity of the Society was contained in these documents, so much would be lost if they were lost. In the same way the autobiography of one of the most influential

[12] G. H. Spinney, "Cheap Repository Tracts: Hazard and Marshall Edition", *The Library*, 4th series, vol. XX (1940), pp. 301–2 and *passim*.
[13] *Add. Ms. 27818*, f614. Letter to Mr Wilson, 18 November 1826.
[14] Charles Shaw, *When I Was a Child, by an Old Potter* (London, 1903), p. 205.
[15] See Francis Place, *The Autobiography of Francis Place*, ed. by Mary Thrale (Cambridge, 1972); Graham Wallas, *The Life of Francis Place* (London, 1898), chap. VII.

radicals of the second quarter of the nineteenth century, William Lovett, begins with a relaxed account of his upbringing but rapidly degenerates into a catalogue of the precious documents interspersed with brief passages of linking narrative.[16] In the 1890s we find one of the last surviving Chartists, G. J. Harney, busily at work collecting the documents of Chartism together for a history which again was not written.

An equally serious, but less obvious task, was to counteract the effect of the accelerating process of industrialization and urbanization. The continuing expansion and reconstruction of the industrial towns meant that the very landscape of radicalism, all the physical points of reference and memory, could be transformed or obliterated. In Manchester, St. Peters Fields, the arena for the most symbolic event in post-war radicalism, became the site for the monument to the triumph of the middle class, the Free Trade Hall, and if the process was not always as pointed, its effect on the capacity of future generations to recall their past was profound. Thus a man like Wilson, looking back from the mid-1880s, to Halifax in the 1830s and 1840s, found that in order to make his narrative comprehensible he had to recreate the town and its surroundings. Look, for instance, at how he goes about describing a demonstration in 1842: "... we made our way over the walls and through the fields, which were not built upon at that time, and came down Range Bank to Northgate. From North Parade to the large building now occupied as an auction room (formerly the Temperance Hall), was one large field known as 'Red Tom's field'. Where the Co-operative Central Stores now stand the field wall would be about four yards high, and, there, I, along with thousands, stood when the soldiers came by; ...".[17]

Alongside the documents and topography, partly dependent upon them, and partly giving them meaning, was the most precious and at the same time most evanescent source of history, the memories of the participants themselves. It is impossible to construct a detailed picture of the oral history of the working class in an era which the tape-recorder cannot reach. By its very nature, no written record exists of the sort of history passed down from one generation to the next by conversation and spoken reminiscence. There is no doubt that such a history existed, and that it was an important means of educating succeeding generations in their political identity. We can see how Wilson gained his knowledge of the political tradition of his community from tales told to him by his mother.[18] And the strength of this oral tradition was illustrated by one of the few local historians to make a determined effort to exploit it. In the late 1870s the Halifax historian Frank Peel set about collecting the reminiscences of surviving Luddites and Chartists. He incorporated their testimony into *The Risings of Luddites, Chartists and Plug-Drawers*,[19]

[16] William Lovett, *The Life and Struggles of William Lovett* (London, 1876).
[17] See p. 200.
[18] See p. 195.
[19] First edition Heckmondwike, 1880, 4th, London, 1968.

and subsequent research has shown the accounts used by Peel to have been remarkably accurate. From the very beginning the radicals were conscious of the significance of this source of history, and set about trying to preserve it. Place interviewed many of the surviving London Corresponding Society members for his projected history. A valuable device was the anniversary or commemorative meeting. Every year for at least forty years after the first great event in working class history, the acquittal of Hardy on the charge of High Treason on 5 November 1794, an anniversary meeting was held in London to keep alive the memory of the triumph. Watson's memoir is taken from the written record of a "Public Tribute" to him on the occasion of his retirement as a radical publisher, and throughout the century the funerals of veteran radicals were used to recall their activities and celebrate the continuity of the radical tradition. The final means of preserving the oral history was of course the autobiography itself. "The commencement of the following pages", wrote William Lovett in the preface to his autobiography, "I must attribute to the solicitations of some of my radical friends, who, when I had been talking of some of the events of my life, of the different associations I have been connected with, and of the various political struggles in which I have been engaged, have urged me to write the facts down; so that the working classes of a future day may know something of the early struggles of some of those who contended for the political rights they may be then enjoying. . . ."[20] These autobiographies were the means of preserving the oral history and in turn they are the major source of information on the unwritten history held in the working class communities.

If these men were concerned with the destruction of their history wrought by the passage of time, they were also directly engaged with the poverty and distortion of the official record which rendered their history so vulnerable to the more impersonal forms of change and decay. A common thread in virtually every campaign throughout the period was hostility to the treatment the working class received from the contemporary press. Hardy's memoir is full of complaints against a press which Place described as being "at this time a poor debased thing, scarcely daring to call its soul its own",[21] and a large part of Watson's career was devoted to an attempt to provide and sustain an alternative working class controlled system of reporting their own activities. The accuracy of the press was important not only for the impact on its immediate readership but also for the quality of the record it bequeathed to later historians. It was a matter which preoccupied William Lovett: "I have yet another reason for adding the documents of the Associations I have taken part in, and for giving a brief account of their proceedings", he wrote in his "Life", "and it is this—That hitherto, little is found in history, or in our public papers, that presents a fair and accurate

[20] W. Lovett, op. cit. (1967 edn.), p. xxxi.

[21] Handwritten introduction to a volume of newspaper cuttings from the 1790s. *Place Coll.*, vol. 36.

account of the public proceedings of the Working Classes; for if the Whig and Tory papers of the day ever condescend to notice them, it is rather to garble and distort facts, to magnify faults and follies, and to ridicule their objects and intentions; the pleasing of their patrons being more important with them than a truthful record. In consequence of this unjust system the historians and writers of a future day will have only garbled tales to guide them—as those of past history have—and hence a caricature is oftener given of the industrious millions than a truthful portrait."[22] The sources are biased and so were the historians who used them. The lesson was brought home to Hardy as the 1790s became history. Protesting at the "mean and malicious sneer against the prisoners" (of 1794) contained in a study on the Tower of London, he attacked the notion that historians were impartial, or of much relevance to working class history: "We learn but little from modern histories, for each historian accommodates the facts to his ideas, almost in the same manner as a cook sauces up his dishes to his palate. We must dine in the taste of the cook. We must read in the humour of the historian."[23] Sixty years later we find the Croydon radical Thomas Frost including an account of Chartism in his autobiography for precisely the same reason: "As I took from that day an active part, and locally a prominent one, in the agitation for the People's Charter, and the movement has been persistently misrepresented by successive writers, and therefore very imperfectly and erroneously understood, some service will be rendered to the cause of truth, and some material afforded for a chapter of English history which has yet to be written, by a brief relation of the progress of the Chartist movement. . . ."[24] The whole of Bezer's narrative is founded on an attempt to rectify misconceptions about the meaning of the 10 April demonstration in 1848 which was seen both by contemporary observers and most later historians as a tragi-farcical attempt by desperate working men to overthrow the constitution. For all the variety of outlook and experience in the autobiographies which deal with working class politics, they are bound together by the common assumption that there was not one but two histories of the working class. There was the history which the autobiographers had experienced and now held in their memory, and there was the history which through a process of distortion and obliteration had been passed down to the reading public of the time in which the autobiographers were writing. The autobiographies are a product of the working man's new sense of history; they are also a large part of the history itself.

The composition of a working man's autobiography rests on three conditions. Firstly, the working man, in the various ways we have outlined, must

[22] Lovett, op. cit., p. xxxii.

[23] *Add. MS. 27818*, f270. Letter to the *Monthly Magazine*, 10 August 1825, complaining about *The History and Antiquities of the Tower of London with Memoirs of Royal and distinguished persons* . . . by John Bayley, Part 2.

[24] Thomas Frost, *Forty Years Recollections, Literary and Political* (London, 1880), pp. 96–7.

decide that he is justified in seeking to summarize and communicate his life's experience. Secondly, he must be capable of the act of literary composition. To possess the confidence and ability to embark upon such a task clearly requires a far more sophisticated degree of literacy than that which is measured by the capacity to sign a marriage register, and all that is certain is that the possession of such skills was confined to a minority of the working class and that there is no reliable means of measuring the size of that minority. There is, however, evidence to suggest that the minority was both substantial and growing. The period covered by these autobiographies ends just before the 1870 Education Act, and in terms of formal education the improvements that took place during the period were both slow and haphazard. Access to schooling did, on the whole, increase, but even the most efficient board or private school would be likely to teach its pupils to copy rather than compose, and of far greater significance was the rapid expansion in the opportunities to practise writing for publication. As we have seen, the working class would look to the puritans for a certain tradition of literary self-expression, but from the 1790s onwards the volume of working class writing appearing in print began to increase dramatically. The expansion was partly a product of the early impact of industrialization on all forms of communication. For a while technical advance brought the availability and cost of literature, and access to the means of publication, increasingly within the grasp of working men, and it was not until after the turn of the half-century that all forms of publication began to become capital intensive and both access and control began to move out of their reach. And in part it was a product of the working men's active response to industrialization and the society which it created. The trickle of addresses and pamphlets which began to appear in the 1790s had become a full flood by the 1830s. Of particular importance was the working class press. Between 1830 and 1836 during the height of the "War of the Unstamped", at least 562 newspapers and journals, containing every sort of prose and poetry, were written, printed, published, sold and bought by working men.[25] The existence of both the writers and the readership was initially dependent on literacy gained either at school or through adult education, but the encouragement and opportunity provided by the embattled press and related forms of literature played the crucial role in turning working men from passive recipients into active creators. It is no accident that all the autobiographers in this volume were involved in some aspect of journalism during their lifetime. Members of all sections of the working class were exposed to the stimulus of literary combat to a greater or lesser extent, and thus whilst there were undoubtedly sections of the class who through their rural isolation, their poverty, or their experience of the most destructive aspects of industrial or town life, remained illiterate, and whilst the majority of the class as a whole remained, in any constructive sense, non-literate, the

[25] See Joel H. Wiener, *A Descriptive Finding List of Unstamped British Periodicals, 1830–1836* (London, 1970).

range of working men, in geographical, economic and occupational terms, who wrote their autobiographies during this period is remarkably wide.

The final condition is that the would-be autobiographer should find the means of publishing his work. It is conceivable that some autobiographies, like some diaries, are simply the means of private record or confession, but it would appear that virtually all extant manuscript working men's autobiographies were meant for publication. Certainly the one manuscript autobiography in this volume, that of Dunning, was addressed to a public audience which it never reached. The possible outlets for the autobiographies fall into four broad categories. Least common, and not represented here at all, was the London-based commercial publisher catering for the middle-class book buying public. On the fringes of the trade there was a market for more sensational forms of the autobiography, of the literally or figuratively anonymous—particularly soldiers' and sailors' memoirs after the Napoleonic wars—and the "confessions", most fictional, of convicted or reformed thieves. Towards the end of the period a handful of outstandingly literate or well-known working men attracted the attention of publishers such as Hodder and Stoughton, but in general such firms restricted their attention to the cabinet minister rather than the cabinet maker. A second category was the autobiographical preface to a book of poetry—a distinct genre which will be covered in a future volume of memoirs of working class poets. Most relevant to the present volume were the third and fourth categories—the various forms of publishing connected with campaigning organizations or movements, and the various forms of publishing based on a particular geographic locality. Of the memoirs in this volume, those of Hardy, finally published by the long-standing radical James Ridgway, Bezer, serialized in the columns of the *Christian Socialist* and Watson, printed in the *Reasoner*, fall into the third; and that of Wilson, published by a Halifax printer, into the fourth group, as, in a sense, does Dunning's, which was written for the same market by a man who was a frequent contributor to his local papers.

The extensive structure of publishing built up by the radical organizations in the early nineteenth century could play a direct role in getting the autobiographies into print, in addition to the general stimulus to composition noted above. A man like Ridgway, who had already published an edition of Hardy's trial, would possess the resources to publish the autobiography, and with 20,000 Londoners attending the funeral of Hardy as the memoir went on sale, he would be assured of a market. Similarly, the radical journals were both able and willing to include such material, and a systematic search through the columns of all the extant journals of the period would undoubtedly bring to light many more short or serialized autobiographies. At best, this method of publication could constitute the ideal relationship between form and content. Ridgway was a veteran of the 1790s and fully in sympathy with Hardy's evaluation of his own life. But where the autobiography appeared in a journal, the relationship was more complex.

Serialization affected the structure of the autobiography. The chronological development is arranged around a number of self-contained episodes, each discussing a single event or theme. As Bezer's work demonstrates, the autobiographer was at the mercy of the fortunes of the journal, few of which lasted any length of time, and Bezer eventually lost the race to reach the end of his life before the *Christian Socialist* itself came to an end. In general the autobiography, both as it was written and as it should be read, was affected by the nature of the journal itself. Most periodicals were the mouthpiece of a relatively narrow ideology or programme, in Watson's case Holyoake's secularist movement, in Bezer's the co-operative movement promoted by the Christian Socialists. Thus the breadth and depth of the autobiographer's life tended to be channelled towards a single destination, a destination with which the autobiographer might not fully identify himself—there is clearly some tension between Bezer's political outlook and that of Charles Kingsley. Then inasmuch as the radical journals were initially the product of growing class consciousness, so their format was available to both sides in the conflict. Middle class propagandists not only launched their own periodicals, but also, appreciating the potential of the genre, sponsored and printed working men's autobiographies. A particular example was the anonymous *Memoirs of a Working Man*, commissioned and published by Charles Knight in his "Penny Papers" series, which contained a denunciation of working class radicalism in the post-war period.[26] Much of the class conflict could be reduced to a debate about the identity of the working man, actual and potential, and consequently the autobiography, the analysis of the working man's identity over time, was as much a weapon in the contemporary debate as a record of past conflict.

By the beginning of the second half of the century the towns which had been created or transformed by the industrial revolution began to achieve a certain stability and with it a new consciousness of locality. If the most lasting monuments to the new civic pride were the great mid-Victorian town halls, the most effective means of sustaining the growing local patriotism was the provincial newspaper which entered a new period of expansion during the third quarter of the century. The newspapers reflected not only an interest in the current life of the town, but, increasingly in the 1870s and 1880s, in its past. The columns of the papers reported the activities of the newly formed antiquarian societies, and, particularly in Lancashire and Yorkshire, dialect societies, and became the forum for exchange of information about the history of the area. As with the radical journals, the local press both stimulated the would-be autobiographer and provided an outlet for his work. And as with journals it exercised a potentially ambiguous effect on the way in which the autobiographers appeared both to themselves and their readership. In one sense their political memories were of the local

[26] The author was a Colchester tailor, Thomas Carter. The first volume was published in 1845 and the second, *A Continuation of the Memoirs of a Working Man*, in 1850.

manifestation of national movements, of class conflicts made all the more bitter by the familiarity of the combatants. Yet the newspaper editors and the middle class antiquarians were interested in them much more as local citizens than local politicians. If the class struggle of the past mattered it was only as evidence of the inexorable triumph of the commercial class which dominated the town. There was thus a persistent tension between Dunning as the old Nantwich inhabitant, and Dunning as the veteran unionist, between Wilson the old Chartist and Wilson the spectator of early Halifax, a tension which, as we shall see, was present during the struggles themselves and was continuously exacerbated by the form in which their autobiographies appeared.

The five autobiographies in this volume have been chosen for a number of reasons. In the first instance it was important that they should be short enough to be reprinted in their complete form. As I hope this introduction makes clear, much of the value of the autobiography is lost if the text is in any way cut or condensed. A reader may be more interested in one passage than another, but the autobiographer constructs his text as a whole in which the parts gain their meaning from their relationship to each other, and neither the editor nor the reader should treat the autobiography as a collection of isolated episodes which can be excluded or reshuffled at will. Then, although none of the five is a literary masterpiece, they are at least adequate as prose works. Watson, Wilson and Dunning are competent and unambitious, with Dunning in particular able to turn the occasional memorable phrase, as, for instance, in his description of one of his fellow unionists as a "light-minded, dancing, public-house man".[27] Hardy's sense of drama in the first section of his autobiography, and of personal injury in the second at times obscures the true stature of both the man and the events he is describing, and it is clear that his adoption of the third person, despite his caveat in the Preface, is at least in part a device to enable him to indulge in more extravagant self-praise than would have been possible in the first.[28] Only Bezer, whose unconventional and energetic style is well suited to his format, seems capable of using language to enhance rather than merely transmit the meaning of his story. Finally, taken together they cover most of the major events and movements of the period and introduce us to a number of important features of the way in which working men viewed their political activity.

The autobiographers have varying notions of their own self-importance. Hardy and Watson acquired fame at a national level during their lifetimes, whereas the prominence of Dunning and Wilson was confined to a local arena, and Bezer was anxious to obscure his personal reputation altogether.

[27] i.e. Matthew Bayley, an officer in the shoemakers' society and one of the two men arrested for administering an illegal oath. See p. 129.

[28] See, for instance, the author's assessment of Hardy's character on p. 70–71.

To this extent we find some divergence in the way in which they handle the problem of their relevance to the readership, with Hardy and Watson tending to draw conclusions from their achievements, and the others, especially Bezer, being more inclined to generalize from their experience. As leaders, however, it should be noted that no position they could or did attain would be likely to remove them from the ranks of their class. Hardy was the first working man to become a national figure, and unlike later leaders he was brought into contact with at least a section of London "Society" as a result. But as the latter part of his autobiography so painfully documents, his sudden projection into the limelight had only a transient effect on his economic situation and in the end probably left him in a poorer state. Watson was one of the earliest working men to try to make a living out of radical activity, by selling, printing and publishing radical literature and becoming the paid storekeeper to the First London Co-operative Trading Association in 1828, which was possibly the first institutional post created by secular working class activity. But as his career, and that of men like William Lovett, who succeeded him at the Association, demonstrated, a life as a "professional agitator" during this period was both insecure and poorly paid, and offered little or no chance of upward social or economic mobility. The "Pitman and Privy Councillor" genre of autobiography belongs to the next generation of working men.[29]

All five, therefore, are presenting themselves as working men, and as working men who spent some significant part of their lives engaged in radical activity. As such they are faced with three tasks as they set out to write their life-histories. Firstly, they have to fit their political life into the context of the rest of their life, and in doing so explain the origin and nature of their political commitment. Secondly, they must decide upon the structure of their work. Unlike a diary, an autobiography is a single narrative in which time is extremely flexible, and the autobiographer must decide how to pace his account, and where to place the climaxes in his story. Thirdly, they cannot escape making some sort of judgement, implicit or explicit, on the lives which they are summarizing.

The proportion of space that was devoted to various areas of the autobiographer's experience, and the relationship that was established between those areas, was controlled by two factors: the autobiographer's conception of his identity and the format in which he was writing. This is nowhere more evident than in the treatment of the most private areas of the individual's life—his early home life, and his emotional life as an adult. Hardy and Watson, as self-conscious public figures, find it necessary to give a brief

[29] See, *inter alia*, Thomas Burt, *Thomas Burt, M.P., D.C.L., Pitman and Privy Councillor. An Autobiography* (London, 1924); George Edwards, *From Crow Scaring to Westminster* (London, 1922); George Barnes, *From Workshop to War Cabinet* (London, 1923); John Hodge, *Workman's Cottage to Windsor Castle* (London, 1931); Henry Broadhurst, *The Story of his life from Stonemason's Bench to a Treasury Bench, Told by Himself* (London, 1901).

account of their family origins, which aside from their relevance to the character of the adult man, stand simply as an assertion of their humanity. The same message is conveyed by the relaxed account of his childhood that prefaces William Lovett's full length autobiography; working class politicians are not one-dimensional fanatics, insurgents existing only at a moment of insurrection, but complete human beings. Bezer's whole autobiography is an attempt to give flesh to the popularly held stereotype of the "Chartist Rebel". Dunning, who of all the autobiographers is the most relaxed in his status as a local character, includes the most discursive account of his family background, describing people and places that his audience will themselves have known. Only Wilson, who is the most concerned to write a complete history of a period and a place, and least concerned with himself, is relatively silent. It is curious to note from the accounts that are given, that all four are largely brought up by their mothers, as, for that matter, are the authors of the two major political autobiographies of the period, Lovett and Thomas Cooper.[30]

In their treatment of their adult emotional life, literary convention plays a more significant role. It was very uncommon for any working man's autobiography during this period to dwell upon courtship and marriage, a reflection not so much of a lack of feeling as of an acceptance of prevailing notions of what should and should not be discussed in print.[31] Hence Dunning devotes just one paragraph to such matters, but seems prolix in comparison with Watson, whose marital affairs occupy one eight-word sentence. In this respect Hardy must be seen as a special case. The death of his wife in childbirth following the attack on his house while he was in prison awaiting trial for high treason elevated his emotional life from the private to the public sphere. Throughout the memoir the event is subordinated to the political drama and treated in such stylized terms, particularly in Citizen Lee's poem which Hardy sees fit to include, that it is difficult to grasp the true impact of the personal tragedy. The one man not only to break through the literary convention but also to establish a convincing balance between his private and his public life is Bezer, and in this achievement he joins the handful of really successful working men autobiographers. His treatment of his father, for instance, makes general points about the iniquity of naval discipline, the inadequacy of the poor-law system, and the potential of Christianity, without diminishing his filial affection or the impact of his father's fortunes on his own circumstances. Similarly his treatment of his courtship and married life is relaxed and at times even amusing, but also

[30] Lovett's father was drowned before he was born. Watson's died when he was two weeks old, Cooper's when he was four, Hardy's when he was eight, and although Dunning's and Bezer's both survived until they were fifteen, they exercised their parental responsibilities only intermittently.

[31] The only major exception is Samuel Bamford's *Early Days* (London, 1849) which deals in some detail with affairs of the heart during his adolescence and early manhood.

forms an essential part of his account of how he eventually became a "Chartist Rebel".

The manner in which these men go about explaining their political commitment is considerably affected by their distance from the events they are describing. Hardy began to write as soon as the London Corresponding Society had finally collapsed, and being intensely conscious of the innovatory nature of the movement and his part in it, provides a full account of the formation of his political consciousness, dwelling upon the influence of both his intellectual environment—reading Price and participating in the debate over the American Revolution—and his personal economic life—his experience as a cobbler of the system of unjust taxation. In the same way Bezer felt he was taking part in a debate over a movement which had only just disappeared from view, and we are provided with an explanation which reaches out into almost every aspect of his experience, the half-century between himself and Hardy being marked by his hostility towards the injustice of capitalist free enterprise rather than government corruption. Watson on the other hand is writing as the veteran of campaigns long since over, even if both he and his audience are still fighting for the cause of freethought. Thus his explanation is relatively narrow, concentrating upon the influence of the post-war radical journals. Dunning and Wilson, the one probably, and the other quite certainly, writing in a secure old age within a largely local perspective, are almost silent on the matter of personal motivation. There are passing references to radical journals, but little else in the way of explicit comment. There is an air of complacency about their accounts. Like Watson, they have become steeped in a radical tradition which, by the time they are writing, stretches back within the compass of Wilson's view alone for over sixty years, and the very permanence of this tradition undermined the need for personal explanation or defence. Chartism was there, so Dunning and Wilson joined it. There is, however, a more positive reason for their silence which has to do with the way they regard themselves as participants. Throughout their autobiographies they stress the extent to which politics involved an entire community. Although Dunning is concerned with his own role in the trial of the union leaders, he emphasizes at every turn the extent to which the entire working class community was involved in the conflict, turning out *en masse*, for instance, to welcome the prisoners back from Chester. Wilson is participating in what is essentially a shared radical tradition. He makes this clear in the opening lines of his memoir: "I was born at Skircoat Green, August 7th, 1824. This village had long been noted for its radicalism",[32] and throughout emphasizes that whatever the numerical size of the paid-up activists, the working class population as a whole, female as well as male, was directly or indirectly involved. The radical tradition rested not with individuals but with the community, and as they were

[32] p. 195.

writing for that community, there was little point in giving the details of their personal commitment.

In the construction of the autobiographies one feature stands out above all others. If we look for the passages in which time is slowed down, when the narrative gathers itself into some sort of climax, then almost invariably we are reading of a conflict with the law or with the forces of the law. Hardy's *Memoir* is completely dominated by the Treason Trials of 1794. The major part of Watson's speech is taken up with the "War of the Unstamped", in the course of which he was four times tried and three times imprisoned. The central event of Dunning's life is the trial of the Nantwich shoemakers, and even his unfinished account of Chartism is preoccupied with the "persecution and imprisonment" of "poor Chartists". The major set-piece description of Wilson's *Struggles* is of the coming of the Plug Plot Riots to Halifax in 1842, and it is clear from references scattered throughout his autobiography that Bezer was building up to an account of his arrest and imprisonment in 1848, what he calls "the Newgate Affair", and was only prevented from reaching his climax by the demise of the *Christian Socialist*.

Given the inherently dramatic quality of such events, it is perhaps not surprising that these men were drawn towards them as they sought to give some shape to their life-histories; nonetheless, their preoccupation does reveal some important aspects of the radical tradition in this period. In the first instance it underlines the degree of personal hardship that a commitment to radical activity frequently entailed. Hardy triumphed, and gloried in his triumph, but having escaped execution he came home to a dead wife and a ruined business. Watson's years in prison had more than earned him the applause his speech received, and though he was himself not directly threatened, Dunning provides us with a convincing account of the atmosphere of fear which prevailed in Nantwich when the authorities decided to attempt a repeat of the Tolpuddle trial and transportations. But all these men survived and, except in Bezer's still angry account, their attempts to heighten the drama of their troubles are frequently undermined by a pervasive air of complacency in the narratives. In this they reflect an essential feature of the relationship between the working class and the law. The law was, and was seen to be, a weapon of class domination, and it was accepted that political conflict would sooner or later mean legal conflict. Even that paragon of "moral force", William Lovett, was jailed for two years, as were the authors of the two other major political autobiographies, Cooper and Samuel Bamford. Benjamin Wilson, writing as a Gladstonian Liberal, offered no apologies for his participation in several riots and later possession of arms. If economic hardship and injustice became unbearable, then illegal activity was both inevitable and justified. Nonetheless, these men never lost the conviction that not only did they possess legal rights as free-born Englishmen, but that with persistence, amounting in Dunning's case to blatant manipulation, these rights could be exercised to further their political demands.

The victories of Hardy, Watson and Dunning were all defensive, yet they were evidence that the working class both had rights and the power to make some defence of their rights, and it is interesting to note that when Dunning and Wilson turned their attention from national to local politics, one of their major tools was the use of statutes and byelaws to attack local vested interests. In this sense the combination of suffering and self-satisfaction we find at the centre of the memoirs is an accurate reflection of the dual role of the law throughout much working class activity during this period.

An autobiography is a single review of the past; its author is faced with the task of making an overall interpretation of his life. As with virtually all the working class autobiographers of this period, these five politicians share two fundamental assumptions about their life's work. In the first instance their analysis both presumes and affirms a basic continuity in their careers. Such a verdict is a product of more than the benign hindsight of old men. The literary model for expressing a major break in personal experience was easily available. As we have seen, the form of the working man's autobiography had grown out of the genre of puritan autobiographies which were constructed around the pattern of sin-conversion-redemption, and in various forms of religious, temperance and other morally improving literature, the model continued to flourish throughout the nineteenth century. It formed the basis of most of the propagandist life-histories that were directed at the working class during this period, including in particular Charles Kingsley's fictional working man's autobiography *Alton Locke*, whose message Bezer was so vigorously attempting to refute.

The rejection of such a model embodied a number of statements about the nature of their career as politicians. At one level it is simply that these men regarded themselves as activists. Historians, trained to catalogue and categorize all the minute variations in forms of working class activity, can sometimes forget that in the eyes of the participants all the forms are bound together by the fact that they are activity. Watson stood before his audience as a man who had begun to struggle for freethought as soon as he had reached maturity, and had continued to do so in various movements in various contexts throughout his life. Wilson had moved from Chartism to Co-operation to local politics to Liberalism, but always he had been engaged with his world, always attempting in whatever manner seemed at the time appropriate, to improve the lot of himself and his class. In this sense at least the old Wilson could confidently face the young Wilson; there had been no break in commitment.

More significantly, the notion of continuity rests on the second major assumption, that the relationship between the beginning and the end of their lives is one of progress. The only one of the five to withhold his judgement on the matter is Bezer. He is under no illusion about the hardship of his youth, but he is inclined to look to the future rather than the present for the fulfilment of his hopes of progress, and it is not surprising that he emigrated to Australia shortly after the composition of his autobiography.[33] For the rest, as for the great majority of the working class autobiographies of the period, history, as seen from the perspective of their own lives and activity, moved forward.

The capacity to make such a judgement was assisted by the changing attitude of the British establishment. Hardy's account of his relationship with the *Times* newspaper is a fine example of this. In his autobiography he complains vigorously about the treatment he received from the press in general and the *Times* in particular, which "teemed with the most wicked and shameful misrepresentation of the views and intentions of the unfortunate prisoner",[34] yet on his death the *Times* treated him as a national hero, carrying a long obituary, an account of his funeral, and then, with fine irony, actually reprinting two passages of the *Memoir* as it came off the press. Times had changed; as the obituary pointed out, the treason for which Hardy had been tried in 1794 was "treason wholly and exclusively consisting of seeking that reform which has been accomplished under the Grey administration".[35] Wilson looked back on a life which saw him buying a gun after the rejection of the third Chartist petition and a generation later voting thanks to Gladstone for carrying a substantial part of that petition. Within the local community the same process took place in a less dramatic fashion. Nothing could have been more bitter than the conflict in Nantwich over the shoemakers' union, with all aspects of the local establishment uniting to crush the union and the union in turn enjoying the support of the rest of the community as it engineered the defeat of the due processes of the law. The true dimension of the dispute is contained in the aftermath when Squire Hammond gratuitously dismissed the father of the suborned witness. Yet Dunning's obituary in the *Crewe Chronicle* claimed that "no-one has deserved better of his townsmen", and that "we shall not be too adulatory if we say that he died without an enemy".[36] This metamorphosis of Dunning's public image was made easier by Dunning's curious capacity, which may be a characteristic of local working class politicians in general, to identify with the locality as a whole in the midst of intensive class conflict. In his autobiography we find him joining Nantwich's military and town bands and playing in the "procession and festivities at Nantwich on the occasions of the accession and coronation of our Queen" in the same paragraph as he describes Squire Hammond's retribution, and then going straight on to describe his leading role in local Chartist activity.[37] But despite such split loyalties, all these men had some reason to claim that whether or not their

[33] He summarizes his attitude in the poem "The Past" which prefaces the autobiography. See pp. 153–4.
[34] See p. 60.
[35] *Times*, 17 October 1832, p. 3.
[36] *Crewe Chronicle*, Saturday, 28 April 1894.
[37] See p. 134.

own idea of themselves had changed over their lifetimes, their image in the eyes of the ruling class, national or local, had done so.

Any interpretation of the past is dependent on the observer's scale of values. The questions of continuity and progress are resolved in the end by the manner in which the observer selects and signifies his experiences. Here two factors predominate. Firstly, all the working class autobiographers, by definition of their activity as autobiographers, are literate men, almost all have been involved in some form of self-improvement, and thus there is a general tendency to place a high value on all forms of literature, and on the agencies which aid its dissemination. When, in his old age, Hardy wrote to Lafayette to congratulate him on the 1830 revolution, he turned to the press as both the engine and the symbol of progress: "Political knowledge is making a great and rapid progress, it is now diffused among all classes. The press—the printing press is performing wonders."[38] In his attempt to describe the backwardness of the times of his childhood, Watson turns first to the prevailing absence of literature: "At that time there were no cheap books, no cheap newspapers or periodicals, no Mechanics Institutes to facilitate the acquisition of knowledge."[39] If such importance is attached to the spread of literature, both during their lifetimes and at the point at which they turn to summarize them, then the arguments for continuity and progress are irrefutable. The autobiographers had always worked for the dissemination of knowledge, with Watson, Bezer and Dunning actually earning their living at it, and throughout the period there had been a dramatic and measurable increase in the availability of the written word. There were problems with its quality, especially after the 1830s and 1840s, but neither the autobiographers nor this introduction has the space to go into them. We must, however, give due recognition to the nature of the sample of working men who wrote autobiographies. Clearly there were substantial sections of the working class population who gained little or no literacy, and whose lives were dominated by more immediate problems of economic survival. The cheap press was not likely to figure so prominently in their scale of values. On the other hand it would be a mistake to confine the relevance of the autobiographies to a small minority of working class intellectuals. It is difficult to think of any working class movement in this period which was not in some way committed to the spread of knowledge and which did not in some way exploit techniques of acquiring, understanding and transmitting various forms of literature. Say working class radical organization and you say committees and sub-committees, minutes and correspondence, newspapers and broadsides, and therefore the sort of self-educated working man who tended to write his autobiography.

The second factor is that these men are politicians, both in the wider sense that they have spent much of their adult lives engaged in disputes with

[38] p. 101.
[39] p. 109.

various forms of national and local government, and in the narrower sense that each of the five has been engaged in the long campaign to reform Parliament itself. They fought as members of an increasingly self-conscious working class against an increasingly defined class enemy, but throughout the period the context of their battle was essentially political. Even Watson, whose commitment to freethought dominated his life, looked back to the state of the government, alongside the state of literature, to characterize the times against which his work should be measured. For all the variety of activities encompassed within the autobiographies and within the history of the class in general during this period, for all the attempts to by-pass direct political conflict through co-operation or trade union activity, it does seem that the one dominant theme is the pursuit of political citizenship. Wilson's summary of his fellow Chartist comrades touches upon all these men: "What they wanted was a voice in making the laws they were called upon to obey; they believed that taxation without representation was tyranny and ought to be resisted; they took a leading part in agitating in favour of the ten hours question, the repeal of the taxes on knowledge, education, co-operation, civil and religious liberty and the land question, for they were the true pioneers in all the great movements of their time."[40] This does not mean that all the Chartists, or all the autobiographers, were heading towards Wilson's destination of Gladstonian Liberalism. Some, like the Uxbridge compositor, poet and autobiographer, J. B. Leno, live to welcome the revival of socialism in the 1880s.[41] But whilst all, as we have seen, were only too conscious of the connection between their political activity and economic experience, none developed the sort of analysis of industrial capitalism that would enable them to relegate political reform to a wholly subservient position in their outlook as activists. When it came to measuring the changes in society over their lifetime, they could not avoid looking at the franchise, and, despite their failure to achieve the total political transformation for which they had once fought, they could not avoid calling the change progress. There is a certain symmetry about the first and last works in this volume, the one completed just after the passage of the First Reform Bill, the other just after the passage of the Third. They belong together, as a beginning and an ending. It is difficult to see Wilson looking forward, and indeed he spent his declining years denouncing the formation of the I.L.P. The task of recasting the relationship between the political and the economic struggle awaited a new generation.

These autobiographies were written out of a sense of the historical status of the working class, and a desire to fill the vacuum in the formal history of the class. But autobiographers are not historians. However much they may tell us of the times through which they lived, the moment their focus shifts

[40] p. 210.

[41] See J. B. Leno, *The Aftermath; with autobiography of the author* (London, 1892). For a discussion of the career of the autobiographer Robert Lowery, which has strong parallels with that of Wilson, see Brian Harrison and Patricia Hollis, "Chartism, Liberalism and the Life of Robert Lowery", *English Historical Review*, 1967, p. 503.

from the individual to a general history of the period, their autobiography suffers. Rather they should be read as fragmentary evidence of the oral history of the working class, all that remains of the memories all working men and all working class communities must have possessed. In this sense we may advance towards an understanding of what succeeding generations knew and thought about their past, and such knowledge constituted the foundation for the emergence, from the 1880s onwards, of the modern labour movement.

Thomas Hardy
(1752-1832)

Thomas Hardy

In 1798, following the final suppression of the London Corresponding Society, Hardy was asked by Francis Place to write an account of its early years. He began work almost immediately, though progress was slow; Place was still urging him to complete it in 1816. In 1807, and again in the late 1820s, he considered publishing the history as a separate work, but in the end deferred to Place who had commissioned the account as part of an ambitious project to write a complete history of radicalism in the 1790s. To that end Place accumulated what was to amount to 7 large volumes of documents and eye-witness accounts, but as early as 1824 we find Hardy anxiously writing to ask, "Is the long looked for history of that much calumniated body of men, the London Corresponding Society, begun yet? I fear your other avocations jostle it aside, or perhaps the extensive plan you have chalked out, requiring such a mass of material to be examined may have delayed it".[1] Hardy's fears were entirely justified. Place did not finish collecting evidence until 1837, and despite continual urging from his friends, especially the old London Corresponding Society leader, Alexander Galloway, the task of editing the material into a publishable form proved beyond him.

For his part, Hardy had delivered a two-part history of the Society to Place by 1825.[2] Part one is a narrative history of the movement from its foundation to the Chalk Farm Meeting on 14 April 1794. It is initially written in the form of letters to a fictitious correspondent, though the device is dropped after the third letter. Using, paradoxically, the first person rather than the third as in the *Memoir*, Hardy strove to produce a proper history, concentrating on the movement as a whole and including much detail on the structure of the London Corresponding Society and on events in other parts of Britain. The second part of the history is simply a fair copy of the Society's minute books covering the period from 3 May 1792 to 2 January 1794. A substantial part of the first two "letters" of the history were read to the 1816 and 1824 anniversary meetings at the Crown and Anchor Tavern, but by the late 1820s Hardy must have despaired of seeing the history published in his own lifetime, and set about recasting his contribution in the form of a

[1] Hardy to Place, 16 October 1824. *Add. MS. 27816*, f. 233.
[2] See "A Sketch of the London Corresponding Society" by Thomas Hardy, *Add. MS. 27814*: Part One, fos. 11–76; Part Two, fos. 88–155.

personal memoir.[3] He included within it some sections of his history,[4] but was much more concerned to discuss his personal role, extending his account backwards to include his life prior to 1792 and forwards to the trial and its aftermath.

The first and only edition of the *Memoir* was followed by a thirty-page Appendix containing the two addresses read to the 1816 and 1824 meetings, together with the text of his speeches to the 1829 and 1830 meetings held at the Golden Lyon Tavern; a letter to Francis Place, dated 6 December 1824, discussing the 1794 Secret Committees and the conduct of his trial; a letter from Place, dated 11 June 1831, asking for more information on the London Corresponding Society; a copy of the warrant committing him to the Tower, with notes by Hardy on the treatment of state prisoners; and three odd letters concerning the Committee for Conducting the State Trials Subscription, with a note from Hardy claiming that neither he nor any other defendant received any money from the Committee. The documents add some detail to the account in the *Memoir*, but are fragmentary and repetitious, and have not been reprinted here.

The "political part" of Hardy's *Memoir* ends with his acquittal in 1794, and indeed he took no further part in the affairs of the London Corresponding Society. However, following the final arrest of the London Corresponding Society committee in April 1798, Francis Place brought him out of retirement to act as treasurer for a committee formed to support the families of the arrested men,[5] and thereafter he was actively involved in London radicalism throughout the remainder of his life. He preferred a less prominent role now, partly because of increasing old age and ill health, and resisted almost all invitations to join committees or stand for elective office. Instead he chose to act behind the scenes, and in this sense was second only to Francis Place as a combined archivist, co-ordinator and instigator of London radicalism. He kept in constant touch with the survivors of the 1790s, including Paine, Tooke, and, when he returned to politics, John Thelwall, exchanging memories and doing a great deal of quiet work to help the families of those who had fallen on hard times. He wrote endlessly to the papers on subjects ranging from the history of the London Corresponding Society and all the current political issues, including Peterloo and Catholic Emancipation, to less serious topics such as the history of the practice of handshaking and the authorship of the Waverley novels, which Hardy believed were written not by Scott, but by "no other than Dr. Greenfield".[6] His commitment to

[3] Place did in fact manage to incorporate much of Hardy's account into a manuscript history which he managed to compose at some point. See "Notes respecting the London Corresponding Society", *Add. MS. 27808*, fos. 2–117.

[4] pp. 26–8 of the *Memoir* is a straight transcription of fos. 14–16 of the manuscript, but otherwise the account is almost entirely rewritten.

[5] See Francis Place, *The Autobiography of Francis Place*, edited by Mary Thrale (Cambridge, 1972), pp. 178–86.

[6] Letter to *The Champion* (Thelwall's paper), 2 August 1820. *Add. MS. 27818*, f. 422.

universal suffrage remained intact, as did his fervent enthusiasm for Bonaparte, "the Child and Champion of Jacobinism", which survived all the vicissitudes of Bonaparte's career, including his final defeat and exile—a prized possession was a piece of one of the Emperor's greatcoats which he acquired in 1816. Although his chief loyalty was to his benefactor, Francis Burdett, for whom he worked in the Westminster elections, he was in close contact with most of the new generation of radicals, including Cobbett, until Cobbett's split with Burdett in 1817, and Wooler of the *Black Dwarf*. In 1822 the London Corresponding Society joined hands with Chartism when Hardy met and befriended the young Feargus O'Connor, writing back to his father, an old friend, that "I see Feargus frequently, he calls almost daily either on Mr. Mackenzie or on me. He is a young man of very fine talents".[7] His funeral at Bunhill Fields on 18 October 1832 was, according to the *Times*, "a species of public ceremonial à la française".[8] At his graveside John Thelwall, the last survivor of the twelve defendants of 1794, addressed an "immense multitude which was variously estimated from 20,000 to 40,000 persons".[9] Four years later a monument to him was erected in the graveyard.

Background Reading

John Binns, *Recollections* (Philadelphia, 1854); Francis Place, *The Autobiography of Francis Place*, edited by Mary Thrale (Cambridge, 1972); John Thelwall, "Prefatory Memoir" in *Poems chiefly written in Retirement* (Hereford, 1801); Henry Collins, "The London Corresponding Society" in J. Saville (ed.), *Democracy and the Labour Movement* (London, 1954); E. P. Thompson, *The Making of the English Working Class* (London, 1963); G. S. Veitch, *The Genesis of Parliamentary Reform* (London, 1913, 1965); Gwyn A. Williams, *Artisans and Sans-Culottes* (London, 1968).

[7] Letter 17 January 1822. *Add. MS. 27818*, f. 491. See also a letter from Hardy to Feargus at the "Bear and Castle, Oxford Street", 16 May 1822, f. 490.

[8] *Times*, 18 October 1832, p. 3.

[9] *Times*, 20 October 1832, p. 3. See also *Gentleman's Magazine*, vol. cii, part 2, November 1832, pp. 480–1.

Mansell Collection

MEMOIR

OF

THOMAS HARDY,

FOUNDER OF, AND SECRETARY TO,

THE

LONDON CORRESPONDING SOCIETY,

FOR

DIFFUSING USEFUL POLITICAL KNOWLEDGE

AMONG THE

PEOPLE OF GREAT BRITAIN & IRELAND,

AND FOR

PROMOTING PARLIAMENTARY REFORM,

***From its Establishment, in Jan.* 1792**

UNTIL HIS ARREST, ON A

FALSE CHARGE OF HIGH TREASON,

On the 12th of MAY, 1794.

WRITTEN BY HIMSELF.

He was a man, from vice and folly free—
No danger could his steady soul appal;
No slave to prejudice or passion, he
Esteem'd his fellow-men as brethren all.

Integrity his shield, and Truth his guide,
Unaw'd, he laboured in his Country's cause;
For that he liv'd, for that he would have died,
A Martyr to her liberty and laws;—
Firm to his purpose, virtuously severe,
He fear'd his God, but had no other fear.

D. MACPHERSON.

LONDON:

JAMES RIDGWAY, PICCADILLY.

M.DCCC.XXXII.

TO

SIR FRANCIS BURDETT, Bart. M.P.

THE FOLLOWING MEMOIR

IS

DEDICATED

BY

HIS GRATEFUL AND MUCH

OBLIGED SERVANT,

THOMAS HARDY.

Advertisement

The duty now devolves upon me, of informing the reader, that Mr. Hardy, having lived to see the last sheet of his Memoir from the press, breathed his last, about eight o'clock on the morning of Thursday, the 11th instant, at his apartments, 30, Queen's Row, Pimlico.

His extreme temperance, added to a strong and robust constitution, preserved him, through a long life, from many of those chronic disorders which, too often, embitter the lives of men of different habits. Some time before he retired from business, in 1815, his health suffered from the anxiety attending a losing concern, but, as soon as that was got rid of, he recovered, and, with the exception of slight rheumatic pains, occasionally, in his legs, he continued almost free from bodily ailments until last year, when, going to the city in a stiff-springed *omnibus*, he was so violently shook, that it brought on a stranguary, which, after much suffering, proved fatal to him.

From the beginning of the last severe attack, about three weeks ago, it became evident that he was approaching his end. Of this he himself was perfectly sensible, and his mind was prepared to meet it as became a man and a Christian.

In his person, Mr. Hardy was of fine proportions, near six feet high, before he began to stoop; large breasted, broad shouldered, and muscular, without the least inclination to corpulency. He was, indeed, such a man, in body and mind, as we may suppose the patriots to have been who followed those immortal heroes, an Alfred and a Wallace, in their attempts to give freedom to their respective countries.

In his manners he was mild, affable, and unassuming; and it may be safely affirmed, that he never made a personal enemy. The leading features of his character were moral courage, benevolence, and integrity, from the practice of which virtues no worldly consideration could deter him, if he saw any chance of being useful to his fellow creatures.

From vanity he was altogether free, his common saying being, that the greatest talents, exercised under the controul of the best judgment, and for the best purposes, did not give a man a right to be vain, for, that when a man did all the good in his power, he did no more than his duty. He, however, allowed that the praise of good men is desirable, forasmuch as it confirms our own approbation of our own best actions.

Ye vain, ye frivolous, ye prodigal, ye proud, behold this good man's mortal career, and learn to amend your lives, learn that man has not been created for himself alone, but for all mankind. Ye false patriots, think of him, blush, tremble, and reform. Ye true patriots, if a momentary temptation to waver should come across your minds, think of Thomas Hardy, and be firm.

Ye who are called noble by descent or creation, contemplate the life of this man, "who held the patent of his nobility immediately from Almighty God,"* and let your actions be suitable to your exalted ranks; learn that virtue is true nobility.

D. MACPHERSON
October 16, 1832

* Burns.

Preface

The greater part of the following Memoir was written upwards of thirty-four years ago. It was begun at the solicitation of some friends; but being too much engaged in business at that time to attend to it properly, I was obliged to lay it aside, and it remained in its hiding place until very lately.

The London Corresponding Society did more in the eight or nine years of its existence, to diffuse political knowledge among the people of Great Britain and Ireland than all that had ever been done before. Its Members *devoted* themselves to the cause of justice and humanity. They laboured zealously, intrepidly, and honestly, although they beheld the guilty arm of power suspended over their heads and ready to crush them, in order to promote the happiness of their fellow citizens.

A correct history of such a Society, the present generation,—who are likely to reap the fruits of its labours—cannot but highly appreciate; and I am happy to say that such a work is in the course of preparation, by a Gentleman every way well qualified for the task,—Mr. Francis Place, who has been upwards of twenty years collecting materials for it.

It is for that reason that many things are omitted in the following Memoir, which would otherwise find a place in it; but brief as these notices are, I earnestly hope they will excite the curiosity of the younger part of the present race to know something of the important Trials for *High Treason*, which took place near forty years ago, and the issue of which saved them from the most absolute and deplorable slavery being entailed upon them before they were born.

I have chosen to write in the third, rather than in the first person, merely, to obviate the necessity of calling the great *I* so repeatedly to my assistance; though I do not, by any means, consider that, what is called, egotism consists in the use, but in the manner of using, that letter.

THOMAS HARDY

Memoir of Thomas Hardy

As every man, whose actions, from whatever cause, have acquired publicity, is sure, in many things, to be misrepresented, such a man has an undoubted right, nay, it becomes his duty, to leave to posterity a true record of the real motives that influenced his conduct. The following Memoir, therefore, requires no apology, and none is offered.

Thomas Hardy* was born in the parish of Larbert,† in Stirlingshire, in Scotland, on the 3rd day of March, 1752. His Grandfather, Walter Hardy, was an Officer in the Army, in what is called the German war, but with what rank the writer could not learn. Before he became a soldier he had a small estate, consisting of some houses, both in Edinburgh and Falkirk, which he mortgaged, and was never able to redeem.‡

His Father, whose name was also Walter, was bred to a sea-faring life in the merchants' service. He married a respectable woman, whose relations were numerous and respectable, and for several years followed his profession with such diligence, that it was supposed when he died, on a homeward

* The first of the name was a Frenchman, who was cup-bearer to John, King of France, and was taken prisoner along with that Monarch, by Edward the Black Prince, and brought to England. At an entertainment, the King of England desired his cup-bearer to fill a cup of wine to the worthiest in company, upon which he presented it to his own master. The cup-bearer to the King of France, taking this as an insult offered to his master, struck the English cup-bearer a blow on the ear, upon which the King of France called out *trop, trop, Hardie;* but the King of England exclaimed, *sera deshormais Hardie!* Upon this he took the name Hardie; and the King of Scotland, who, at that time, was also prisoner in England, upon being set at liberty, carried him along with him to Scotland, and gave him the lands of Corregarff in Mar, where they flourished, until a quarrel happening with the Clan of Grant, the Hardies murdered the Chief of that Clan, and, in consequence, their estates were forfeited. They were followers of the family of Huntly.

Motto of the Hardies:—*Sera deshormais Hardie.*

† About a mile from the forest of Torwood, famous in Scottish history as the place where, in the hollow trunk of an extraordinary large oak tree, many of the exploits of that great man and true patriot, Sir William Wallace, were planned. The writer remembers having often visited *Wallace's tree,* above sixty years ago; and he has learnt, with regret, that a Goth, into whose hands the estate fell, has since destroyed every vestige of it.

‡ His Grandson, Thomas, who was his legal heir, after he came of age, took some measures to recover them: with this view he had some communications with Mr. Livingston, the person on whom they devolved after the death of him who had advanced the money on them; but not being in circumstances to incur law expenses, he was obliged to give the matter up, although the first professional gentlemen, both in Stirling and Edinburgh, assured him that the case was quite clear.

voyage from America, he left enough to enable his widow and three children to live comfortably in that cheap part of the country.

The death of Walter Hardy happened in 1760, when his eldest son, Thomas, was no more than eight years of age; and, unfortunately, as is too frequently the case, his affairs having got into bad hands, his widow found herself unable to give Thomas an education suitable to the clerical profession, according to the original intentions of her deceased husband and herself.

Her Father, Thomas Walker, a shoemaker by trade, on learning the hapless state of Mrs. Hardy's affairs, took Thomas under his own care and protection, and put him to school to learn reading, writing, and arithmetic. At that time the price of tuition was no more than a penny a week; before he left school it rose to three-halfpence, and now it is a shilling.

When he arrived at a proper age, his Grandfather taught him his own business. After having learnt as much as he could from his kind relative, he went to Glasgow, that beautiful and populous city, to improve himself in his trade. At that period the traffic between that city and America was very great, and many adventurers went and established manufactories of various kinds. One of these adventurers, a Mr. Ingram, who had projected a shoe factory at Norfolk, in Virginia, was returned, principally with a view of engaging workmen to go out with him.

He engaged many; and Thomas Hardy entered into an agreement with him to superintend the concern for five years. The terms were flattering; the agreement was signed on both sides, and they were to embark in a few days; but his relations interfered and prevented his going, urging that he could not legally enter into an agreement, being then under twenty-one years of age. Very soon after, the town of Norfolk was burnt to ashes, in one of the mad fits of the British Government, in the beginning of the American war. His first project being thus frustrated, he left Glasgow, and went to the iron works at Carron, where he followed the bricklaying business for some time. The Carron Company having just then established their manufactory for cast iron, were much in want of hands to carry on their buildings, and gave great encouragement to bricklayers.[1] While here working with several others, on the second story of a large house that was being built for Mr. Roebuck, one of the proprietors, an accident happened that had nearly cost him his life;

[1] Here Hardy will have gained a preview of the Industrial Revolution. The Carron iron works, founded in 1760, was attracting world-wide attention on account of its size, efficiency, and use of the revolutionary coke-smelting process. The employers were paternalistic, but stamped on combinations of workmen. He will also have witnessed the endemic instability of the early industrial undertakings. The firm very nearly went bankrupt in 1772, at about the time Hardy was working there, causing David Hume to report to Adam Smith that "the Carron Company is reeling, which is one of the greatest Calamities of the whole; as they give Employment to near 10,000 People. Do these events anywise affect your Theory? Or will it occasion the Revisal of any Chapters?" (quoted in R. H. Campbell, *Carron Company*, Edinburgh, 1961, p. 133). The Roebuck here will have been Thomas, general manager and brother of John, one of the three founders. Thomas went bankrupt in 1772 and John a year later.

the scaffold gave way, and they were precipitated into the cellar, covered with boards, bricks, and mortar. One man was killed, and others much hurt: Hardy was carried home, much bruised; but with proper care he soon recovered, but returned no more to the bricklaying business.

He recommenced the trade of shoemaking with James Wilson, who had just settled in that part of the country from London; and having much conversation with his master about the metropolis, his curiosity was excited, and he determined to see it. With that view, he engaged a passage on board the Stirling, Carron smack, *Stewart Boyd* master, and, in eleven days, arrived in London, 23rd April, 1774, where he was a total stranger, with no more than eighteen-pence in his pocket:[2] however, before that was expended, he found employment. He had a letter of introduction from his late master, to Mr. John Kerr, a most worthy character, with whom he lodged the first night, and with whom, and with his amiable family, he maintained afterwards the most friendly intercourse. The acquaintance of Mr. Kerr procured him that of others, of dispositions and turns of mind similar to his own. Hardy was, from his earliest years, of a sedate and serious turn of mind; avoiding all those scenes of dissipation, which, too often, lead astray the youthful and unwary, to the ruin of both their morals and their constitutions. It must, however, be owned, that a disposition to what is falsely called a life of pleasure, affords adventures, which, when afterwards related, conduce greatly to the entertainment of certain readers; but such as peruse these pages must expect nothing of the kind.

The life of a plain industrious citizen affords nothing of the light or the ludicrous circumstances which compose a great part of the frivolous reading of the present day.

Being of a contemplative and serious turn of mind, Hardy, soon after his settling in London, became acquainted with many of the middle and lower classes of Dissenters: among these he had a number of highly respected and intimate friends, by whom he was much valued on account of his peaceable disposition and suavity of manners. He became, and continued many years, a member of the congregation which met in Crown Court, Russell Street, Covent Garden, under the ministry of Mr. Cruden.[3] In 1784, some transactions, to which he was a party, took place in that congregation, and which may not be improper here briefly to relate. The Society was a numerous and

[2] A time-honoured progress which was to be repeated a generation later by the Cornish-born William Lovett, who inherited Hardy's political legacy in London. In his autobiography he records how "I left home on the 23rd of June 1821, and in the course of a few days . . . I arrived in the great city, with the clear sum of thirty shillings in my pocket; knowing no one, nor being known to any". (William Lovett, *The Life and Struggles of William Lovett*, London, 1967, p. 17).

[3] An outpost of the Presbyterian Church of Scotland founded in 1718. This was a natural church for an expatriate Scot to seek out, and Hardy retained his links with both the London Scottish community and the Presbyterian church throughout his lifetime. He was one of the few leading members of the London Corresponding Society to be a practising Christian.

highly respectable one, and paid their Pastor a considerable salary. At this period a vacancy occurred, by the death of Mr. Cruden, and candidates from various parts of England and Scotland, continued, for near two years, to preach in their turns with little approbation. One, however, at length appeared, who gave great satisfaction to the people, a Mr. James Chambers, from Scotland, a very eloquent and powerful preacher. Hardy, being zealously attached to the congregation, and having its interest much at heart, observed, with regret, that many of the members were leaving it, on account of its unsettled state. He, therefore, wrote privately to Mr. Chambers, to know if he would accept a call, if one were given him. Mr. Chambers replied by letter in the affirmative, provided the call was signed by a majority of the whole body. He communicated this circumstance to a friend; and they having consulted two or three others, again wrote to him, and again received a satisfactory reply. They then called a meeting of as many as they could inform of the business. The meeting was held in a large private room, and a greater number attended than was expected from so short a notice. Hardy was appointed chairman, and he opened the business by informing them, in a few words, the purpose for which they were called together. After a good deal of conversation, they adjourned, having appointed another meeting, which was still more numerously attended. At that meeting a deputation was appointed to wait upon the Elders or Managers, to request that they would call a general meeting of the Church, to consider the propriety of giving Mr. Chambers a call.

With this request the Elders refused to comply, alledging, or, at least, insinuating, that there was something wrong in his character; but what is was they would not satisfy the deputation. By the people, who very much esteemed Mr. Chambers, this was deemed calumny; and the consequence was, that the congregation became divided into two parties, the Elders, and their adherents on the one side, and the friends of Chambers, the greater number, on the other.

A correspondence was commenced immediately with many Ministers and others in Scotland, who knew Chambers, in order to learn if his moral character was good; and many certificates of his unblemished reputation were received.

In the mean time, the Elders were ransacking all quarters, in order to discover something to justify them in their objections, and to verify their insinuations: and they, at last, succeeded in discovering that he had two wives then living, one in Scotland, and another in England. Upon this, a meeting of both parties was thought requisite, and also to have Mr. Chambers present, that the affair might be publicly and properly discussed. The result was, that both sides became pretty well satisfied of the truth of what had been alledged against Chambers. Thus ended a controversy, which had been carried on smartly for nearly two years, and which had threatened the dissolution of the Society; the people contending that they had a right to the man of their choice, and the Elders as strenuously resisting that right. This circumstance illustrates the saying, "how small a spark kindleth a great fire."

Another disagreeable circumstance happened one Sunday at the Chapel of the same congregation, of which Hardy was also the innocent cause. Happening to meet Lord George Gordon, with whom he was intimate, he asked his Lordship to come next Sunday, to hear a young man from the Highlands of Scotland, preach. Lord George said he would, and seemed even anxious to hear him; but it happened, through some accident or disappointment, that Mr. Bean, the gentleman of whom Hardy spoke, did not preach that day, but another in his place, who was not very acceptable to the congregation.

This man *read* his sermon in a monotonous manner, and without the least animation, which so displeased Lord George, that he interrupted him in the midst of his discourse, by telling him, that it was contrary to the rules of the Kirk of Scotland for the Minister to *read his sermon from the pulpit;* and this he proceeded to prove from the Confession of Faith, and Directory for public worship.

However lightly they might have thought of the preacher, so extraordinary an interruption gave great offence to many of the congregation, and much confusion consequently ensued. Lord George knew no person present, very few of them knew him, and, unfortunately, Hardy happened to be detained at home by the illness of one of his family. Lord George seeing none whom he knew, called loudly for Hardy, who had invited him there, and who he supposed had played him a trick; the congregation, on the other hand, thought that Hardy had sent Lord George to the meeting to create a disturbance, so that poor Hardy between them was in an awkward situation; yet it must be confessed, though he was perfectly ignorant and innocent of the whole affair, that the conclusion which each of the parties had drawn, though hasty, was not unreasonable.

Hardy, as already mentioned, was very intimate with Lord George Gordon, but was, by no means, an approver of any of his wild schemes: so far from it, that he often told him, with honest bluntness, both verbally and by letter, how much he differed from him in opinion on many subjects. Nevertheless, he always entertained, and expressed a sincere respect for the many virtues, and amiable qualities of that misguided, but much injured man; and was of opinion, that his life fell a sacrifice to the malice of his persecutors. Here, however, it may not, perhaps, be prudent to state who they were, whether ecclesiastical or political, or probably both.

At the period of his arrival in London, the American war was commenced, and then, as well as now, politics were the general topics of conversation in almost every company. His heart always glowed with the love of freedom, and was feelingly alive to the sufferings of his fellow creatures. He listened with attention to the arguments he heard advanced for and against the conduct of the Administration towards the Colonies; and as he was then unwilling to believe it as bad as it was represented by the partizans of the American people, he found himself frequently involved in disputes in their defence. In those disputes, however, he felt rather diffident of his own knowledge on the subject. This was the state of his mind with respect to the American war, until he met with and read Dr. Price's celebrated Treatise on Civil Liberty.[4] The arguments brought forward in that masterly work, were, to him, so convincing, that he found himself compelled to adopt its principles. He saw that it was not only necessary for the happiness of the trans-atlantic patriots themselves, that the struggle should terminate in their favour; but that even the future happiness of the whole human race was concerned in the event. From that moment he became one of the warmest and most sincere advocates for the *right* cause.

In the year 1781, he married the youngest daughter of Mr. Priest, a carpenter and builder in Chesham, in Buckinghamshire, with whom he lived, in spite of all the tricks of fortune, in the most perfect state of connubial happiness. She bore him six children, who all died young—the last of them, still-born, found a grave with its hapless mother, who died on the 27th of August, 1794, in the unfortunate manner which shall be hereafter related. For many years after his marriage he followed his business with various success, and refused several advantageous offers which had been made to him if he would go to America; but he was strongly attached to his native country, and besides something always happened, in a manner to him unaccountable, to overthrow every momentary inclination of his own, and every effort of those who endeavoured to persuade him to emigrate.

In the latter end of the year 1791, a proposal was made to him, as it was pretended, very much calculated to advance his circumstances, to enter into a partnership with a currier and a leather cutter, who undertook, if he would engage in the manufactory of boots and shoes, to furnish leather, and to find a market for as many as he should make. To this proposal he agreed, and for that purpose took the house, *afterwards so well known*, No. 9, Piccadilly, and began with that active industry which nothing could ever depress, to fulfil his part of the contract he had entered into; when, lo! one of those instances of treachery, too common, but too little attended to, in corrupt and luxurious communities, threatened to overwhelm him and his family in utter ruin. Before he was well settled in the house he had engaged, his pretended friends deserted him, broke through the agreement they had made, sent in their bills at a short date, which, to avoid law expenses, he paid when due. The only excuse that can be offered for such conduct is, that their own affairs were not so prosperous as they expected. In this affair he experienced the great value of a good character; for having no capital of his own, he must,

[4] Published in 1776, it sold almost 200,000 copies. Price and his fellow dissenters argued that traditional English liberties were being undermined by the corruption of George III's government and the unrepresentative nature of Parliament.

unavoidably, have given up business, had not unsolicited friendship come forward, with timely aid, which enabled him to carry on his trade until the memorable period at which he was arrested for High Treason, which circumstance shall be more particularly noticed presently.

However, notwithstanding every personal effort of his own, and the support of his friends, he soon began to feel the heavy pressure of the daily accumulating taxes, and the consequent rise in the prices of all the necessaries of life. He knew the country to be productive, and its inhabitants to be industrious and ingenious; therefore, the distress which he saw every where around him could not arise from the fault of the soil, or of those who occupied it, and the cause must be sought for somewhere else. It required no extraordinary penetration, once the enquiry was begun, to be able to trace it to the corrupt practices of men falsely calling themselves the representatives of the people, but who were, in fact, selected by a comparatively few influential individuals, who preferred their own particular aggrandisement to the general interest of the community.

The next enquiry naturally arose—Was the cause of the people hopeless? Must they and their posterity for ever groan under this intolerable load? Could not the nation, by a proper use of its moral powers, set itself free? Hardy thought it could; and he projected the plan of "the London Corresponding Society", as a means of informing the people of the violence that had been committed on their most sacred rights, and of uniting them in an endeavour to recover those rights. Why the Father of that Society remained unknown, except to two or three persons, until after the State Trials, is thus accounted for. He saw, with pleasure, that it was bidding fair to overturn a long established system of corruption and oppression, and he was afraid that it might operate to its prejudice were it made publicly known, that so obscure an individual was its founder. He saw his intentions to do good in the course of being fulfilled, and he never had any vanity to gratify. He was often asked who began the Society, but for the above reason he always evaded the question. Some said it was J. Horne Tooke; others, that it was Thomas Paine; but neither of them had any hand in it.

So prevalent, however, was the opinion, that the Attorney General, in his opening speech, on Hardy's trial, made use of the following words, which may be found in the report of that trial, taken in short hand by Mr. Ramsay, and published by Mr. Ridgway, page 57.[5] "The London Corresponding Society was modelled by some of the leading Members, and owes its corporate existence, and was formed under the Constitutional Society." It has been already shewn that this must have been an error; for, in fact, the Constitutional Society had ceased its meetings for several years, and was not

[5] Published in 1794; Ridgway was also the publisher of the *Memoir*. At least four separate accounts of the trial were published in 1794–95, one of them printed by order of the London Corresponding Society, which is some indication of the public interest in the trial.

re-opened until three months after the London Corresponding Society had been modelled by Hardy, as above: and it was at their first meeting, after being re-opened, that they received a copy in *manuscript* of the address and resolutions of the London Corresponding Society. The envelope was signed by Hardy, but the address itself had no signature; and as the Constitutional Society resolved to publish it, it is probable that Mr. Tooke put Hardy's name to it before it was entered in the books, and sent to the newspapers. That circumstance is sufficient to account for the mystery which so puzzled the Attorney General, why the name of *Thomas Hardy, Secretary,* was in the hand writing of *Mr. Tooke.* The address thus signed was seized among the papers of Mr. Adams, Secretary to the Constitutional Society; and from that circumstance and others, equally mistaken, jumbled together, the Attorney General inferred and asserted, that the London Corresponding Society was modelled by the Constitutional Society—meaning Tooke, and Felix Vaughan. Gurney's Report has the same in substance, at pages 69, 77, and 78.

At this period he had some leisure from his usual employment, and he occupied the time in re-perusing a collection of political tracts, published by the Society for Constitutional Information, in the years 1779, 1780, 1781, 1782, and 1783, which had been presented to him by a Member of that Society, T. B. Hollis, Esq. This drew his attention more closely to the subjects on which he had been accustomed to think and talk a great deal during the American war. He drew up some rules, with a preamble to them, for the management of the Society which he had projected. These rules he submitted to three friends, whom he engaged to supper with him one night, with a view of obtaining their opinions on the subject. His friends highly approved of them, as proper fundamental regulations for a Society, whose efforts were to be employed in endeavouring to restore to Britons those civil rights of which they had been deprived by the unholy union of force and fraud, at various periods, and by all parties that had obtained power—Whigs, then, as well as Tories.

These outlines being agreed upon between him and his three friends, they, next, resolved to meet weekly in future at a public house, and to invite as many of their friends as they thought were likely to exert themselves in promoting the object of the Society.

"What great events arise from little things!"

This Society, consisting at first of no more than four members, plain homely citizens, soon acquired an influence, and encreased to a magnitude too well known to require any particular description.

However, it is necessary to follow its progress a little. In the beginning of January, 1792, the first meeting was held at the sign of the Bell, in Exeter Street, in the Strand, when there were present only nine persons, all acquainted with each other. They had finished their daily labour, and met there by appointment. After having had their bread and cheese and porter for supper, as usual, and their pipes afterwards, with some conversation on the hardness of the times and the dearness of all the necessaries of life, which they, in common with their fellow citizens, felt to their sorrow, the business for which they had met was brought forward—*Parliamentary Reform*—an important subject to be deliberated upon, and dealt with by such a class of men. Hardy then produced the rules and preamble which he had drawn out; and after they had been read twice, it was proposed that all who wished to become members should subscribe them, and engage to endeavour, by all the means in their power, to promote the objects the Society had in view. To this proposal all present, except one man, readily agreed. This man said he would take a week to consider of it; and he also became a member at the next meeting. Hardy presented a book which he had bought for the purpose, that those who became members might put down their names, and pay one penny, which was to be continued weekly, as one of the rules expresses.

There was some conversation about what name should be given to the Society; some would have it called "The Patriotic Club," some the "Reformation Society," when Hardy shewed them some cards upon which he had written "The London Corresponding Society, No. 1, 2, 3, &c.;" and that denomination was unanimously adopted. Hardy was then appointed Secretary and Treasurer. There were eight persons who had subscribed the rules, and paid a penny each, consequently there was eight pence in the treasury,—a mighty sum! Next weekly meeting, nine more joined the Society, which encreased the fund to two shillings and one penny. The third meeting brought an accession of twenty-four new members, which made the treasury rich to the important amount of four shillings and one penny.

The first correspondence of the Society was the following letter, addressed by Hardy to the Rev. Mr. Bryant, of Sheffield. It was private; but, on reading that gentleman's answer to the assembled members, the transaction was adopted as that of the whole body. The letter is here inserted, because, on the trial, the Attorney General, now Lord Eldon, lamented very much—he is good at lamentations—that he had not possession of it, and because the reply which it elicited tended very much to animate the Corresponding Society in the great cause of *Parliamentary* Reform.

London, 8*th March*, 1792.

Reverend Sir,

I hope you will pardon that freedom which I take in troubling you with the following sentiments; nothing but the importance of the business could have induced me to address one who is an entire stranger to me, except *only* by report. Hearing from my friend, Gustavus Vassa, the African, who is now writing memoirs of his life in my house,[6] that you are a zealous friend to the abolition of that cursed traffic, the Slave Trade, I infer, from that circumstance, *that you are a zealous friend to freedom on the broad basis of the RIGHTS OF MAN.* I am fully persuaded that there is no man, who is, from principle, an advocate for the liberty of the black man, but will zealously support the rights of the white man, and *vice versa.*

The reason why I write to you, at this time, is this. There are some tradesmen, mechanics, and shopkeepers here in London, forming a Society for a Reform in Parliament, which, in our opinion, is of all other things most deserving the attention of the public. We are more and more convinced, from every day's experience, that the restoring the right of voting to every man, not incapacitated by nature for want of reason, nor by law for the commission of crimes, together with annual election, is the only reform that can be effectual and permanent. It has been a long, and very just complaint, that a very great majority of the people of this country are not represented in Parliament; that the majority of the House of Commons are chosen by a number of voters, not exceeding twelve thousand; and that many large and populous towns have not a single vote for a representative: such as Birmingham, containing upwards of 40,000 inhabitants; Manchester, above 30,000; Leeds, above 20,000; besides Sheffield, Bradford, Halifax, Wolverhampton, &c. &c. &c.; since that estimate of the inhabitants was made, their number has been more than doubled. The views and intentions of this Society are directed towards ascertaining the opinion, and to know the determination, as far as possible, of the unrepresented part of the people. From these considerations we have taken the name of *The London Corresponding Society*, for restoring the right of suffrage to the unrepresented of the people of Great Britain. The following are our leading rules. That the number of our Members be unlimited. That no one can become a Member unless he be proposed by one of the Members and seconded by another. That he be above the age of twenty years, and resident in Great Britain one year. And to be esteemed a Member of the Society, it is requisite that he pay, at least, *one penny* a week, towards defraying the necessary expenses of the Society. I have here given you some of our reasons and motives for associating, and our terms of admission. Since we did associate, we have heard that there are Societies also forming in Sheffield for promoting the same important cause.[7]

As I do not know either the President, or the Secretary, and presuming you are a Member, I trust you will oblige me with all the information you

[6] The freed slave, Gustavus Vassa, had in fact published his autobiography, *The Interesting Narrative of the Life of Oloudah Equiano, or Gustavus Vassa the African, written by himself* in 1789. However, he may have been preparing one of the several new editions which appeared during the decade.

[7] Sheffield was the home of the country's first popular society, the Sheffield Constitutional Society, which was founded a month before the London Corresponding Society in December 1791. At the time of this letter its membership numbered about 2,000. Mr Bryant later sent a reply, which greatly encouraged the society.

judge prudent, concerning the government of your Society, as ours is not yet perfectly organized. Any information from you, or the Society at Sheffield, tending to facilitate the grand and ultimate end, or even any advice, will be gratefully received by him who begs leave to subscribe himself,

Reverend Sir,
Your most obedient and most
Humble Servant,
THOMAS HARDY.

4, *Taylor's Buildings,*
St. Martin's Lane.

On the 2nd of April, 1792, the London Corresponding Society came before the public with an address and resolutions, in which their principles and views were clearly and unequivocally stated. This first address was written by Mr. Margarot; and it was judged requisite and proper that some person should sign it as Chairman; more especially as it was their first public act. It was proposed to several persons to allow their names to appear, but some objected, and others pleaded private reasons, best known to themselves, in excuse.[8] However, as the Society deemed it necessary to have a name, it was at last proposed to Hardy to allow his to appear. He had no other objection than the probability that it might prove prejudicial to the Society, to have their first document published under the sanction of so obscure a name. This objection was overruled, and his name alone, as Secretary, appeared to the first Address and Resolutions, of which the following is a true copy:—

LONDON CORRESPONDING SOCIETY,

Held at the Bell, Exeter Street, Strand.

MAN, as an individual, is entitled to liberty—it is his birthright.

As a member of society, the preservation of that liberty becomes his indispensable duty.

When he associated, he gave up certain rights, in order to secure the possession of the remainder;

But, he voluntarily yielded up only as much as was necessary for the common good:

He still preserved a right of sharing in the government of his country;—without it, no man can with truth call himself FREE.

Fraud or force, sanctioned by custom, with-holds that right from (by far) the greater number of the inhabitants of this country.

[8] In his manuscript history, Hardy is more explicit about the pressures upon the society's members: "who was to sign this address became the next question? Some objected because they were serving masters who might perhaps discharge them from their employment—others that if their names appeared to any address and resolutions of any society for a reform of parliament, they might lose customers." (*Add. MS. 27814*, f. 29.)

The few with whom the right of election and representation remains, abuse it, and the strong temptations held out to electors, sufficiently prove that the representatives of this country seldom procure a seat in Parliament, from the *unbought* suffrages of a free people.

The nation at length perceives it, and testifies an ardent desire of remedying the evil.

The only difficulty, therefore, at present is, the ascertaining the true method of proceeding.

To this end, different and numerous Societies have been formed in various parts of the nation.

Several likewise have arisen in the Metropolis; and among them, (though as yet in its infant state) the LONDON CORRESPONDING SOCIETY, with modesty intrudes itself and opinions, on the attention of the public, in the following Resolutions;

1. *Resolved*,—That every individual has a right to share in the government of that Society of which he is a Member—unless incapacitated:

2. *Resolved*,—That nothing but non-age, privation of reason, or an offence against the general rules of society, can incapacitate him.

3. *Resolved*,—That it is no less the RIGHT than the DUTY of every citizen, to keep a watchful eye on the government of his country; that the laws, by being multiplied, do not degenerate into *Oppression*; and that those who are entrusted with the Government, do not substitute *Private Interest* for *Public Advantage*.

4. *Resolved*,—That the people of Great Britain are not *effectually* represented in Parliament.

5. *Resolved*,—That in consequence of a *partial*, *unequal*, and therefore *inadequate Representation*, together with the *corrupt* method in which Representatives are elected; *oppressive taxes*, *unjust laws*, *restrictions of liberty*, and *wasting of the public money*, have ensued.

6. *Resolved*,—That the only remedy to those evils is a fair, equal, and impartial Representation of the people in Parliament.

7. *Resolved*,—That a fair, equal, and impartial Representation can never take place, until all *partial privileges* are abolished.

8. *Resolved*,—That this Society do express their *abhorrence* of tumult and violence; and that, as they aim at Reform, not anarchy; reason, firmness, and unanimity are the only arms they themselves will employ, or persuade their fellow-citizens to exert, against ABUSE OF POWER.

Ordered,—That the Secretary of this Society do transmit a copy of the above to the Societies for Constitutional Information, established in *London*, *Sheffield*, and *Manchester*.

By Order of the Committee,
T. HARDY, Secretary.

April 2, 1792.

A copy of these Resolutions was sent to the Society for Constitutional Information, as already mentioned, and they were, by that Society, published in the newspapers. They were afterwards published by the London Corresponding Society itself, in the form of hand-bills, and thousands of them distributed in London, and throughout the country.

It was about this period that Hardy became acquainted with a gentleman, whose acquaintance and friendship was a real honour—J. Horne Tooke—that steady and intrepid champion of freedom; that unflinching supporter of Parliamentary Reform; and with many others of the friends of that cause, which promised peace and happiness to their fellow men. These virtuous men have been since falsely represented by successive governments and their hirelings, as traitors and enemies to their country; a dark and shameful blot on the annals of this civilized land, that its destinies should be confided to the management of men, either so ignorant or so wicked! The discerning and unprejudiced part of the nation, however, see clearly who are, and who have been the real enemies of their country; who have been aiding and abetting the robbery and murder of their fellow creatures, both at home and abroad. And these are the men who have been active in slandering and persecuting the friends of justice and humanity. He acquired the acquaintance of Thomas Paine, also, about the same time; a man whose political writings, especially his celebrated "Rights of Man," seemed to electrify the nation, and terrified the imbecile government of the day into the most desperate and unjustifiable measures.

The next transaction of the London Corresponding Society, was a congratulatory Address to the National Convention of France, of which the following is a copy. It was confided to the French Ambassador, who was, soon after, suddenly ordered to quit this country. In the Convention it was received with rapturous applause, as the first address from this country; and was afterwards one of the documents brought against the prisoners tried for High Treason. The National Convention distributed printed copies throughout all the Departments of France, where it caused a very great sensation.

The London Corresponding Society's Congratulatory Address to the National Convention of France.

"Frenchmen,

"WHILE foreign robbers are ravaging your territories, under the specious pretext of justice, cruelty and desolation leading on their van, perfidy, with treachery, bringing up their rear; yet mercy and friendship, impudently held forth to the world as the sole motives of their incursions, the oppressed part of mankind forgetting, for a while, their own sufferings, feel only for yours, and with an anxious eye watch the event, fervently supplicating the Almighty Ruler of the universe to be favourable to your cause, so intimately blended with their own.

"Frowned upon by an oppressive system of controul, whose gradual, but continued encroachments, have deprived this nation of nearly all its boasted liberty, and brought us almost to that abject state of slavery, from which you have so emerged, 5,000 British citizens,[9] indignant, manfully step forth to rescue their country from the opprobrium brought upon it by the supine conduct of those in power. They conceive it to be the duty of Britons to countenance and assist to the utmost of their power, the champions of human happiness, and to swear to a nation, proceeding on the plan you have adopted, an inviolable friendship. Sacred from this day be that friendship between us! and may vengeance to the uttermost, overtake the man who hereafter shall attempt to cause a rupture.

"Though we appear so few at present, be assured, Frenchmen, that our number encreases daily; it is true, that the stern uplifted arm of authority at present keeps back the timid, that busily circulated impostors hourly mislead the credulous, and that Court intimacy, with avowed French traitors, has some effect on the unwary, and on the ambitious. But, with certainty, we can inform you, friends and freemen, that information makes a rapid progress among us. Curiosity has taken possession of the public mind; the conjoint reign of ignorance and despotism passes away. Men now ask each other, What is freedom? What are our rights? Frenchmen, you are already free, and Britons are preparing to become so.

"Casting far from us the criminal prejudices artfully inculcated by evil-minded men, and wily Courtiers, we, instead of natural enemies, at length discover in Frenchmen our fellow citizens of the world, and our brethren by the same Heavenly Father, who created us for the purpose of loving and mutually assisting each other; but not to hate, and to be ever ready to cut each others throats, at the commands of weak or ambitious Kings, and corrupt Ministers.

"Seeking our real enemies, we find them in our bosoms, we feel ourselves inwardly torn by, and ever the victims of a restless, all consuming aristocracy, hitherto the bane of every nation under the sun! Wisely have you acted in expelling it from France.

"Warm as our wishes for your success, eager as we are to behold freedom triumphant, and man every where restored to the enjoyment of his just rights, a sense of our duty, as orderly citizens, forbids our flying in arms to your assistance; our government has pledged the national faith to

[9] At the time of the address the membership of the London Corresponding Society was probably no more than 200, but it increased rapidly during the autumn to number some 1,500 by the end of the year, by which time it could possibly claim another 4–5,000 active but unpaid-up supporters. (G. A. Williams, *Artisans and Sans-Culottes,* London, 1968, pp. 68–70.)

remain neutral:—in a struggle of liberty against Despotism, Britons remain neutral! oh shame! But we have entrusted our King with discretionary powers!—we, therefore, must obey;—our hands are bound, but our hearts are free, and they are with you.

"Let German despots act as they please. We shall rejoice at their fall, compassionating however their enslaved subjects. We hope this tyranny of their masters will prove the means of reinstating, in the full enjoyment of their rights and liberties, millions of our fellow creatures.

"With unconcern, therefore, we view the Elector of Hanover join his troops to traitors and robbers; but the King of Great Britain will do well to remember, that this country is not Hanover.—Should he forget this distinction, we will not.

"While you enjoy the envied glory of being the unaided defenders of freedom, we fondly anticipate, in idea, the numerous blessings mankind will enjoy; if you succeed, as we ardently wish, the triple alliance (not of Crowns, but) of the people of America, France, and Britain, will give freedom to Europe, and peace to the whole world. Dear friends, you combat for the advantage of the human race. How well purchased will be, though at the expense of much blood, the glorious, the unprecedented privilege of saying mankind is free! Tyrants and tyranny are no more! Peace reigns on the earth! And this is the work of Frenchmen!

"The desire of having the concurrence of different Societies to this Address, has occasioned a month's delay in presenting it. Success, unparallelled, has now attended your arms. We congratulate you thereon. That success has removed our anxiety, but it has no otherwise influenced our sentiments in your behalf. Remember, Frenchmen, that although this testimony of friendship only now reaches your Assembly, it bears date the 27th September, 1792."

(Signed by Order)
MAURICE MARGAROT, President.
THOMAS HARDY, Secretary.

We now arrive at a period which draws the subject of this Memoir forth from the humble occupation of a shoemaker, in which he had hitherto laboured with great credit to himself, to take his stand by the side of those immortal heroes, in whose praise the tongues of Britons will never cease to speak with rapture and grateful veneration. With that patriotic band who broke the ruffian arm of arbitrary power, and dyed the field and the scaffold with their pure and precious blood, for the liberties of their country,—Hampden, Russell, Sidney; ye intrepid martyrs to freedom! All hail to your ever glorious memory! Alas! how near was the page of our history to being again stained with the record of another bloody tragedy, similar to that which terminated your bright and honourable career! But, thanks to the firmness and integrity of twelve honest Britons, the page which was again intended for so foul a record has been preserved pure, and, for the happiness of millions, has been made the splendid recorder of the triumph of truth and justice.

But to return to the subject, from which the warmth of honest feeling has caused us to digress. Before the end of the year 1792, such is the prevalence of truth, and such is the weight and force of her arguments, the London Corresponding Society, to which Hardy was still Secretary, formed an intimate connexion, and had frequent correspondence with every Society in Great Britain, which had been instituted for the purpose of obtaining, by legal and constitutional means, a Reform in the Commons' House of Parliament. The correspondence with these Societies, and with others which continued to be daily forming, in all parts of England and Scotland, was regular, until they were deranged in November, by the starting up of a Society, hostile to liberty, under the denomination of "An Association for protecting property against republicans and levellers," which met at the Crown and Anchor Tavern. This Society was not merely countenanced, but actually appointed by the Ministers of that day, for the express purpose of calumniating the best friends of the country, that they might plunder and tyrannize, uncontrolled, over the people, in which, in a great measure, they succeeded. John Reeves, Charles Yorke, and Mr. Devaynes, were at the head of the Association.

In this deranged state of the London Corresponding Society, they published an Address to the Nation, vindicating their character from the base lies propagated against them by the new Association, every member of which was interested in preventing Reform.[10] The whole body, with their connexions, were, in fact, plundering the nation of millions, which has since been clearly proved; so that if a Reform had taken place at that time, these few worthless individuals would have been reduced to comparative poverty, and the nation saved. Mr. Margarot signed the Address as Chairman, and Hardy as Secretary. The copies were printed in the form of large broadsides, and posted up in various parts of London. As a preliminary to what was to be expected to follow, the bill-sticker was apprehended, and afterwards tried, found guilty, and sentenced to six months imprisonment and a fine, which was paid by the Society. The Address is here given at length, that the present generation may see the severity with which liberal principles were dealt with in the days of their fathers, and that if these fathers did not recover the liberty that had been wrested from their ancestors, it was not for want of struggling, and braving every danger in the cause. It was written by Felix Vaughan, Esq. Barrister at Law, and Member of the Society.

[10] The Association's most effective tactic was to persuade London J.Ps. to threaten publicans and tavern keepers with the loss of their licence if they "suffered any of these reforming societies to meet in their houses". This action severely disrupted the functioning of the society. (*Add. MS 27814*, f. 40.)

ADDRESS
OF THE
LONDON CORRESPONDING SOCIETY,
To the other Societies of Great Britain,
UNITED FOR THE OBTAINING A
REFORM IN PARLIAMENT.

FRIENDS, AND FELLOW COUNTRYMEN,

UNLESS we are greatly deceived, the time is approaching when the object for which we struggle is likely to come within our reach.—That a nation like Britain should be free, it is requisite only that Britons should will it to become so; that such should be their will, the abuses of our *original Constitution*, and the alarm of our aristocratic enemies, sufficiently witness.—Confident in the purity of our motives, and in the justice of our cause, let us meet falsehood with proofs, and hypocrisy with plainness.—Let us persevere in declaring our principles, and Misrepresentation will meet its due reward—Contempt.

In this view the artifices of a late ARISTOCRATIC ASSOCIATION, formed on the 20th instant, call for a few remarks, on account of the declaration they have published relative to other Clubs and Societies formed in this nation; it is true that this meeting of *gentlemen* (for so they style themselves), have mentioned no names, instanced no facts, quoted no authorities; but they take upon themselves to assert, that bodies of their countrymen have been associated, professing opinions favourable to the RIGHTS OF MAN, TO LIBERTY AND EQUALITY; and moreover that those opinions are conveyed in the terms NO KING! NO PARLIAMENT!—So much for their assertions.

If this be intended to include the Societies to which we respectively belong, we here, in the most solemn manner, deny the latter part of the charge; while, in admitting the former, we claim the privilege, and glory in the character of Britons. Whoever shall attribute to us (who wish only the restoration of the lost liberties of our country) the expressions of NO KING! NO PARLIAMENT! or any design of invading the PROPERTY of other men, is guilty of a wilful, an impudent, and a malicious falsehood.

We know and are sensible that the wages of every man are his right; that *difference of strength, of talents, and of industry, do and ought to afford proportional distinctions of property, which,* when acquired and confirmed by the laws, *is sacred and inviolable.* We defy the most slavish and malevolent man in the meeting of the 20th instant, to bring the remotest proof to the contrary. If there be no proof, we call upon them to justify an insidious calumny, which seems invented only to terrify independent Britons from reclaiming the *rightful Constitution of their country.*

We admit and we declare, that we are friends to CIVIL LIBERTY, and therefore to NATURAL EQUALITY, both of which we consider as the RIGHTS OF MANKIND—could we believe them to be "*in direct opposition to the laws of this land*," we should blush to find ourselves among the number of its inhabitants; but we are persuaded that the abuses of the constitution will never pass current for its true principles, since we are told in its first Charter that all are EQUAL in the *sight of the law*, which "*shall neither be sold, nor refused, nor delayed, to any free man whatsoever*." Should it ever happen that "RIGHT AND JUSTICE" are opposed by expence, by refusal, or by delay, THEN IS THIS PRINCIPLE OF EQUALITY VIOLATED, AND WE ARE NO LONGER FREEMEN.

Such are our notions of those rights, which it is boldly maintained are "*inconsistent with the well-being of Society*." But let us not suffer men who avow no principles of liberty, whose favourite cry is INEQUALITY OF PROPERTY, to estrange others of our countrymen from aiding us in serving the community, and from recovering to the nation that share of its sovereignty, which has unhappily been sacrificed to CORRUPT COURTIERS and intriguing BOROUGH MONGERS.

If our laws and constitution be just and wise in their origin and their principle, every deviation from them as first established must be injurious to the people, whose persons and property were then secured; if, at the Revolution, this country was adequately represented, it is now so no longer, and therefore calls aloud for REFORM.

If it be true that the people of Britain are superior to other nations, is it that our taxes are less burthensome, or that our provisions are less expensive? Is it from the various productions of our soil that we are rich? Is it owing to the majority of our numbers that we are strong? Certainly not! France has the advantage in all these respects, and up to this period she has never been our superior in wealth, in power, in talents, or in virtues. But let us not deceive ourselves; the difference between us and that nation was, formerly, that our Monarchy was limited, while theirs was absolute; that the number of our aristocracy did not equal the thousandth part of theirs; that we had Trial by Jury, while they had none; that our persons were protected by the laws, while their lives were at the mercy of every titled individual. We, therefore, had that to fight for, which to them was unknown, since we were MEN while they were SLAVES.

The scene indeed has changed: like our brave ancestors of the last century, they have driven out the family that would have destroyed them; they have scattered the mercenaries who invaded their freedom, "and have broken their chains on the heads of their oppressors." If during this conflict with military assassins and domestic traitors, cruelty and revenge have arisen among a few inhabitants of the capital, let us lament these effects of a bloody and tyrannous MANIFESTO; but let us leave to the hypocrite pretenders to humanity, the task of blackening the misfortune, and attributing to a whole nation the act of an enraged populace.

As we have never yet been cast so low at the foot of despotism, so is it not requisite that we should appeal to the same awful tribunal with our brethren on the Continent. May our enmities be written in sand, but may our rights be engraven on marble! We desire to overthrow no property but what has been raised on the RUINS OF OUR LIBERTY! We look with reverence on the landed and commercial interests of our country; but we view with abhorrence that MONOPOLY of BURGAGE TENURES, unwarranted by law or reason, in this or any other nation in Europe.

Let us then continue, with patience and firmness, in the path which is begun; let us then wait and watch the ensuing Sessions of Parliament, from whom we have much to hope, and little to fear. The House of Commons may have been the source of our calamity; it may prove that of our deliverance. Should it not, we trust we shall not prove unworthy of our forefathers, WHOSE EXERTIONS IN THE CAUSE OF MANKIND SO WELL DESERVE OUR IMITATION.

M. MARGAROT, *Chairman.*
T. HARDY, *Secretary.*

The signing of this Address, though it was so public, and its principles, it is to be hoped, were those of every rational being, was brought against Hardy as an act of High Treason. Other documents, equally devoid of treason, were also brought against him, some of which shall be hereafter noticed; but to notice them all would be to republish the Attorney General's speech, which took him nine hours to deliver.

In the Spring of the year 1793, petitions were promoted by the different Constitutional Societies in their respective towns and neighbourhoods, not in their capacities of members of the Societies, but as members of the community deprived of their rights, and desiring that those rights might be restored to them.

These petitions were presented to the House of Commons, for the purpose of strengthening Mr. Grey's motion for Reform. Some of them were read and animadverted upon with great asperity by many of the members of that House, for speaking with a bolder tone of remonstrance than was agreeable to the prejudices and opinions of a great majority of them. These, of course, were all rejected. Others, less offensive, were ordered to lie on the table, or, in other words, were consigned to oblivion without observation.[11]

In October, 1793, a Convention of the different Societies of Scotland was held in Edinburgh, with the view of obtaining the Reformation of Parlia-

[11] At the beginning of May 1793 petitions from all parts of the country were presented to the House of Commons, and on 6 May Charles Grey, the future Whig Prime Minister, presented a petition for reform on behalf of the Society of the Friends of the People. A motion to refer it to a committee was rejected by 282 votes to 41.

ment; previously to which Mr. Skirving, the Secretary, wrote to Mr. Hardy Secretary to the London Corresponding Society, requesting that Society to send delegates to the Convention in Scotland, and also a request that he and the other members would use their influence with other English Societies to do the like. A similar letter was sent, by Mr. Skirving, to the London and Sheffield Constitutional Societies, with a similar request, all of which requests were complied with; and these three Societies, on the 9th of November, 1793, sent delegates accordingly.

It is almost unnecessary to say any thing upon a subject so well known but as the thread of our story requires to be preserved unbroken, we shall be as concise as possible. The Convention met in Edinburgh on the 19th of November, 1793; the delegates of the three English Societies being of the number that attended. They proceeded to business with a regularity, decorum, and dignity, by no means unworthy of the imitation of *assemblies* of a much longer standing. They met with no interruption for upwards of a fortnight. Their proceedings were open to the public at large, and their resolutions debated and adopted in the presence of all who chose to attend A short time after the meeting of the Convention, Mr. Margarot, delegate from the London Corresponding Society, received authority from the United Societies of Norwich to act for them; and Mr. C. Brown, from the Sheffield Society, received a similar commission from the Society at Leeds. Every week fresh Societies were springing up, even to the utmost parts of Scotland, and sending delegates to Edinburgh to the Convention. The eyes of the whole nation were so anxiously and steadily fixed upon its proceedings, that the servants of Government became alarmed, and all at once, in defiance of justice, the law of Scotland, and in the face of Magna Charta, and the Bill of Rights, the Magistrates of Edinburgh, attended by a posse of constables, thief catchers, and others, armed with bludgeons, pistols, and hangers,[12] invaded the Convention, and insisted on dispersing it, which, after some struggle, they effected. What followed, is well known. The English delegates were all held to bail, and some of them indicted. Margarot and Gerald were tried for sedition; and with Skirving, the Secretary to the Scottish Societies and Convention, Thomas Muir, and F. Palmer, were convicted, and sentenced to fourteen years' transportation to Botany Bay.[13]

The English Societies, whose rights had been thus wantonly trampled upon, in the severe and unjust punishment inflicted upon their delegates, held frequent meetings, and passed some strong resolutions on the subject, expressive of their indignation; and after many consultations and communications, it was at length resolved to call another Convention to be held

[12] i.e. short swords.

[13] Muir had in fact been arrested, tried and sentenced to 14 years' transportation back in August, and the Unitarian minister Thomas Fyshe Palmer had been sentenced to 7 years' transportation in September. Margarot and Skirving were tried in January and Gerrald in March 1794. (Hardy's 'Gerald' is either an alternative spelling or a mis-spelling.)

in England, and to which the Scottish Societies should be requested to send delegates. The English Ministers being advised, through their *spies* and *informers*, that this measure was about to be adopted, took the alarm, and employed such means to prevent it as reflect disgrace upon their memories, and astonished, not only Great Britain, but also all Europe.

On the memorable 12th of May, 1794, at half-past six o'clock in the morning, Mr. Lazun, junior, the son of the King's messenger of that name, and who was himself afterwards made an assistant messenger, as a reward for his activity on that occasion, gave a thundering knock at the door, No. 9, Piccadilly, before the shop was opened; and Hardy, having no suspicion of what had been prepared for him, jumped out of bed, and went, half-dressed, to see what could be the matter at that early hour. Upon the door being opened, Lazun rushed in, followed by John Gurnel, the King's messenger, P. Macmanus, and John Townsend, Bow Street officers—better known by the appellation of thief takers—Mr. John King, private Secretary to Mr. Dundas, and two or three others whose names Hardy did not learn. Lazun seized him, and proceeded to search his pockets, where he found some letters and papers, besides his pocket book, containing two bills of exchange to the amount of £196. Hardy desired to know by what authority he was thus treated, when Lazun shewed him a paper, which he called a warrant for his apprehension, on a charge of High Treason: but before he could read more than a few lines, the young upstart in authority, re-folded, and put it again in his pocket. He observed, however, something about High Treason, connected with his own name, but had not an opportunity then of observing by whom it was signed.[14]

Lazun was very active in rumaging all the drawers, even those containing Mrs. Hardy's clothes. He demanded the key of a bureau, which happened to be locked, and when he found he could not obtain it, he threatened to break it, and proceeded to put his threat in execution by trying to force it open with the poker. Mrs. Hardy entreated him to desist, and Mr. King called in a smith, who was in waiting, with a box full of all sorts of pick-locks, and skeleton keys. This man did his business very expeditiously. He picked the lock of the bureau, and those of some trunks, and the party soon had four large silk handkerchiefs filled with letters and other papers; among which were many of Hardy's private letters from friends in America, and at home. Mr. King then called a hackney coach, which was in attendance, into which Mr. Hardy and the four bundles of papers were put, accompanied by Gurnel and Townsend, and carried to the messenger's house in King Street, corner of Charles Street, Westminster. The rest of the party remained behind, at No. 9, Piccadilly, and, not content with manuscripts, took as many books and pamphlets as nearly filled a *corn sack*, without *marking* one article.

[14] Daniel Adams, the Secretary of the Society for Constitutional Information, was arrested the same morning, and the next day a further twelve leading radicals were seized, all of whom, except John Lord, being later charged with high treason.

The feelings of poor Mrs. Hardy, on that occasion, may be easier imagined than described. In an advanced state of pregnancy, sitting in bed all the time, and unable to dress before so many unwelcome visitors, whom she could hardly consider in a better light than that of robbers.[15]

Hardy remained in the custody of Mr. Gurnel, by whom, and his family, he was civilly treated, from the 12th to the 29th of May. During that time he underwent several examinations before the Privy Council, consisting of Messrs. Pitt, and Dundas, the Duke of Montrose, the Marquis of Stafford, Lords Grenville, Hawkesbury, and Salisbury, the Lord Chancellor, the Attorney and Solicitor General, White, Solicitor to the Treasury, John Reeves, of notorious memory, Falkner, &c.

The first examination took place at eleven o'clock on the morning on which he was taken; when, being asked by Mr. Dundas his name and occupation, he gave a ready answer. He was then asked many questions to which he could not reply; and many letters and papers were shewn to him which he had never seen before, and of which, of course, he knew nothing; but the letters and papers he had written and signed, he readily acknowledged. On Tuesday and Wednesday his examination was continued; but he was not again called before the Council until Monday, when he was questioned about guns, pikes, and other warlike instruments. Of such instruments he knew nothing. It is impossible that so many Societies as then existed, could be without some violent characters, among which might be included the Government spies; but whatever such unworthy persons may have hinted, in any of the numerous Societies, about arms, Hardy, and the real patriotic part of them, abhorred the very idea of having recourse to violence of any sort. All their efforts were directed to the recovery of the lost rights of themselves and of their fellow citizens—in fact, to the attainment of Parliamentary Reform, by constitutional and peaceable means.

On the very day of Hardy's capture, a Message from the King was brought down to the Commons, by Mr. Dundas, announcing that the seditious practices which had been for some time carried on by certain Societies in London, in correspondence with Societies in different parts of the country, had lately been pursued with increased activity and boldness, and had been avowedly directed to the object of assembling a general convention of the people, in contempt and defiance of the authority of Parliament, and on principles subversive of the existing laws and Constitution, and directly tending to the introduction of that system of anarchy and confusion which had *fatally prevailed in France*. That, in consequence, his Majesty had given directions for seizing the books and papers of the said Societies in

[15] According to the London Corresponding Society's account of the episode, when she protested at her husband's arrest, one of the officers replied: "I hope you will have the pleasure of seeing him hanged before your door." (*An Account of the Seizure of Citizen Thomas Hardy* . . . , 1794, p. 1.)

London, which had been seized accordingly; and that these books and papers, appearing to contain matters of great importance to the public, his Majesty had given orders for laying them before the House of Commons; and his Majesty recommended it to the House to consider the same, and to take such measures thereupon as might appear to be necessary, for effectually guarding against the further prosecution of those dangerous designs, and for preserving to his Majesty's subjects the *enjoyment of the blessings* derived to them by the Constitution happily established in these kingdoms.

On the 14th, a Committee was appointed for examining the papers, which Committee was afterwards accused, and not without apparent reason, of falsifying and garbling the documents. On the 16th, Mr. Pitt brought up the Report, and moved "for leave to bring in a bill to empower his Majesty to secure and detain all such persons as shall be suspected of conspiring against his person and Government.": which, after an animated debate, during which the House divided thirteen times, was granted. After another debate, in which the minority, though small, displayed splendid talents, the bills passed, of course. On the 17th, a similar Message was presented by Lord Grenville, from his Majesty, to the House of Lords, when the Ministers were attacked by the Duke of Grafton, and Lord Stanhope. The latter nobleman defended the Societies. "These papers," said he, "are written by a set of men, honest in their intentions, though not rich, nor of high rank. They may, from a defect of education, have been somewhat inaccurate in their expressions—(the Ministers laughed at this); but their intentions were clearly legal, as their professed aim was to obtain a redress of grievances by legal means".

The bill for suspending the Habeas Corpus passed the Lords on the 22d of May, and was protested against by the following noblemen:—Earl Stanhope, Duke of Bedford, the Earls of Albemarle, Lauderdale, and Derby.

In spite, however, of all these severe measures, it is pretty clear, had this country remained at peace, that nothing short of an extensive and efficient Reform would have satisfied the people. The Ministers were "wise in their generation;" they saw this, and, with a view of diverting the public mind from the subject, plunged the country into a destructive war, which has caused an accumulation of debt and misery, dreadful to contemplate. The industrious have complained, and have had oppression added to oppression. They have been answered as Rehoboam answered the people of Israel:—"My Father hath chastised you with whips, but I will chastise you with scorpions." And what was the consequence? The people said, "what portion have we in David? neither have we inheritance in the son of Jesse. To your tents, O Israel; now see to thine own house David. So Israel rebelled against the House of David unto this day."—1 Kings, chapter xii. verses 16, 19.

But to resume our subject. Hardy was, on the 29th of May, 1794, committed to the Tower, on a warrant from the Privy Council, on a charge of High Treason, with orders that none should be admitted to see him, except such as brought a precept for that purpose, from those under whose authority he was committed. After some days had elapsed, the faithful partner of his bosom, who has been already mentioned as far advanced in a state of pregnancy, obtained permission, by virtue of such precept, to pay him a mournful visit, and was allowed after to see him twice a week; but not to remain with him more than two hours at a time; sometimes no more than one, and that always in the presence of the Gaoler, one of the Wardens, or a Serjeant, whom the Gaoler ordered to prevent any private conversation inaudible to him. If they happened to whisper, they were told to speak up, that they might be heard.

In the mean time, the newspapers, particularly the TIMES NEWSPAPER, teemed with the most wicked and shameful misrepresentation of the views and intentions of the unfortunate prisoner.[16] He was loaded with every degree of calumnious accusations, with a view of inflaming and prejudicing the public mind against him. Even his innocent and unprotected family was persecuted with the most dastardly and unmanly rancour. The following well known fact will evince this beyond contradiction. It happened on the 11th of June, 1794, the night on which the illumination took place in London, to commemorate Lord Howe's victory over the French fleet. On that night a large mob of ruffians assembled before his house, No. 9, Piccadilly, and without any ceremony began to assail the windows with stones and brick-bats. These were very soon demolished, although there had been lights up as in the adjoining houses. They next attempted to break open the shop door, and swore, with the most horrid oaths, that they would either burn or pull down the house. The unfortunate Mrs. Hardy was within, with no other protector than an old woman who attended her as nurse. Weak and enfeebled as she was, from her personal situation, and from what she must have suffered on account of her husband, it is no wonder that she should have been terrified by the threats and assaults of such a crowd of infuriated desperadoes. We have seen the readiness with which the military have been sent to the aid of the civil power, to preserve crimping houses, but neither civil nor military power interfered to preserve the property of this persecuted man, nor that of the exalted patriot, Lord Stanhope, from the violence of a lawless mob, more than suspected of having been hired for the base purpose.

Mrs. Hardy called to the neighbours who lived at the back of the house, and who were in a state of great anxiety for her safety, in case the villains

[16] Hardy seems to be unduly sensitive here. The *Times* was certainly giving active support to the government's campaign of repression, including, in addition to factual reports of the arrests and interrogations, a series of squibs, patriotic songs and cod advertisements directed against the cause of reform. But apart from describing Hardy at the time of his arrest as "a tall thin man; much marked in the face with the small pox; his manners low and vulgar; and in dress and habit quite a *Sans Culotte*" (13 May, p. 2), the newspaper's personal abuse was reserved for renegade members of the establishment like Earls Stanhope and Lauderdale. The only L.C.S. member to receive personal attention was the gentlemanly Horne Tooke. A man like Hardy was simply beneath the contempt of the paper.

should have effected their purpose of breaking into the premises. They advised her to make her way through a small back window, on the ground floor, which she accordingly attempted, but being very large round the waist, she stuck fast in it, and it was only by main force that she could be dragged through, much injured by the bruises which she received: and as, when brought to bed, soon afterwards, the child was dead, it may reasonably be concluded that it lost its life by the violent compression which the unfortunate mother suffered in that afflicting business.

The unceasing and merciless system of defamation which continued to be pursued against her husband, had such an evident effect upon the mind of Mrs Hardy, that her health began rapidly to decline; yet she strove to appear as cheerful as possible, and continued her visits to the Tower, as often as she was permitted, until the very day of her death. On the 27th of August, 1794, she was taken in labour, and delivered of a dead child. She declared, soon afterwards, that she found her own death fast approaching, and that she believed it to be entirely owing to what she had suffered in her person, and in her mind, on account of the confinement of her husband. About two o'clock of the same day she had parted with her husband, in as good spirits as was possible in her situation—took her last farewell—it was her last—for they were doomed never to see each other again in this vale of tears.

The following is the beginning of a letter which Mrs. Hardy was writing to her husband, a few hours before she died, August 27th, 1794; but a summons of eternal importance to her own soul obliged her to drop the pen without finishing it.

"My Dear Hardy,

"This comes with my tenderest affection for you. You are never out of my thoughts, sleeping or waking. Oh, to think what companions you have with you! None that you can converse with either on temporal or spiritual matters; but I hope the Spirit of God is both with you and me, and I pray that he may give us grace to look up to Christ. There all the good is that we can either hope or wish for, if we have but faith and patience, although we are but poor sinful mortals. My dear, you have it not in——"

To describe the state of the unfortunate prisoner's feelings, on receiving the mournful account of his loss, next morning, would be impossible. Let us think better of human nature than to suppose it necessary. The reader who can peruse the tragic story without a double emotion of indignation and pity, is not to be envied his feelings.

The following beautiful poem, written by "A friend to the distressed Patriots," appeared some time afterwards, and merits a place here. The author, Citizen Lee, went to America, in 1796, and died soon after. He wrote many beautiful poems, which have been published in several volumes. Free for ever be the land which afforded an asylum and a grave to the patriot bard!

ON THE

DEATH OF MRS. HARDY,

Wife of Mr. Thomas Hardy, of Piccadilly;

IMPRISONED IN THE TOWER ON A CHARGE OF HIGH TREASON.

She expired in Child-bed, on Wednesday, August 27, 1794; and declared, in her last moments, that she died a martyr to the sufferings of her husband.

Exalted hero! glory of my verse;
THY WEIGHTY SUFFERINGS! would the Muse rehearse!
With melting lays obtain the listening ear,
And draw from Pity's eye the pearly tear.
I see thee, fetter'd in tyrannic chains,
Thy spirit laden with a thousand pains;
Yet heedless to the mighty load of woe,
No plaint is heard, no tears are seen to flow;
The pleasing hope of bringing SLAVES RELIEF,
Inspires thy gen'rous soul, and lulls thy grief.
On Heav'n reclining, still thou hop'st to see
All tyrants dead, and heav'n-born LIBERTY
Her gentle sway extending all around,
Each human forehead with her LAURELS crown'd!
But why art thou enchain'd? What hellish might
Presum'd to rob thee of thy dearest right?
To rob the world? So good a man confin'd,
He suffers not alone, but all mankind!
'Twas TYRANNY'S FELL DEED; his haggard eyes,
Saw truth in thee, reflected from the skies;
Bright as the morning planet, with her light,
Chasing the shadows of retreating night;
And trembled lest the SECRETS should be known,
That are in HELL conceal'd and prop his Throne,
With the strong energy of fear imprest,
Thee, SON OF HEAV'N! his iron hands arrest:
Grasp not alone the common joys of life,
But ev'n the brightest gem, THY LOVING WIFE:
Inhuman monster! smiling at the smart,
That nature shot thro' each united heart.
BEHOLD THE SCENE, the piercing scene appears!
Imagination drops a pitying tear.
Bereft of thee, thy tender partner pines,
Thinks of thy state, and dangers new divines:

'Till in her bosom black despair conceives,
Nor beam of hope the pungent pain relieves;
Tho' thy misfortunes all her efforts claim,
The hand of nature bears upon her frame:
Feeble, and unassisted, hear her cry,
"*For thee, O husband! 'Tis for thee I die!*"
The martyr falls—Angelic guides convey
The spirit to the climes of endless day.
Ah! now the cruel tidings reach thine ear,
Thy dauntless courage melts into a tear:
Thy joints relax, thy fearful face grows wan,
And all the stoic softens into man:
For one soft moment other cares resign'd,
Ev'n LIBERTY, her image fills thy mind;
Yet in the cause thy soul unmov'd remains,
And from th' OPPRESSOR'S ROD new vigour gains.
How great thy sufferings! how amazing great!
Thy patience future poets shall relate!
Man shall record with gratitude thy name,
The winds from pole to pole shall waft thy fame.
And (if the Muse her object may pursue,
And set futurity to mortal view;)
Ere thou rejoicing yield'st thy fleeting breath,
Thy wife to follow thro' the paths of death;
FREEDOM SHALL REIGN! from earth thou shalt arise;
And bear the tidings to th' impatient skies.
And will ye deign to hear my mean applause,
Ye friends of man, and pillars of the cause!
Who, firm as rocks, amid the storm have stood,
And dar'd all dangers for the public good;
Ye, who with HARDY NOW are doom'd to feel
The lawless vengeance of ambitious zeal!
How would my heart with gen'rous rapture glow,
Could my weak strain alleviate your woe;
Inspire some noble bosom to a deed,
Humanity and Nature's dictates plead,
To PITY YOUR MISFORTUNES; and impart
His needful succour:—Every feeling heart,
Eager must yield the strongest aid it can,
To *prop* the *cause* of *God*, of *Angel*, and of *Man!*

A Friend to the distressed Patriots.

One would have naturally supposed that the wretches, who had so long amused themselves by sporting with the feelings of this unfortunate couple, would have been disarmed of their malignity, by the death of a much injured and amiable woman, and would have stopped in the midst of their shameful career; but the diabolical rancour of their minds was not to be thus satisfied. It is scarcely credible, that in a country celebrated for its humanity and liberality, such conduct should have been still pursued; yet so it was; for on the very day, or the day but one after the death of Mrs. Hardy, calumnious paragraphs appeared in the TIMES NEWSPAPER.[17]

Hardy's place of confinement was a small room above the western gate of the Tower. Mr. Thelwall's room was next, and Mr. Tooke's below. Here he remained for about ten or twelve days after the mournful event already narrated, without taking his accustomed walks—for the prisoners had been permitted to walk on the ramparts and parade some hours each day, for some time before—in a state of mind impossible for tongue or pen to describe, deprived of the faithful and beloved partner of his bosom, the participator of all his joys, and the kind and tender alleviator of all his sorrows; and without that variety of objects and occupations which divert the minds of men in Society, in a certain measure, from continually brooding over their afflictions; his mental sufferings must have been extreme. At length his fellow prisoners not meeting him in their daily rounds, his friend, Mr. Tooke, found means, privately, of advising him not to confine himself so closely, but to walk out and meet his friends in the different rendezvous which they had appointed; that, by seeing, and privately conversing with them, it might relieve his spirits, and enable him, with more fortitude, to meet the tremendous trial which awaited him; for, about this time, there were some hints in the public papers that they were to be tried for High Treason.

The Special Commission of Oyer and Terminer, for enquiring into, and hearing and determining of all High Treasons, and misprison of Treason, in compassing or imagining the death of the King, &c. was dated the 10th of September, 1794. The volume of written evidence was so enormous, that the Attorney General[18] was upwards of nine hours in opening the case to the Jury. Never was such a host of Crown Lawyers employed against any person tried for High Treason; and they certainly did justice to their employers, for they strained every nerve, in order to criminate their intended victim. The whole weight of the arm of power was employed to crush him; for if his ruin could be once accomplished, the other eleven who were in the indictment with him, were reckoned upon as an easy sacrifice.

It appears that the Government felt so confident of a conviction, that they

[17] Presumably a reference to a mock "Lamentation of Little Cato and his Senate for the loss of Robespierre" which appeared in the paper on 28 August, but although, in his bereaved state, Hardy may have read much into lines such as "How sorrowful our Party appears! We are become as widows who have lost the comfort of their mates, and the tears of distress moisten their eyes", the piece is in fact about the death of Robespierre (on 28 July) and contains no direct reference to Hardy or his wife.

[18] Sir John Scott, later Lord Eldon, who as Lord Chancellor took a leading part in suppressing radical activity during most of the first quarter of the nineteenth century.

had prepared eight hundred warrants, three hundred of which were actually signed, in order to be ready to be executed that very night and the next morning, in case a verdict of guilty were returned. Who the persons thus marked for destruction were, Hardy did not learn, but he is compelled to believe the authority upon which he states the damning fact. No means, however unjustifiable, were spared, that could effect his ruin. Letters written by others to different persons, without his knowledge or consent, and which he had never seen or heard of, until they were produced in Court, were attempted to be read in evidence against him, and one of that description was actually admitted.

The following papers, which he found means of conveying privately to his brother-in-law, Mr. Walne, two days previously to his removal from the Tower, will shew what desperate means Hardy's blood thirsty enemies had recourse to, in order, if possible, to take away his life, so plainly, that it needs no comment.

"On Thursday last, Mr. Kinghorn, the Gentleman Gaoler, and Underwood, a Warder, came into my room. Mr. Kinghorn seemed much agitated, and asked me to step with him to the Governor's, where he said a gentleman was waiting, who wished to speak with me. I inquired who it was, and what it was about? Mr. Kinghorn replied, that he did not know, but believed it to be something about subpœnas. Not suspecting that a trap had been laid for me, I went readily with him, and two Warders, to the Governor's house on the parade. In the dining-room into which I was shewn, one of the clerks of Mr. White, Solicitor to the Treasury, was sitting alone. When we entered, he arose from his seat, with what might be taken for an innocent smile on his countenance, and, addressing his discourse to me, said, 'Mr. Hardy, Mr. White omitted to inform you, when he delivered the indictment, that your Solicitor, by applying at the Crown Office, may have subpœnas for your witnesses without any expense to you.' All that I said in reply was, very well, and with a low bow returned with the Gaoler and the two Warders, in order to return to my room. In my way back I met Mr. Clarkson, my Solicitor, and told him where I had been, and what orders I had to give him. He replied that he had received a letter from Mr. White, the day before, to the same purport. While we were standing together talking, another of Mr. White's clerks, with a woman on his arm, came close up to us, and the female stared very hard at me. They walked on a few paces, then returned, and stared as before. I then recollected having seen the same couple standing opposite the Governor's door, apparently watching me as I came out. These two clerks were with White when he delivered the indictment; and this is the Miss Jane Partridge, of Nottingham, one of the witnesses for the Crown. They have had recourse to this artifice, to give her an opportunity of identifying my person. Before I had returned to my room five minutes, the same man whom I saw at the Governor's house came up to Thelwall, who is in the next room to me, and told him the same he had told me. This conduct caused some suspicion. Why should there have been such parade about my going to the Governor's, and yet the same message be delivered to Thelwall in his own room? We have enquired, and find that no such message has been sent to any of the other prisoners. There must, therefore, be some design in it.

"The mystery has been unfolded. Mr. Joyce, of Essex Street, informs us, that this woman has been brought to the Tower on purpose to see me; and it seems she is satisfied that I am the person who travelled with her from Nottingham to London, in the stage coach, about two years ago; and what she is to swear to is this: that I said to her in the coach that I would no more mind cutting off the King's head than I would shaving myself. Take particular notice of this woman; if she swears to such words, she perjures herself, for I never was at Nottingham in my life, nor farther north from London, by land, than Hampstead or Highgate."

Tower, 20th October, 1794.

How to counteract the evidence of this very wicked, or very much mistaken woman, was a very material point, and to be immediately considered. The circumstance was, without delay, communicated to the friends of the prisoners, and they set actively to work, and found persons who could prove satisfactorily that Hardy was not out of London one whole day, for more than a year before, and after the time she was to swear to.

The hand of Providence is evident in the manner in which the testimony that Jane Partridge was to give was discovered. What evidence the other witnesses for the Crown were to give, had been pretty well ascertained; but to what circumstance she was to bear witness, puzzled the friends of the prisoners. It happened, that the same evening she had been at the Tower to see Hardy, she drank tea with a party of young ladies, among whom there chanced to be the sister of Mr. Wardle, one of those in the indictment, but not in custody. Here Miss Wardle learnt the nature of Jane Partridge's evidence, and immediately communicated the circumstance to Mr. Joyce, of Essex Street, who went instantly to the Tower, and informed Hardy. Thus, great danger was averted; for had nothing been known of the nature of her evidence before her coming into Court, it would then be difficult to rebut it: there would be no witnesses prepared to prove that Hardy had not been at Nottingham, and, consequently, could not have travelled with Jane Partridge from that town to London. When the trial came on, and she was ordered into Court, she fainted in the room where the Crown witnesses were. When recovered, she was again called in, and again fainted. Whether the managers of the prosecution thought it best to dispense with her evidence, from a fear of its containing some fatal self-contradictions, or whether they found it impossible, from the effect that conscious guilt had upon her, to obtain that evidence, we know not, but she was no more called. It is clear, however, were her nerves as strong as her heart, as those of her employers were corrupt and wicked, that she would have ventured her eternal salvation by trying, falsely, to swear away the life of a man whom she had never seen, until she went to the Tower for that purpose.

It is to be hoped she lived to repent of her iniquity. If she is still living, it may be some consolation to her mind to know, that the man whom she would have destroyed forgives her.

A full report of the trial is already before the public. It lasted *nine days*, on the last of which, after the fullest investigation that ever took place in this or any other country, Hardy was pronounced "NOT GUILTY,"* by the unanimous voice of as respectable a jury as ever was empannelled. A jury, which, with unremitting patience, underwent a fatigue and confinement unparallelled in the annals of our courts of justice. A jury, on whose awful voice depended the liberties of eleven millions of their fellow citizens. A jury, whose integrity established on a firm basis the first and most important pillar of the English Constitution,—THE TRIAL BY JURY, which had been greatly on the decline, and much tampered with, for some time before, and thereby entitled themselves to the grateful acknowledgments and applause, both of the present and of future generations.

Having thus seen the subject of our Memoir delivered by twelve honest men from the power of his merciless persecutors, it will not, we trust, be deemed altogether foreign to our purpose to say a few words respecting the others who were in the same indictment with him.

Mr. Tooke was the subject of vindictive persecution and prosecution, because he had been from early life an ardent supporter of the rights of his fellow men. His talents were of the first order, and he distinguished himself as an active and formidable champion in favour of, what was then called, *Wilkes and liberty*. On that occasion his oratory and writings were equally admired, for their energy, perspicuity, independence, and constitutional spirit.

In spite of the oppressions and violence of the Court, Mr. Wilkes, in 1768, became a candidate for the county of Middlesex. On that occasion, Mr. Horne rode throughout the whole county, canvassing for him, which was the principal cause of his being elected. Mr. Horne was brought to the bar of the House of Commons, for a letter signed "*Strike but Hear*," published in The Public Advertizer, 14th of February, 1774, in favour of a petition of W. Tooke, Esq. respecting the enclosing of an estate. Shortly afterwards, by

* On hearing of the acquittal of Hardy, John M'Creery, the printer and poet, wrote the following lines:—

Twelve true hearted men held the balance of fate,
While these Shylocks were whetting the knife:
Of th' existence of thousands they lengthened the date—
Their VERDICT was FREEDOM and LIFE.

virtue of an Act of Parliament, he took the name of Tooke, at the desire of the same gentleman, who adopted him, and left him that estate which he had preserved from being swallowed up to satisfy the cormorant appetite of the law, at a time when he expected no other advantage from such essential services, than the conscious satisfaction of having procured justice to be done to a fellow citizen, about to be injured under the mask of legal forms. It is gratifying to see such eminent virtue and talent meet with their well merited reward, in such a very unequivocal testimony of friendship and gratitude, as was thus given by Mr. Tooke to Mr. Horne, now Horne Tooke.

Mr. Tooke's trial lasted six, Thelwall's four days; and the prosecutors, finding they could not obtain a conviction, declined proceeding with the trials of the other nine.

Mr. John Thelwall is well known, and highly esteemed as a public lecturer on politics, classical literature, and general education, in London, and various other parts of England and Scotland. He is also the author of many valuable works in prose and verse, and still lives highly and deservedly respected by a great number of his countrymen.

Stewart Kyd was an eminent barrister, author of a great law work, and of several political productions.

Augustus Bonney, an attorney of great repute.

Jeremiah Joyce, a man of great worth, and highly esteemed by all who knew him; was some years in the family of the late Earl Stanhope, as tutor to his sons. He was the author of several excellent sermons, some political tracts, and various valuable works on the arts and sciences.

Thomas Holcroft, a celebrated novelist, dramatic writer, and traveller.

The other five were John Richter, Thomas Wardle, Matthew Moore, Richard Hodgson, and John Baxter: all excellent men, and sincere and active promoters of Parliamentary Reform.[19]

As severe sufferers in the same great cause, it is to be hoped that a very brief notice of those gentlemen who were tried at Edinburgh, will not be deemed out of place here. They were all men of education and talents, and their only crime was being sincere in a cause from which Mr. Pitt had become an apostate. The proceedings against them in the Court of Justiciary of Scotland, excited universal odium throughout the country, and were execrated in terms of indignation by several Members of both Houses of Parliament.

Skirving and Gerald did not live long after their arrival at Botany Bay. Palmer, and another, purchased a vessel which had been a prize taken into Botany Bay, and intended coming home in her; but she was very leaky, and they were obliged to put into, as it happened, the very port to which the vessel belonged, where she was re-seized with her cargo, consisting of poor Palmer's whole property. Here all his sufferings closed soon after.

[19] Richter was a banker's corresponding clerk, and at Hardy's trial Wardle and Moore were described as "gentlemen", Hodgson as a hatter and Baxter as a labourer.

Mr. Margarot was a man of a strong philosophical understanding, ready wit, undaunted courage, and incorruptible integrity. He was the only one, of the five, who returned to his native country. He died about fifteen years ago.[20]

Mr. Thomas Muir, younger, of Hunter's Hill, was a man animated by strong enthusiasm, insomuch that even some Reformers blamed him for the indiscretion of his zeal; but it must be admitted that the zeal that is required to reform a system of abuses, ought to be intense, and should obtain forgiveness for any slight excesses it may run into. The following letter, written by Hardy to a friend, with a print of Muir, and containing quotations from his address to the Jury, and the Lord Justice Clerk, will clearly evince the rectitude of his intentions, and that he did not think his punishment, by any means, an ignominy.

"DEAR SIR,

I was very much gratified when you informed me, the other day, that you had in your possession a box of manuscripts, letters, and papers, of that excellent man, the late Thomas Muir, who was cruelly sentenced by the Court of Justiciary, of Edinburgh, on the 31st of August, 1793, to 14 years transportation, to the inhospitable shore of Botany Bay. For what? What was his crime? Strange to tell—for a life of virtuous conduct up to that hour. Hear what he says to the Jury at the close of his celebrated defence. "This is now, perhaps, the last time that I shall address my country. I have explored the tenor of my past life. Nothing shall tear me from the record of my departed days. From my infancy to this moment, I have devoted myself to the cause of the people. It is a good cause; it shall ultimately prevail; it shall finally triumph. Say then, openly, in your verdict, if you do condemn me, which I presume you will not, that it is to this cause alone, and not for those vain and wretched pretexts stated in the indictment, intended only to colour and disguise the real motives of my accusation. Weigh well the verdict you are to pronounce. As for me, I am careless and indifferent to my fate. I can look danger, I can look death in the face, for I am shielded by the consciousness of my own rectitude. Nothing can deprive me of the resolution of the past. Nothing can destroy my inward peace of mind, arising from the remembrance of having done my duty."

After the Judge had delivered the sentence, Mr. Muir rose, and said:—"*My Lord Justice Clerk, I have only a few words to say. I shall not animadvert on the severity or the leniency of my sentence. Were I to be led this moment from the bar to the scaffold, I should feel the same calmness and serenity which I now do. My mind*

[20] The Place Papers contain three letters to Hardy from Margarot in New South Wales, the second two, written in 1798 and 1799, complaining bitterly that he has received no letters or parcels from Hardy or any other L.C.S. members. But on Margarot's return to London Hardy took a leading part in organizing a subscription for him and was present at his funeral on 19 November 1815. (*Add. MS. 27816*, fos. 86, 89, 108, 112, 113 and 115.)

tells me, that I have acted agreeably to my conscience, and that I have engaged in a good—a just and a glorious cause, a cause which sooner or later must, and will prevail; and, by a timely reform, save this country from destruction."

With this I send a print of Thomas Muir for your acceptance.

When the Surprise transport was lying off Portsmouth, at Motherbank, in which these persecuted patriots, *Muir*, *Palmer*, *Margarot*, and *Skirving*, were sent to Botany Bay, I was on board of her at the time, and saw Mr. Banks, who was an eminent statuary, take a cast from Muir's face, from which he afterwards made a bust, and from which the present engraving is taken. It is a good likeness.

Accept, Dear Sir, the best wishes of

3rd March, 1821. THOMAS HARDY."

To Mr. Witherspoon, Cheapside.

Muir escaped from Botany Bay, on board a South Sea Whaler; was shipwrecked on the coast of South America, and after a variety of hardships reached the Havannah. His misfortunes did not end here. He took a passage on board of a Spanish vessel for Europe; and this country being at that time at war with Spain, they were attacked by a British frigate, off Cadiz. In this rencounter a splinter struck Muir on the cheek, part of which it carried away, and destroyed the sight of one of his eyes. The Spanish vessel was boarded, and he was recognized, while lying among the wounded, by a British officer, as an old acquaintance, and this circumstance enabled him to get to Spain. At the invitation of the National Convention, he went soon afterwards to France, where the Government granted him a pension, which he enjoyed until his death.

The particulars of his eventful life have been recently published.[21]

It was a most fortunate circumstance that the public prosecutor made choice of Hardy as the first victim to be sacrificed to ministerial vengeance. Had the friends of Reform themselves the election, a better could not have been made. Perhaps there never was a man, in any country, brought to the bar of a Court of Justice, for an imputed great crime, who could find so many respectable and creditable persons to testify to the uniform goodness of his private and moral character. So numerous, indeed, were they, that his learned, eloquent, and excellent counsel, Erskine, and Gibbs, deemed it unnecessary to bring any thing like the whole of them forward.

During the whole of the trial, the conscious rectitude of his own heart shone conspicuously through that index of the mind, the face. There the court, the jury, the learned bar, and the anxious and highly interested auditory, might plainly read the integrity of the honest man; the inflexible firmness of the patriot, proud of having been called to answer, even with his life, for his exertions in the cause of freedom; for his efforts to obtain for

[21] See P. Mackenzie, *The Life of Thomas Muir* (Glasgow, 1831).

himself, and fellow countrymen, a restoration of those inestimable rights which had raised the British name to that pre-eminence it had so long held among surrounding nations, and the abandoning of which would have degraded it to a level with the most slavish of them.[22]

The room in which he was confined in Newgate, during his trial, was in the inner prison, and he had, every morning, to walk through the yard in which the felons were allowed to walk. They were heavily ironed, some with single, and some with double fetters. They were upon each side, and as he walked through the middle, he found that even men of that description could distinguish between a man suffering for the assertion of honest principles, and those suffering for a breach of those moral restraints that bind society together.

They all expressed their good wishes towards him, in one way or other, and congratulated him on his good spirits.

When he passed the room in which Mr. Kyd was confined, every morning, they shook hands through the iron grating. On the third day, he said cheerfully to Kyd, "Now, Kyd, this day, death or liberty;" but he was mistaken, for his persecutors protracted the struggle as long as they had any hopes of success.

Mr. Ridgway, Mr. Symonds, and others, were confined on the State side of the prison for libels, or, in other words, for publishing the truth. As he passed here every morning, on his way to the court, they crowded to the gate, anxious to shake hands with him, and to express their good wishes. One morning as he passed the gate in high spirits, he said to Ridgway, "We are going to have another long spell at it to-day." On the Sunday before the trial finished, as he was walking in the yard with Mr. Kyd, and some others of his fellow prisoners, Mr. Kirby, the Keeper of Newgate, asked him if he would like to see the condemned cells—he accepted the invitation, without any hesitation, and went along with Kirby, accompanied by his friend Kyd. The poor unfortunate men were then walking in a small yard opposite the doors of their melancholy dwellings; consequently the cells were empty. What conversation took place, or what remarks were made by Hardy on those horrible places, it is unnecessary to repeat; but we may conceive that the sight was not very pleasing to a man in his situation, when it was uncertain whether he might not be lodged in one of them himself in two or three days.

Immediately on the words "NOT GUILTY" being pronounced by the foreman of the worthy jury, the Sessions House, where the court sat, was

[22] In the face of this grandiloquent self-praise it is perhaps necessary to point out that Hardy was indeed on trial for his life. Only ten days before his trial opened, Robert Watt had been executed in Edinburgh on a similar charge. Watt may well have been an over-zealous government double agent, but all that was known for certain at the time was that in the wake of the loaded trials and heavy sentences which had crushed the Scottish radicals, the government was bent on making a similar example of the leadership of the London societies.

almost rent with loud and reiterated shouts of applause. The vast multitude that were waiting anxiously without, caught the joyful sound, and like an electric shock, or the rapidity of lightning, the glad tidings spread through the whole town, and were conveyed much quicker than the regular post could travel, to the most distant parts of the island, where all ranks of people were anxiously awaiting the result of the trial.

After these extraordinary effusions of joy had a little abated in the court, Mr. Kirby, the Gaoler, advised Hardy to go through the prison to the debtor's door, where a coach was in readiness to convey him, according to his directions, to the house of his brother-in-law, Mr. Walne, in Lancaster Court, in the Strand; for he had no house of his own left to go to, nor family to welcome him home. Although he went into the coach as privately as possible, and drove down Snow Hill, yet he was observed by some persons, and the circumstance was announced to the multitude, who turned it into another direction, drove it along Fleet Market; and when they came to the end of Fleet Street, the concourse of people was very great, though it was a bleak rainy afternoon in the gloomy month of November. Here they stopped the coach, took out the horses, and drew it along Fleet Street, the Strand, Pall-Mall, St. James's Street, Piccadilly, the Haymarket, and back again to Lancaster Court, where he alighted. He addressed the people from the window in a short speech, after which they gave three cheers, and quietly dispersed, leaving him to enjoy the evening with some particular friends, among whom were the Rev. Dr. Bogue, and Rev. James Steven. During the procession, the people frequently stopped, and shouted at different places, such as Charing Cross, Carleton House, and St. James's Palace. At No. 9, Piccadilly, his former comfortable habitation, they stopped a few minutes in *solemn silence.*

The joy that appeared in every countenance of the vast multitudes of people who thronged the windows of the houses, in the streets through which the procession passed, was truly gratifying. In fact, the general joy that the acquittal of Hardy diffused throughout the country, was never exceeded, perhaps never equalled. It was heartfelt and extensive; the triumph of freedom was complete over those who wished to crush it at one blow; and every liberal-minded man felt himself, and not without reason, as if unexpectedly relieved from some terrible impending danger.[23]

Shortly after a public meeting, at which Earl Stanhope presided, was held at the Crown and Anchor, to celebrate the result of the State Trials. All parts

[23] Hardy's account is confirmed by the *Annual Register*: "The satisfaction of the public on the acquittal of Mr. Hardy, which took place on the 5th of November, was for this reason great, and expressed without restraint. . . . The trial of Mr. Hardy lated eight days; during which the anxiety of all men how it would terminate, was visible not only in the metropolis, but in every place throughout the kingdom. When the circumstances of the trial were known, the verdict of the jury impressed the public with the highest sense of the importance of that strongest bulwark to justice and liberty, that had been felt for many years." (*Annual Register*, 1794, p. 279.)

of the house were filled, and it was calculated that the assemblage consisted of no fewer than a thousand persons. This meeting was addressed by the noble chairman, by Sheridan, and other gentlemen, with animation and effect; and the friends of Parliamentary Reform have met annually on the 5th of November, to commemorate the acquittal of Thomas Hardy from a charge of High Treason, on the same day of the month, 1794. On these occasions it is expected, when a gentleman's health is drank, that, on returning thanks, he will make a speech; but Hardy, not being an orator, has, of late years, previously committed to paper what he had to say on his health being drank. Three such addresses, with their dates, will be placed at the end of this sketch, and in which will be found an interesting account of some circumstances relating to the London Corresponding Society, not mentioned in the Memoir.

We shall close the political part of this Memoir with the following address to the jury, the counsel, and his friends in general; and we hope that the reader, who has thus far accompanied us, will find it consistent with the proper feeling evinced by Hardy throughout the whole of his imprisonment and trial. It was published in all the Newspapers of the time.

ADDRESS TO THE PUBLIC.

"WITH a heart overflowing with gratitude, I now sit down to the most pleasing task which I have experienced in the course of my life. Little did I imagine that the public efforts I have made, in support of that cause which I deemed it my duty to promote to the utmost of my power, would have excited, in so great a degree, the most lively emotions of affectionate regard in the bosoms of thousands to whom I am unknown, but by name.—But so it has happened, and I feel myself labouring under a weight of obligations, which I am ardently anxious to discharge, as far as my ability will permit.

"Untutored in any language but that of truth, I proceed, without fear of the attack either of prejudice or malevolence, to pay the debt I owe, as far as I am able.

"TO MR. ERSKINE and MR. GIBBS, the two learned Counsel appointed for my defence, I beg permission, in this public manner, to return my best and warmest acknowledgments.—Any words in my power to use, would fall far short of expressing what they TRULY DESERVE, and what I REALLY FEEL they deserve. I have, however, this animating reflection in my mind, that every defect in my powers of expression to do them justice, is abundantly compensated by the force and eloquence of their own respective exertions, and that their transcendant talents and integrity cannot fail to stand recorded, not only on the minds of the present race, but will receive additional lustre in every progressive movement their names shall make through the progress of time.

"TO THAT PUBLIC, whose servant I have always been proud to acknowledge myself, I am equally at a loss for words to express the grateful sensations of my heart.—The feeling manner in which they have sympathized in my sufferings, while it gives a delight to my heart which no language can describe, almost disables me, from the overflowings of that source of sensibility, to perform my duty;—but the softness of nature gives way to the impetus of gratitude, and I beg leave to say to a generous public,

BE PLEASED TO ACCEPT MY THANKS.

"Acquitted by the unanimous voice of a jury of my country, from the charge of a crime at which my soul revolts, and my nature shudders, I find it impossible to express my gratitude to THEM in any degree adequate to what I feel. I must, therefore, intreat them for a moment to suppose themselves in my situation, and CONCEIVE what they would have said to me, had I, in similar circumstances, been their arbiter, and given the same decision in their behalf. I have no doubt but, in the consciousness of the rectitude of their own hearts, they feel a far greater reward than any in the power of mortal man to bestow;—but what I can I will:—I SINCERELY AND FERVENTLY THANK THEM.

"Small, indeed, is the return for the preservation of life and honour;—it is only the grateful effusions of a plain and poor man, but it comes warm from the heart, and, like the widow's mite, is ALL I HAVE TO GIVE.

"Restored to my friends and country after an absence of several months, in the course of which, all my family have descended into the peaceful tomb, I find my business ruined, and I have the world to begin again. I therefore take this opportunity of informing my friends, in particular, and the public in general, that I intend to resume my occupation, and to support myself as heretofore, by honest industry. I have not yet been able to find an eligible situation for opening a shop; but as soon as I can accomplish that object, I shall take the liberty of making it known, and have no doubt of receiving that encouragement and support which injured innocence never yet has failed to obtain in this generous and liberal island.

"THOMAS HARDY."

Lancaster Court, Strand,
Nov. 11, 1794.

It has already been mentioned that Hardy had many flattering offers made to him, if he would go and settle in America,* and it is no wonder, on

* When Mr. Adams, the first Ambassador from the United States, was in this country, his son-in-law, Col. Smith, was his private Secretary. With that gentleman Hardy was very intimate, and supplied him with boots and shoes while he remained in England. Colonel Smith held out great encouragement to him if he would go and carry on his business in America. Hardy called on him one day, at the beginning of the London Corresponding Society, and shewed him the first Address, with which he was well pleased, and for his encouragement, said to Hardy, "Hardy, the Government will hang you." Though this prophecy was afterwards too near being fulfilled, yet he still lives a monument of the excellence of the TRIAL BY JURY.

his acquittal, finding himself pennyless, his whole property having been expended in defending himself from the base charges exhibited against him, and his trade totally ruined, in consequence of his imprisonment, that he should have formed a resolution of bidding an everlasting adieu to a country where he had been thus maltreated: to a country where he had been so incurably wounded in his dearest affections; where he saw the most exalted virtues treated as the greatest crimes; where he had been persecuted to the imminent danger of his life, for what he himself, and all such as he could consider upright men, deemed his *virtuous* efforts, to restore to his fellow countrymen the inestimable blessing of a FREE PARLIAMENT, fairly chosen by the people.[24] For these reasons, and they were sufficiently weighty, he finally determined to expatriate himself; but all human intentions must yield to the overruling power of the Omnipotent, who, in his wisdom, thought fit it should be otherwise. Though moneyless, he was not friendless; for, in fact, his friends were numerous, and some of them were sanguine in their hopes that, if he would recommence business in London, he would soon realize an independent fortune, which they said would prove some recompense, though an inadequate one, for all his wrongs and sufferings. He suffered himself, therefore, to be persuaded; altered his resolution, and recommenced business, in Tavistock Street, Covent Garden, on the 29th of November, 1794.

The public were certainly much interested in his favour; and the orders which he received, for the first two weeks, employed himself, and another man, merely to take measure, and to enter them in the book. Many paid for their orders at the time of giving them; some ordered two pair of shoes, and paid a guinea, and a few paid a guinea for one pair; and these the newspapers magnified to a thousand, at a guinea a pair. Multitudes of people, of all ranks and sexes, in carriages, and on foot, came to congratulate him; and crowds of persons were continually collected about the door and the windows, out of curiosity to see him. The shop, though large, was always full, from morning till night, and thus continued for, perhaps, two or three months, when it fell off gradually.

He employed, at first, six shopmen, to assist in carrying on the business; and it was, at one time, apparently encreasing; but when the public curiosity was satisfied, it began to decrease, and, at the end of six months, he found occasion for no more than two shopmen, and, within twelve months, for only one.

[24] Hardy's obituary in the *Times* gives a rather more graphic account of his emotional and physical reaction to his experiences: "The first use he made of his liberty was to proceed to the churchyard (St. Martin's) where his wife's remains were deposited. On approaching the grave he immediately fell and embraced the cold earth . . . he was lost in the agony of his grief; it was with difficulty that he could be removed; and such was the effect upon his wounded feelings and dilapidated frame and most 'constructively' destroyed prospects, that for a considerable time there were entertained apprehensions regarding his own life." (*Times*, 17 October 1832, p. 3.)

After his business had thus fallen to the level of ordinary trade, he found that, what with a large house, high rent, and high taxes, he was retrograding as rapidly as he had at first progressed. There were many unfounded reports spread abroad of the patronage which he received from a variety of quarters, which, though many wished and believed them true, operated greatly to his disadvantage. For instance, it was said, his landlord, the Duke of Bedford, had given him the house he inhabited rent free; that another nobleman had made him a present of five hundred pounds; and another had settled a hundred a year upon him. In consequence of these, and similar rumours, many gentlemen, who had intended to befriend him, thought it unnecessary, as they were led to believe he was already liberally provided for by the noble and the wealthy. They, therefore, turned their benevolence into other channels, and bestowed their favours upon others who they thought stood more in need of them—and, alas! many there were who had really need of support from the benevolent, at that time. So very injurious did these reports prove, that one of his leather merchants, in little more than a year, refused him credit. This was the son of the worthy Alderman Newman, who had so kindly called upon him the second day after his acquittal, and generously offered him credit, if he designed to go into business again, which kind offer he accepted. Another of his leather merchants actually served him with a copy of writ for a sum under ten pounds, which had been standing two months longer than the usual time of credit.

His journeymen, too, believing that he had greater profits on his goods than others had, struck for higher wages; but as they are a class of intelligent men, who can readily appreciate any question that is clearly stated to them, the following letter convinced them of the propriety of returning to their work at the same wages. The circumstance, however, which no doubt was owing to the unfounded stories which were afloat, was of some inconvenience to their employer, who was very busy at the time.[25]

36, *Tavistock Street*, 24*th April*, 1795.

"Fellow Citizens

"It is with no small degree of pain, I now address you on a subject of considerable importance to me, and, I think I may add, of no less importance to you, as a body.

[25] The London shoemaking trade at this time was based on a complicated division of labour with shoemakers specializing in many different types of shoe, and the various stages of manufacture again subdivided among different categories of journeymen. There was a basic division among the employers between small masters who gave irregular employment to at most a handful of journeymen and apprentices, and large shopkeeping masters who could employ a workforce of several hundred and become extremely wealthy. In the heady atmosphere which pervaded after his acquittal Hardy may have hoped that he was to make a permanent transition from the former to the latter category, but it was not to be, though he was later to be admitted to the Cordwainers Company which traditionally represented the large masters. The journeymen were known for their militancy but their capacity to

"I presume you are not unacquainted with the very peculiar situation I have been in since the beginning of last May. Six months of that time I was immured in a prison; and it must be fresh in the memory of every one of you the cruel persecution I suffered, and the probability there was of my being hurried from the prison to the scaffold; but thank God it has been ordered otherwise, for the happiness of individuals, and the peace of the nation. Immediately on my regaining my liberty, I had some thoughts of leaving that country in which I had been so maltreated; but I found a great number of my friends, and friends also to the happiness of mankind, solicitous that I should remain in London, and go into business again, as I might be sure of a very extensive trade among those who felt for my situation, and were friendly to the cause I had espoused and suffered for. Accordingly, I was prevailed upon, took the house I now occupy; and, certainly, I have done a great deal of business within the last five months. Numbers employed me from real friendship; some came to see me from motives of curiosity, and gave orders, whom it is not likely I shall ever see again. Others, who came from the mere novelty of the thing, honestly told me that they did not mean to continue after the first orders, but to return again to their old shoemakers: very few have given me a second order. The whole of my customers are among what is called the middling and lower class of the people, who cannot, or who do not choose to give a high price for their shoes and boots. They must, also, have them strong, or, to use a common phrase, they must have a pennyworth for their penny. Not so the generality of the higher ranks of society, who care not how light their goods are, nor how high the prices. I have to inform you that my price for boots is £1. 8*s*., and for shoes 8*s*. 6*d*.; some lower. When I opened this shop, I advanced the journeymen sixpence a pair on the shoes and boots above what I formerly used to give, which some of you may remember. Bootcloser's wages I also advanced.

"I have chosen to give you an open and candid statement of facts, which you, as a collective body, are to judge of betwixt me and those whom I formerly employed; and I think you have sufficient discernment to discover why I could not comply with the demand of my workmen.

"I ask no favour; I only wish for that which is just between man and man.—I have here to remark, that, according to my feeble ability, I have always been an enemy to all injustice and oppression, and for my opposition to them have suffered persecution; but I am still determined, as far as I can, to resist injustice or oppression, from whatever quarter they may be attempted, whether by my declared enemies, or my professed friends, though I should fall in the conflict.

---

sustain a high level of wages was undermined by the prevalence of piece-work and by increasing competition from cheap ready-made shoes imported from other parts of the country.

"These few hasty thoughts I leave to your deliberation; and if there is any thing which I have not stated of which you wish to be informed, I am ready to explain, or give every reasonable information in my power to any two or three intelligent men you may depute for that purpose. I conclude, with sincerely wishing you, and all mankind, health and fraternity.

"THOMAS HARDY."

To the Society of Journeymen
Boot and Shoemakers

Though this letter dispelled the delusion under which the journeymen had laboured, with respect to their employer's growing fortunes, yet others continued still in that delusion. Soon after the State Trials, in 1794, John Redman, Esq. of Hatton Garden, made a will, in which he put Hardy down for a legacy; but, in a subsequent one, made about four years afterwards, his name was omitted, for which no reason can be assigned, except that the testator, like many others, thought the bequest unnecessary. This is the more likely, as Mr. Redman, as long as he lived, continued to employ him as his shoemaker. A few days after that gentleman's death, Dr. Cooke called upon Hardy, in Fleet Street, and congratulated him upon the fortune that had been left him: though he did not then know but it might be true that such was the case, yet, having been amused with so many stories of great things, for some years past, he did not feel much elated at the intelligence. He merely thanked the Doctor for his good wishes, and observed, that if it was large it should be applied to benevolent purposes, and if small, it would assist him in carrying on his business, for he then had need of assistance—and if it should prove as unreal as the other gifts and legacies he had been promised, and said to have received, he could jog on his old way without it: for his happy temper enabled him to take all things very easy, whether adverse or prosperous. Another legacy, which *another gentleman* was reported to have left to him, turned out to be as unsubstantial as the last.

One disappointment, in the legacy way, is particularly worthy of remark. A gentleman, of large fortune, in Derbyshire, of the name of Kant, soon after the State Trials, in 1794, made his will, and in testimony of his approbation of the ability, patriotic exertions, and splendid eloquence, displayed by Mr. Erskine, in his defence of Hardy, bequeathed him an estate worth upwards of thirty thousand pounds. Hardy himself was, also, handsomely mentioned in the will, to which Mr. Kant afterwards added a codicil. He died about seven years afterwards, and his attorney came up to London with the will inclosed in a letter, written by the gentleman himself at the time of making it. After Mr. Erskine had read the letter, he asked the attorney if he had taken the proper legal steps to make the codicil valid. He replied, no: then said Mr. Erskine, "By God you have lost me the estate." Mr. Erskine sent for Hardy a few days afterwards, told him what had happened, and said that the will was void, through the ignorance, or villainy, of a stupid country attorney. Thus ended the last of the legacies.

That the rumours which were afloat, respecting the generous and liberal support which Hardy was receiving from the wealthy friends of liberty, should have been so readily, and so generally believed, may seem somewhat strange; but the following letters will, perhaps, in a great measure, account for some, if not for all of them. There the nucleus will be seen; and we know that rumour, in its nature, very much resembles a snow-ball, which gathers fresh matter rapidly as it rolls along.

"FRIEND LAUDERDALE,[26]

"I cannot help addressing you by that familiar and endearing title. You have boldly exerted yourself in defence of the rights, and done what you could to promote the happiness of the people, both in your place in the Senate, and on other public occasions, in opposition to an all-powerful and an all-devouring Oligarchy.—From such conduct, persevered in, you deserve the title of Friend to your country. When I have said this much, I am not sensible that I have said any thing more than the truth. Give me leave now to turn your attention to a few facts which concern myself, and which you have either forgotten, or are perhaps unacquainted with. Of some of those, however, I know you are not ignorant, and I think they cannot have escaped your memory.

"Upwards of two years ago, a few days after my acquittal from the charge of High Treason, Mr. Jaques, the coal merchant, called upon me with a message, to wait upon you the next evening. He told me, also, that he understood from you, that something handsome was to be done for me. This intelligence, no doubt, was very pleasing; especially from the quarter from which it came, and as my circumstances were then in such a state as required the assistance of friends. I readily embraced the flattering invitation; with a chearful heart I set off to wait upon you, and was soon admitted into the room where you, Colonel Maitland, and Dr. Moore,* were sitting. After some very friendly and familiar conversation about the trial, the treatment I met with during my confinement, the state of my mind during the trial, and my own opinion as to the event of it, with a variety of things, which were the common topics at that important period, important to me, at least. You then informed me that you, and several gentlemen, considering me as a very much injured and persecuted man, had determined to present me with a sum of money, in order to assist me

* The father of the brave General Sir John Moore.

[26] The Earl of Lauderdale (1759–1839) was a leading member of the small group of Foxite Whigs who were still putting up a token resistance to Pitt's campaign of repression. He was a founder of the Society of the Friends of the People and the father of the radical M.P. Colonel James Maitland.

in beginning business again, (as a proof of their sincerity.) You told me, at the same time, that you had already in your hands for this purpose no less a sum than one hundred pounds, and that next day you were going down to the Duke of Bedford's, where you expected to make it considerably more, from him and his friends. You desired me to call upon you the next day but one, when you would return from Woburn, and you would inform me what success you had. When I was about to depart, Colonel Maitland said to you, that you might as well let Hardy have that hundred pounds now, but I replied, that I had no immediate use for it just at that time, and that, until I got a house and shop, it might remain in your hands.—It was so settled, and I took my leave. Agreeably to your appointment, I did call on the next day but one, but it was said you was not at home. *Your Butler*, with whom I was intimate, informed me that it was your desire that I should call in the evening; I did so, but was told that you was just gone out. I was desired to call again in the morning, and even then you was engaged, and could not be spoken with. I was told, however, that if I came again in the evening, about six or seven o'clock, you would then be at leisure. I did call, but, as usual, you could not be seen; you had got company—so from morning to night, and from night to morning, alternately, for several weeks, did I continue this fruitless pursuit, till I was quite ashamed of being so troublesome to the servants. I felt, too, that the trouble I myself had was too much to intitle me to suppose, that I would at last be successful, notwithstanding your friendly and unsolicited professions towards me. I, therefore, determined to call no more, though I should beg for my daily bread. This resolution I formed and kept. I heard no more about that business till some time, I think, in last January, excepting from a variety of people, both in London, and from different parts of the country, and even from Ireland, who were profuse in their congratulations, on the many civilities and marks of friendship, which they were told I had received from you and the Duke of Bedford, &c.

"Some time in January, 1796, to the best of my recollection, I accidentally met with you, in company with Mr. Grey, and Mr. Tierney, at the Crown and Anchor Tavern: I dare say you may recollect the circumstance. You left them, and took me aside, and asked me very kindly how I did, and told me to call upon you next morning, or any other time that was most convenient, as you had forty pounds in your hands for me—twenty that Earl Derby gave, and twenty that you meant to give yourself; and that if I did not see you, Mr. Bowmaker, (your Steward,) would account with me. You then left me, and joined the company of Mr. Grey, and Mr. Tierney again, and went up stairs to the Whig Club Meeting. Two days afterwards I called at your house in Leicester Square, but received the same sort of answer which I had been accustomed to receive before. You was not at home. I called many times for several weeks, but could not meet with either you or Mr. Bowmaker; till at last, either by accident, or convenience, I know not which, neither is it material to me, I met with Mr. Bowmaker, and stopped with him about two hours conversing, very dryly, indeed, about the public news, &c. expecting every moment when he would mention something of the business to me, as I understood from your Butler you had made your Steward acquainted with it. When I found that he took no notice of it, and my patience being by this time exhausted, I mustered courage enough to inform him what you had told me at the Crown and Anchor Tavern. He replied that he did not know any thing of it, but that he should speak to you about it that same day, and desired me to call again the next morning. Agreeably to his appointment I called, expecting to meet with him, but he happened, also, not to be at home, but had informed the Butler that he had not an opportunity of speaking to his Lordship; but I was to call the next morning. Time after time was I put off with these sorts of answers, for several weeks, 'till at last I was told, (to save me the trouble of calling so frequently), that Mr. Bowmaker was going into the City, about two or three o'clock that same afternoon, and would call upon me as he passed.

"That answer, I assure you, was a considerable relief to me, for, at that period, time was a little more value to me than it is at present, or has been ever since; and as it left me without a pretence of again troubling you or your servants, I have ever since carefully avoided mentioning the subject.

"Various are the constructions which may be put upon the commencement, the progress, and the termination of this business, so far as you are individually concerned; I would really wish to put the most favourable construction upon it if I knew it; I cannot see how I can have deserved to be tantalized in the manner I have described, which is a literal statement of facts, of which you cannot be altogether ignorant. I have been buoyed up with the hope of friendship, and have found myself left in the possession of the name only; and the report of it throughout the nation, instead of being of service to me, has operated very materially to my injury. Many who I knew had designed to befriend me, hearing of your liberality, and that of others, were, in fact, induced to turn their civilities another way, concluding that a man who was so handsomely and powerfully supported by the rich and the noble, stood in no need of the countenance which their slender ability enabled them to bestow. One Nobleman, they were told, had given me a free house to live in—another had settled upon me a hundred a year for life—and a third had presented me with a purse of five hundred guineas; and a thousand stories, equally absurd, ridiculous, and improbable, were industriously spread abroad. Some people rejoiced at my good fortune, while others, of a different temper, were filled with envy at seeing fortune apparently smiling so abundantly upon me—and it was stated with confidence by all, that I should not have occasion to remain in business above two or three years; that I was making a fortune rapidly, &c.

Sorry am I to be obliged to say, that the contrary with me is a lamentable truth.

"Your proffered kindness certainly was unexpected, and unmerited on my part; but being so handsomely offered, and, after a lapse of two years, remaining unperformed, it appears to me that I cannot be too presuming in considering myself to have a fair claim to some sort of explanation; without this, I must be led to suppose that since the first time you spoke to me, some particular part of my conduct has deprived me of that esteem which I had flattered myself I possessed in your mind, and put a stop to those liberal and generous exertions in my behalf, which you were good enough to think my unjust persecution demanded; or, perhaps, you may have been led into the same error as many others, by believing what is so confidently, though falsely asserted, that I had such an overflow of business, that it was of little use either to assist or employ me. If those *real* friends, who, amidst the foolish and ridiculous reports that are so industriously circulated, did assist and employ me, and continue still so to do, had argued in this way, it is not difficult to conceive where I would have been long ere now.

"Whatever may have been your motives respecting me, from first to last, I hope I shall stand excused for troubling you with the perusal of this long address. I have ruminated, for some time, upon the propriety of this measure, and it has been with the utmost reluctance that I at last resolved upon it. In carrying that resolution into effect, I conceive that I am doing a duty to myself, by endeavouring to procure an explanation of a conduct for which I cannot account; and, perhaps, it may ultimately turn out that I am doing justice to you at the same time; for I cannot allow myself to imagine, that the facts which I have stated, (which have hitherto been buried in my own breast,) can lay claim to the sanction of your name.

"THOMAS HARDY.

23rd *January*, 1797. "36, *Tavistock Street*."

To the Earl of Lauderdale.

No notice was taken of this letter, until his Lordship was, two years afterwards, reminded of the circumstance, by the following letter.

"My Lord,

"It is by the desire and advice of some friends, to whom my situation and circumstances in life are no secret, and to whom I long since made known the promises, which, at different times, I have received from your Lordship, that I now address to you a few lines.

"I need not, I am sure, remind you, that when first you did me the favour of an interview, near four years ago, you assured me, in the presence of Dr. Moore, and Col. Maitland, that you had already received for me, from your friends, the sum of £100., in order to assist me in re-entering on my business; nor can there be occasion to say any thing respecting the second interview, when you told me that you had received £20. from the Earl of Derby for me. These sums, to you, are, no doubt, trifling, but to a person in my situation, struggling against difficulties, of which you can have no conception, they, (or either of them,) are of real moment.

"My friends have, therefore, urged me to recall these circumstances to your recollection, in the full persuasion that you will have the goodness, as speedily as may be, to direct your steward, or agent, to realise those expectations, which I was so confidently led to indulge from your promises. But if, (which I cannot well bring myself to believe,) I have been flattered with hopes of assistance, never to be afforded, or by assurances of sums of money, received for my use, which have never been subscribed, I hope it will not be reckoned too great a favour for me to expect, that the real state of the case may be fairly, and, at once, explained to me. I will only add, that I have formerly been told by Mr. Perry, who is supposed to be much in the secrets of those gentlemen with whom you act, that money had been raised for me; and that very lately, I could scarcely gain credit to my assertions, when being put into a situation, which obliged me to declare, that I had never received any assistance through your Lordship's hands."

"THOMAS HARDY.

August 24, 1798. "161, *Fleet Street*."

To the Earl of Lauderdale.

On the 4th of September following, Hardy received *forty pounds, twenty from the Earl of Lauderdale himself*, and twenty from the Earl of Derby, accompanied by the following Note.

"*Edin., Saturday.*

"Sir,

"I have this day received yours; I have always forgot to send you £40., which, however, I now enclose you; except Lord Derby, I could collect from nobody; it is, therefore, £20. from him, and £20. from myself. I am very ill in bed, and can hardly write.

"Yours, &c. &c.
LAUDERDALE.

"On reading your letter a second time, I see you say I had received £100. for you, in which you are completely wrong, £20. was the whole, and this, together with my own, you might have received at any time.

"Pray acknowledge the receipt."

On the receipt of this sum, Hardy wrote Notes of acknowledgment, of which the following are copies.

"My Lord,

"I received your letter, enclosing a draft for £40., £20. was from the Earl of Derby. Accept my warmest thanks for your Lordship's kindness to me. Sincerely hoping that your health may be speedily restored, and that your country may long be benefited by your exertions in the cause of public liberty and happiness,

"I remain, with great respect,
"Your obliged and obedient servant,
"THOMAS HARDY.

September 7, 1798. "161, *Fleet Street.*"
To the Earl of Lauderdale.

"My Lord,

"Having received £20. from your Lordship, through the hands of the Earl of Lauderdale, I beg leave to offer you my most grateful acknowledgments for this act of kindness. Be assured, that while I have life, I can never forget the goodness of those gentlemen who have so generously stepped forward to assist me in sustaining the difficulties in which I was involved by a public prosecution. Hoping that my country may long enjoy your exertions for her liberty and happiness,

"I remain, with the greatest respect,
"Your much obliged and obedient servant,
"THOMAS HARDY.

September 11, 1798. "161, *Fleet Street.*"
To the Earl of Derby.

While upon pecuniary matters, it will be proper to insert here the following correspondence, which took place between Thomas Hardy, The Right Honourable Henry Dundas, the Duke of Portland, and The King.

"Sir,

"On the 12th of May, 1794, various effects of mine were seized, and carried away from my house, No. 9, Piccadilly, by a messenger, under a warrant, bearing your signature. I make this application to you, to demand their immediate restitution.

"THOMAS HARDY.
"36, *Tavistock Street, Covent Garden.*
"*October* 12, 1796."

To the Right Hon. Henry Dundas.

"Sir,

"I repeat the demand which I made to you last week; namely, that you would restore to me immediately my property, which was seized in my house, No. 9, Piccadilly, on the 12th of May, 1794, by a warrant, bearing your signature.

"THOMAS HARDY.

"36, *Tavistock Street, Covent Garden*."

October 22, 1796.

To the Right Hon. Henry Dundas.

"MR. DUNDAS has received Mr. Hardy's letter, which he has transmitted to the Secretary of State for the Home Department, to whom the consideration of the subject exclusively belongs.

"*Parliament Street, Oct.* 23, 1796."

To Mr. Hardy,
36, *Tavistock Street.*

"THOMAS Hardy learns, by a note from Henry Dundas, dated the 30th of October, 1796, that the Secretary of State for the Home Department is acquainted with the demand which he made, by two applications, to Henry Dundas, (supposing him to be Secretary of State for the Home Department,) for the restoration of the property seized from him in his house, No. 9, Piccadilly, on the 12th of May, 1794, by a warrant, signed, Henry Dundas. Thomas Hardy has waited above a fortnight since the last application, and he now demands, from the Duke of Portland, as Secretary of State for the Home Department, that the property seized, under the above mentioned warrant, be immediately restored.

"36, *Tavistock Street, Covent Garden.*
"*November* 8, 1796."

To His Grace the Duke of Portland, Secretary of State for the Home Department.

TO THE KING IN COUNCIL.

"SIRE,

"YOUR Ministers have bereaved me of my wife and my child;—they have attempted to take away my life, and, failing in their plots, they have done every thing in their power to destroy my good name in society.—After such accumulated wrongs, my present complaint may be thought unworthy of notice. There was, indeed, a time when I could have addressed you as a father—a husband—a man—I could have called on you, on the pledge of these relations, to pity my sufferings;—that time is past:—I ask now only for justice;—I petition the King for justice; for I am too poor to obtain it in his courts of law.—Your Ministers have robbed me of my property—it is now in their hands. It is not enough that I languished in a gaol—that my small means were expended in my cause—that I was sent pennyless into the world.—Their malice was not contented—they withheld from me that which may appear trifling in your eyes, but is not so to a poor man. I have no other resource left, than to desire you, Sire, to command your Ministers to restore to me every thing which, by the warrant of the Secretary of State, was, on the 12th of May, 1794, taken from my house in Piccadilly.

"THOMAS HARDY.

"36, *Tavistock Street, Covent Garden.*

December 5, 1796.

"The King will perceive, by the subjoined correspondence between Thomas Hardy, Henry Dundas, and the Duke of Portland, that Thomas Hardy refrained from troubling the King till the necessity of the case could amply plead in his justification."

Having received no answer to this last application, he made several unsuccessful attempts to bring the business before Parliament. His want of success, in these attempts, was owing to the circumstance of Mr. Fox, and the other distinguished Members of the Opposition, having *withdrawn* from the House of Commons, which, according to the principles of our Constitution, ought, in a peculiar manner, to represent the people—as finding it in vain to oppose their integrity and splendid talents to the strong tide of corruption.[27] He, therefore, gave up all hopes of redress. Such was the result of the above correspondence, if correspondence that can be called, where the greater number of one party's letters are never answered by the other.

As a last resort, he published the whole correspondence, on the 13th of November, 1797, in the London Courier newspaper, that the public might see that no man's property nor person were safe, even in his own house, from the rapacity and lawless violence of men armed with usurped power. He was plundered of property of considerable value, among other things, of his pocket book, as already mentioned, which, with other papers, contained two inland bills of exchange: one of them was on J. Callender, for £136.; the other, for £60., was accepted by G. Sutton, Esq. M.P. and became due on the 25th of January, 1794. When it was presented for payment, he did not honour it; but declared that "he had not a sixpence to take it up with, and should not be in possession of money until June, when the Parliament would be prorogued!!" About a week afterwards, the bill was again presented, and the same answer returned; it was then that Hardy threatened to compel payment, to which Sutton's reply was, "You cannot arrest me; I am a Member of Parliament!!" Hardy then saw that there was no alternative but to wait until June, when the *Honourable Gentleman* should have received his half yearly salary, for voting on all questions as the Minister directed him: but before June, (12th May,) he and the bills were both secured, by the warrant of the Secretary of the State; and from that day to this he has not

[27] The Foxite Whigs withdrew from the House of Commons following the defeat of Grey's motion for Reform in May 1797.

seen the bills, nor any other part of the property he had been robbed of; nor has G. Sutton had the honesty to pay his bill that was then due.* This is but a small sample of the robberies committed by Mr. Pitt's Administration.

While speaking of robberies, sanctioned by legal sophistry, though not exactly in chronological order, this may not be an improper place to mention two instances in which Hardy was robbed without that sanction. A short time after his arrival in London, some thieves broke into his room, stole his clothes, and left him almost naked; but being then a single man, he soon procured more by his industry, and forgot his loss. The next instance was a little more serious: the first Christmas after he was married, the same description of lawless people broke into his house, when he and Mrs. Hardy were visiting at a friend's house, took all their clothes, and almost stripped the shop of its contents of boots and shoes. He was thankful that they had left the bed and clothes behind. By persevering industry he overcame this loss also; and after struggling some years against wind and tide, to use a seaman's phrase, he had the harbour of prosperity full in view, when he was attacked by more powerful *Buccaneers;* or, to drop the metaphor, when he was plundered by thieves of a worse description, under the authority of GEORGE THE THIRD'S PRIVY COUNCIL!

When his property was completely destroyed, his person nearly sacrificed to their wicked designs, and he was again sent into the world almost as bare as he came into it, without a home, and without the dear partner of his joys and sorrows to welcome him, and to rejoice in his escape from a cruel, sanguinary, and unjust prosecution. This is repetition, but the wrongs which have called it forth were repeated; and, surely, the magnitude of those wrongs may well plead an excuse for it.

It is already manifest, that the stories so commonly believed of the Eldorado that was pouring in upon him in Tavistock Street, were entirely without foundation. These rumours gave rise, however, to one thing which grieved him very much, because it was impossible for him to act according to his inclination in respect to it. He received many letters and petitions from poor distressed people, to which it was out of his power, in all instances to attend. To many of the most distressing he did attend, but it was painful to his mind to be obliged to dismiss others with only his good wishes, which was like saying to them, in the language of Scripture, "Be ye warmed, and be ye filled."

* The reader will recollect that this was written in 1796. On Mr. Margarot's departure for Botany Bay, where he was sent, it cannot be too often repeated, for fourteen years, by the arbitrary and unjust sentence of the Court of Justiciary, he left the two bills with Hardy; and, on his return, after seventeen years absence, he applied to Mr. Litchfield, Secretary to the Treasury, for the two bills, or payment for them. After a good deal of searching and enquiries, they could not be found; and Mr. Margarot insisted on payment, or else he would lay his case before Parliament. Probably Government considered it better to pay the money privately, than to bring so disagreeable and disgraceful a subject, then partially forgotten, again before the public. Be that as it may, Margarot got his money from Government.

But the public delusion did not confine itself to pecuniary matters alone. Hardy was exalted, by public credulity, to a level with the first practitioners of the law, and, strange as it may appear, many persons, and among them, some men of learning and ability, applied to him for the solution of some very knotty perplexities, and intricate points of law; conceiving, no doubt, that as he had passed unhurt through such an ordeal, he must be a very clever fellow. Some of them did not know that he was only a shoemaker, and incapable of giving an opinion on any point of law. To all that applied to him about law, his uniform advice was, not to go to law upon any account, when it was possible to avoid it.

Whatever difficulties he had to struggle with, during the latter part of his time in Tavistock Street, he did not, for some time, communicate to any of his friends, otherwise they would have readily relieved him. Indeed, had his particular friends given ear to the absurd stories that were in circulation, and, in consequence, neglected to support him with their custom, he would have found himself, at the end of two years, worse off than ever; but, fortunately for him, they were too much of matter of fact men to be so misled. He had many real friends, even among those who differed widely from him in political opinions. These candidly told him, that they did not employ him on account of his politics, but because they thought him a persecuted and injured man. He refused money, at the time of his recommencing business, out of delicacy, from gentlemen, who, no doubt, offered it generously and freely. Such refusals, he had afterwards reason to believe, were construed to his disadvantage. Towards these gentlemen, however, he felt, and confessed his gratitude, as much as if he had availed himself of their favours.

A gentleman in Fish Street Hill, whose name we are not at liberty to mention, sent his son, two or three days after Hardy had settled in Tavistock Street, with ten guineas, saying that it might be useful to him in his then circumstances, and that he would call and have a pair of boots or shoes when he wanted them. The young man called several times, but would not tell his name nor residence, and it was near a year afterwards that it was discovered. Before that sum was worked out, he sent another ten guineas, and another equal sum before that was worked out. Some time afterwards he sent twenty guineas, and so on, always taking care to send a sum of money before the last was worked out. Himself, and his sons, two fine young gentlemen, continued to employ him as long as he remained in business; but to this day he will not allow his name to be mentioned, as it ought to be, a FRIEND. To another particular friend, in Lombard Street, he is much indebted, whom, as well as several others, we wish we were at liberty to name.

One thing, however, though it did not exactly balance the benefits accruing from the patronage of his real friends, was much against him at this period. A number of persons who *called* themselves his friends, and professed great zeal in the cause of Parliamentary Reform, employed, but have omitted to pay him to this day. Others borrowed money, and proved equally forgetful. The sums lost by this class of *pretended* friends, amounted, in the first year, to upwards of three hundred pounds, and has since encreased to a much greater sum. He was blamed for giving credit to such persons; but it is not easy to distinguish between the sincere and the designing: experience alone will teach this. Besides, he was himself naturally sincere and unsuspicious, which exposed him, more than men of a different character, to these sorts of depredations; and if such qualities are at all censurable, it must be confessed that there is a good deal of censure due to him.

Next to his pretended friends, may be ranged those who were covertly, and those who openly professed themselves his enemies; for though the tide of public opinion ran strongly in his favour, it could not be expected that the tools of his persecutors would refrain altogether from abuse. Accordingly he was attacked, by the hireling Ministerial press, in newspapers, and anonymous pamphlets; and although one would hardly think it possible, who did not know the constitution of that House in Mr. Pitt's days, there were Members of Parliament found possessed of so little decency and common sense, as, in their places in the House of Commons, to apply the most unjustifiable epithets to him, and the other prisoners who had been honourably acquitted. The newspapers did not stick at any falsehood. The following extract is a fair, or rather foul, specimen of the methods which they pursued, to injure the character of a man, who, certainly, never did any thing to deserve such treatment at their hands.

"TO THE EDITOR OF THE COURIER.

"Sir

"On Wednesday, the 25th of October, the following Letter, and Statement, by '*An Old Inhabitant of Fleet Street,*' appeared in the '*True Briton.*' Knowing the greater part of the statement to be absolutely false, and having good reason to suppose it a malicious attempt to injure me in the opinion of the public, I thought it a duty which I owed to my friends, as well as to myself, to expose its falsehood and its malice; and accordingly desired the Editor of that Paper to insert the following Letter, which, however, he refused to do. I have, therefore, to request *you*, as a REAL friend to Truth, to assist me in rescuing my character from the attack of a malignant and cowardly Assassin, by giving a place in '*The Courier,*' to the following Letter, from,

"Sir,
"Your constant Reader,
"THOMAS HARDY."

"TO THE EDITOR OF THE TRUE BRITON.

"Sir,

"Not being in the habit of reading your Paper, I did not see the following Letter, and pretended Statement, which appeared in it on Wednesday last, till two or three days afterwards, when it was shewn to me by a friend.—I do not wish to obtrude myself unnecessarily on the notice of the public; but I feel it a duty which, as a member of Society, I owe to myself, to repel an ill-founded, and apparently malicious and cowardly attack upon my character, in as public a manner as it has been made. I claim, therefore, from you, as a matter of right, that you will re-insert in your Paper the Letter and the Statement, together with the answer and observations which I have subjoined. I claim this as a right, which you cannot refuse me, consistently with your duty, as the Conductor of a Public Print, more especially of a Print which, by its title, assumes to itself the peculiar character of '*True.*'

"RIOT IN FLEET STREET.

"TO THE EDITOR OF THE TRUE BRITON.

"SIR,

"THE Riot at *Citizen* HARDY's house, in Fleet Street, having been the subject of much conversation, and but imperfectly represented in the Public Prints, I send you the following Statement, which I, as an Eye-Witness to the whole proceeding, can assure you is authentic.

"I am, Sir, your constant Reader,
"And very humble Servant,
"AN OLD INHABITANT OF FLEET STREET."

October 20, 1797.

"On Friday evening, the 13th instant, when the first account arrived of the glorious and truly important victory, gained by the gallant Admiral Duncan over the Dutch Fleet,[28] a number of people paraded the streets, calling for 'Lights,' &c. A party of them being assembled at Drury Lane Theatre, for the same purpose, three or four *ill-looking fellows* began to harangue them on the impropriety of rejoicing at an event, which, they said, "would only tend to prolong the War;" and one of those *Seditious Emissaries* struck a lad a violent blow on the head with a bludgeon, merely for saying 'DUNCAN for ever!—No Jacobins!'—The Mob then surrounded them; and on examination they proved to be *Citizens* ASHLEY, HARDY, and others, Members of the *London Corresponding Society.* The people then expressed their indignation at these *spiteful Pseudo Reformers*, in a violent manner, and saluted them with hisses and groans, which were but a prelude to a shower of stones, mud, &c. which obliged the *Gentlemen* to decamp towards Prince's Street, with great precipitation, amidst the execrations of the spectators. Being *rather quick* in their flight, they escaped; and, *like men of courage, when out of danger*, they *valiantly* knocked down an aged and decrepid mendicant, and two or three boys, who were amusing themselves by letting off fireworks, and, like *victorious heroes*, they triumphantly marched off.

[28] The destruction of de Winter's invasion fleet at Camperdown on 11 October.

"The account of this *gallant action* was immediately carried to the Mob, who vowed revenge; but on Saturday night the *victorious Citizens* rested in peace. On Monday night, *Citizen* HARDY's house was filled with a set of Ruffians, armed with cutlasses, sword-sticks, bludgeons, &c. calling themselves Constables! Every house in Fleet Street was illuminated, except *Citizen* HARDY's; of course a number of people collected opposite his house, and called for 'Lights!' The Ruffians inside immediately sallied out, and indiscriminately assaulted every person who had not the good fortune to escape. After the first shock, however, the Mob rallied, and growing formidable, by increase of numbers, they repelled the *Corresponding Army*, and broke most of *Citizen* HARDY's windows, amidst the cries of 'DUNCAN for ever! HARDY for ever! No Jacobins! No Lights, &c. &c. &c.'

"*Citizen* HARDY, finding his reforming sham Constables of no service, sent for the Military, and the Mob dispersed. This is a true statement of the affair: and it is hoped the Magistrates will prevent the *Corresponding Constables* from *breeding another riot*, as they were the sole cause of that above related."

"It may be true, for ought I know to the contrary, that the Riot at my house has been *imperfectly* represented in the public Prints; but I can take upon myself to say, that no other representation of it has been so replete with falsehood as that which is given in the above statement by 'An Old Inhabitant of Fleet Street,' which he, as an eye-witness to the whole proceeding, *says* he can assure you is authentic.

"Of my *own* positive knowledge, this statement is so far from being authentic, and such as an eye-witness who had any regard to truth would have given, that the greatest part of what relates to *me* is absolutely false; and, judging as a plain man of mere common sense, I believe that by far the greater part of the *whole* is a malicious fiction.

"It *may* be true, that a party of those who paraded the streets on Friday evening, the 13th instant, calling for 'Lights,' may have assembled at Drury Lane Theatre for that purpose; and it may possibly be true, though I do not believe it, because it is not probable that three or four such persons as this eye-witness calls *ill-looking fellows*, and *seditious emissaries*, may have begun to harangue the *mob*, on the impropriety of rejoicing at an event which, they said, 'would only tend to prolong the war:' but I am sure it cannot be true, that 'one of them struck a lad a violent blow on the head with a bludgeon,' merely for saying 'DUNCAN for ever! No Jacobins.' The men whom this 'Old Inhabitant' stigmatizes with the name of *seditious emissaries*, are not accustomed to carry *bludgeons*, or to use the arguments of *blows:* they leave such practices, and such conduct, to the *mob*, of which, if I may judge from the spirit of his statement, this eye-witness, probably, makes now and then a distinguished member. For the same reasons, I am sure it cannot be true, that these three or four *ill-looking fellows* afterwards 'knocked down an aged and decrepid mendicant, and two or three boys who were amusing themselves by letting off fireworks.'—The whole of this story carries in itself its own refutation. The ill-looking fellows are described to be only *three* or *four:* had their number been so small, it needed not to have been put in the alternative; an eye-witness to the whole proceedings might have stated precisely the exact number; but taking them to be *four,* it is not likely that one of so small a number, even of such *valiant* heroes, would have ventured to strike a lad a blow on the head with a bludgeon, in the presence of a *mob,* who are described to have been so numerous as to *surround* them; nor is it likely that when thus *surrounded,* and discovered to be *Citizens* ASHLEY, HARDY, &c. they would have been *permitted* to *escape* without some personal marks of mobish vengeance for the violent blow in the head with a bludgeon. The 'Old Inhabitant of Fleet Street,' indeed, states, that the hisses and groans with which they were at first saluted, were but a prelude to a shower of stones, mud, &c. which obliged the *gentlemen* to decamp with great precipitation; but how does he reconcile this to what he had just before related, that the mob *surrounded* them, and that, on *examination,* they were discovered to be *Citizens* ASHLEY, HARDY, &c.? If they were *surrounded,* and *examined,* there was hardly occasion for a shower of *stones, mud,* &c. which rather implies that the *ill-looking fellows* were at a *distance* from the mob: had they been *surrounded,* and *examined,* it is more probable they would have been *bludgeoned* than *stoned:* but, supposing them to have been *surrounded,* it must have required something more than *mere quickness* of *flight* to enable them to escape; they must have used something more *valiant* than swiftness of foot to break the *ring* with which they were *surrounded:* but the eye-witness says nothing of that kind. Suppose, however, they escaped, and knocked down the mendicant and the boys, how was the account of this *gallant action* immediately conveyed to the mob? Did the eye-witness, endowed with *quickness* of *pursuit,* equal to the *ill-looking fellows' quickness* of *flight,* convey the hasty intelligence? But the 'intelligence' was immediately conveyed to the mob, and the mob vowed revenge.' Had this been the case, it is probable that the *victorious Citizens,* instead of resting in peace on *Saturday* night, and enjoying their *triumph* till Monday, would, on *Friday* night, have suffered the threatened *revenge.*—So much for the *probability* of this 'authentic' account.

"The fact, so far as I am myself concerned, is this:—I do not *know* that there were either illuminations, or mob, on the evening of Friday the 13th, but by information which I have received since; and I was not, the whole of that evening, beyond the threshold of my own door; and, notwithstanding the confident assertion of the 'eye-witness to the whole proceeding,' who would have you suppose he is so well acquainted with my *person,* I was not one of the *three* or *four ill-looking fellows* surrounded, and *examined* by the mob at Drury Lane Theatre: and I am sure that the 'Old Inhabitant of Fleet Street,' if his countenance bears any relationship either to the wickedness of his heart, or to the weakness of his head, would, on examination, be found the *worse-looking fellow* of the two.

"Of the next paragraph, which pretends to state the transaction of Monday night, every syllable which relates to *me* is false, excepting the few words of it which state that most of my windows were broken. During the whole of Monday, the 15th instant, there certainly was not one *ruffian* in my house, unless the 'Old Inhabitant of Fleet Street' may have been there. I do not know, but from subsequent information, that every house in Fleet Street, but my own, was illuminated; but I know, that that exception gave no right to a lawless mob to break my windows to pieces. The fact is, that a mob, whether *composed* of such persons as the 'Old Inhabitant of Fleet Street', or *instigated* by such persons, did on that evening begin to collect about my door, and to express a disposition to riot: about eight o'clock, therefore, an hour before my usual time, I had my shop shut up, to prevent the windows of it being broken through. There was not at any time, nor till a considerable time after, any person in my house but myself and my ordinary inmates. I had formed no positive determination as to illuminating or not, till a little before nine o'clock, when hearing a violent knocking at the street door, I went down stairs and opened it; a considerable number of people were there; I asked what they wanted; a baker's man asked me if I did not intend to illuminate; I told him he had no right to ask me that question, and desired him to go about his business: a voice from the crowd cried out, 'That's right, HARDY; don't illuminate;' on which I shut the door. It *might* have been *prudent* for me, in the *first instance*, to illuminate; but I did not like the idea of compulsion: I do not relish the government of a mob, though I cannot say I rejoice much in the success of a war which its abettors pretend to have been undertaken for the purpose of suppressing anarchy and confusion.—From the mixed cries of 'DUNCAN for ever,' and 'HARDY for ever,' I supposed the crowd was composed of different sets of people; and I have since been told, and I believe it to be true, that a number of my friends, apprehensive that my person and property were in danger, assembled from different quarters, with a determination, at the risk of their lives, to defend both; and I have understood that they did so most manfully; but there was no person in my house, ruffian, or otherwise, armed with cutlass, sword-stick, or bludgeon, or that assumed the character of constable. It is true that after the affair was over, some of my friends were received into the house, and partook of such sober refreshment as it afforded; and this circumstance, perhaps, the eye-witness, if indeed he had *any fact* in contemplation, has converted into an assertion, that on Monday night my house was filled with a set of ruffians, armed with cutlasses, sword-sticks, bludgeons, &c. calling themselves constables! To my friends, on that occasion, I am assuredly much indebted. A few *such* trusty friends, on a similar occasion, on the 11th of June, 1794, might probably have prevented the fatal effect which afterwards ensued: the candles which were then placed in my windows proved NO PROTECTION to the HELPLESS and the INNOCENT! and I have had too much experience of the wicked and persecuting spirit of such men as the 'Old Inhabitant of Fleet Street,' not to be satisfied that a few candles placed in my windows, would have proved at least as feeble a protection on the *late* occasion as they did on the *former*.

" '*Citizen* HARDY,' says the 'Old Inhabitant of Fleet Street,' 'finding his sham constables of no service, sent for the military, and the *mob* dispersed.' —It is true, that when the conduct of the misguided populace gave me every reason to suppose that nothing short of making one grand illumination of my house was their diabolical object, I did, less from personal consideration than to render easy the minds of my neighbours, send for a party of the London Militia, who did not, however, arrive till after the contest was decided in favour of my friends. Notwithstanding this, I think it an act of justice due to the Gentleman to whom the application was made, to state his conduct on that occasion:—Sir WATKIN LEWES, to whom my friend carried my message, had a Military Officer with him. When my friend explained his business, this Officer said, 'I suppose Mr. HARDY has put no lights in his windows; go home and tell him to put lights in his windows, and the mob will disperse.' Sir WATKIN LEWES prevented my friend's reply by saying, 'Sir, we have nothing to do with a man's political principles; our duty is to protect every Citizen of London who requires our protection; tell Mr. HARDY that I shall send the Guard immediately.'

"The 'Old Inhabitant' concludes with a hope, that 'the *Magistrates* will prevent the *Corresponding Constables* from *breeding* another riot, as *they* were the sole cause of the above related.' I am not disposed to quibble on the structure of a sentence, or I might accuse the 'Old Inhabitant' of asserting that the *Magistrates* were the sole cause of the riot. I impute no fault to the Magistrates; had they suspected an intention to produce one, they probably would have prevented it; and I hope, that if, unfortunately, any peaceable inhabitant of this City shall hereafter be so shamefully attacked as I have been, the Magistrates will shew that the Police of the City does not permit such outrages to pass with impunity. There is no doubt but the 'Old Inhabitant' means to assert, that those whom he calls the *Corresponding Constables* were the cause of the riot. The assertion is absolutely false, and *maliciously* false: the riot was most unquestionably *bred* by such men as the 'Old Inhabitant,' who seem to know no better mode of supporting *order* and *regular* Government than by encouraging the disorders of an unruly mob!"[29]

"THOMAS HARDY,

October 30, 1797. "*No.* 161, *Fleet Street.*"

[29] Hardy's version of the conflict is supported by an account in the autobiography of another L.C.S. member, John Binns, although according to Binns, the defence of the house was more organized than Hardy suggests: "On the night to which I refer, Hardy would not

But his traducers did not confine their abuse to pamphlets and papers; they gave vent to it on all possible occasions. A single instance of this kind, as it is rather a laughable one, may be mentioned. In the Summer of 1795, when his business became so slack as to admit of his absence for a short time, he took a journey to Leicester, at the invitation of several friends then personally unknown to him, but from whom he had received considerable orders before. At Northampton, one gentleman, who had travelled in the coach from London, left, and another took his place. This latter gentleman happened to take up one of Hardy's shop cards, which a lady had laid down on the parlour table where the passengers breakfasted. As soon as he perceived what it was, he threw it down again with the greatest indignation, accompanying the action with some indecent and opprobrious expressions not fit to be repeated; and added, that the jury which had acquitted him consisted of a set of villains, &c. One of the ladies present, observed, that he subjected himself to severe punishment, by animadverting, in such unbecoming terms, on the decision of an English jury. This reproof silenced him, and he spoke very little more during the journey. When he did speak a few words, it was in such a cross and ill-natured manner that he became a subject of amusement to the passengers. The rest of the company were very cheerful, and the silent gentleman's remarks, and the ready and well-merited reproof which these remarks had received, introduced the trials as the subject of conversation, in which Hardy, who was personally unknown to any of the company, joined.

When the passengers were parting at the Bell Inn, Leicester, he stepped up to the crabbed gentleman, took him by the hand, and said to him, "Friend, be so good as to tell your acquaintance, that you have had the mortification to travel in the same coach with that Hardy whom you have been so illiberally abusing. I am that Hardy—farewell!" He stood with astonishment, and went away without saying a word, to all appearance, really mortified; to the great amusement of the other passengers.

Mr. Phillips, now Sir Richard, the bookseller, then resident in Leicester,[30]

---

allow his windows to be illuminated, and they were not only threatened to be broken, but the more radical royalists declared they would sack his home. These threatenings were noised abroad, and about 100 men, chiefly members of the society, many of them Irish, armed with good shillelahs, took post early in the evening in front of and close to the front of Hardy's home. As night approached, an immense crowd gathered in the street; many and violent were the attacks and efforts made to get possession of the house, and many were the wounds inflicted by fists and sticks. There were no fire-arms used nor stones thrown, except at the windows. About 11 o'clock at night a troop of horse were sent to keep the peace, and soon after the crowd dispersed. I never was in so long-continued and well-conducted a fight as was that night made by those who defended Hardy's house against such overwhelming numbers." (John Binns, *Recollections of the Life of John Binns*, Philadelphia, 1854, pp. 42–3.)

[30] Richard Phillips opened a bookshop in Leicester in 1790 and in 1792 founded the *Leicester Herald* as a platform for his radical views. He was sentenced to 18 months imprisonment in January 1793 for selling Paine's *Rights of Man*, and a year after Hardy's visit moved to London where he founded the *Monthly Magazine*, to which Hardy regularly contributed during the first two decades of the nineteenth century.

was the first who called upon, and introduced him to many other kind friends. The next day he set out for Nottingham, with his good friend, Thomas Simpson, to whom he was introduced by Mr. Phillips. At Nottingham he remained a week, and was kindly and hospitably treated by some of the principal people of the town, from whom he received considerable orders.

From Nottingham he crossed the country to Derby, where he stayed two or three days with some friends, and then returned to London, highly pleased with his journey.

The next Summer he took a journey to Suffolk, and stayed a few days at Bury St. Edmunds, where he was kindly received by Mr. Buck, Mr. Vardy, and several other friends. From Bury he went to Norwich, where he met with some friends whom he knew, and by whom he was introduced to many others, some of them the principal people of the town, who treated him with particular kindness and attention. He next went to Yarmouth, and returned to London by Woodbridge, and Ipswich, at each of which places he met with such civilities and kindness as he never can forget.

Finding that he could not, with any hopes of advantage, continue in such an unfrequented situation as that in which he had recommenced business, he removed into Fleet Street, in September, 1797. There he became a Freeman of the Cordwainers Company, and Liveryman of the Needlemakers Company, and carried on his business with some success until 1815, when he retired; in what circumstances will appear sufficiently plain from the following correspondence.

"Dear Sir,

"I shall never forget the kindly manner in which you expressed your wish to serve me, when I had the pleasure of meeting you in the Committee Room, during the last election; and it was to me quite unexpected. I am sensible that you will excuse me for troubling you with the following facts, which concern myself, and which I shall state as briefly as possible. A few years before I left Fleet Street, I found my business gradually declining, owing to several causes. The general failure of trade, and bankruptcy of tradesmen about that time, the great cause of which, many worthy men, and their families knew, and felt to their sorrowful experience. Of the consequences of that general calamity I had my share, for almost every month I suffered a loss, less or more, by bankrupts, or by some compounding with their creditors, and by others exiling themselves. I had also outlived so many of my friends, who were in the habit of employing me, but who had passed that bourne from whence no traveller returns; and, likewise, my getting old, and old fashioned, so that I could not keep up with the rapid changes of fashion which the young require, and are fond of, and which it is quite necessary for tradesmen to attend to, however trifling they may be. In the last year or two, my difficulties rapidly increased, and I also found my health much impaired, from anxiety, losses, and crosses, which at last decided me to wind up my business, and dispose of it in the best way I could, while I had some little property remaining. I made no one acquainted with my circumstances, and I believe no one suspected that I was going behind; for with those with whom I had any dealings, my payments were regular, although, towards the close, I had great difficulty to keep my credit good. It was always a happy thing for me that my wants were few, and they are still diminishing, and my family small, only my dear Sister and myself. After collecting all debts due to me that I could possibly get, which amounted to but a small sum, compared to the debts now totally lost, some from real inability to pay, and others from causes not so excusable: when I had disposed of all belonging to the business, with the lease of the house, and settled all claims on me, *I retired*, at Midsummer, 1815, with a clear £700. The next consideration was, how this sum was to be disposed of to the best advantage for our future subsistence. It was too small a sum with which to purchase an annuity for myself and Sister. I therefore calculated, that from the then state of my health, that my life was apparently fast drawing to a close, and that by confining my expenses, so as not to exceed £100. a year, as having no other income, it would be more, perhaps, than sufficient, without being troublesome to my friends, for I was very unwilling to let my situation or circumstances be known. But when I was relieved from the cares, perplexities, and precariousness of a losing concern, my mind became easy and contented, and I soon recovered my health. And now, upwards of seven years and a half afterwards, there is but a little of the £700. remaining; but, perhaps, it may be enough; for if I see the third of next month, March, I shall then enter on my 72d year. And when I take a review of past occurrences, I find that I have abundant cause to be grateful.

"Be so good, dear Sir, to accept of my sincere wish, that you may long live in health and happiness, to enjoy the beneficial effects, which I hope are beginning to appear, of your long and honest efforts, with others, to benefit your country.

"THOMAS HARDY,
"30, *Queen's Row, Pimlico.*"

4th February, 1823.
To Sir Francis Burdett, Bart.

"DEAR HARDY,

"I SHALL have great pleasure in rendering you assistance, having great regard for you, as an honest, sensible, ill-treated man. I wish you to be more explicit as to your desires, and, in the mean time, beg of you to accept the enclosed*

"With great regard,
"F. BURDETT."

St. James's Place, February 8th, 1823.

*£10.

"*St. James's Place, May 9th*, 1823.

"Dear Hardy,

"I told you long ago to set your mind at rest, and have written a line to Mr. Friend,[31] in answer to one he sent me concerning you. I propose to him to get an annuity for you of £100. a year, which I take to be about as much as would make you and your Sister comfortable; I will advance one half, and five other persons who know and respect your understanding and integrity, will advance £10. a piece. The money will be placed in Mr. Friend's hands, and you will be pleased to draw it out just as you have occasion for it.

"I am laid up with the gout, which makes writing painful, but would not lose a moment in setting your mind at ease. I hope your Sister is well.

"Yours, very sincerely,

"F. BURDETT."

"Dear Sir,

"I do assure you it is with grateful satisfaction I have to acknowledge your liberality to me, as mentioned in your letter on Friday last. From the moment you told me to make my mind easy respecting my future subsistence, and knowing so well your disposition to do good, I was sure that you would fulfil your benevolent intentions, therefore I hope you will excuse me when I state that my writing to Mr. Friend, afterwards, did not arise from any doubt on that head, but because I thought that the burden of my support ought not to rest on one friend only, however able and willing that friend may be. A few minutes after I received yours on Friday, I had a note, by the twopenny post, from Mr. Friend, desiring me to call on him. I have not yet seen him, for I have not been out for this week past; but as the weather is getting more favourable for invalids, I hope to be able to call on him in a few days. Will you be so good as to offer to those five Gentlemen whom you mentioned, my sincere thanks for their kindness to me. I hope you are now fast recovering, and have dislodged that troublesome and cruel enemy the gout. Be so good, dear Sir, as to accept my sincere good wishes for a speedy restoration of your health.

"THOMAS HARDY."

To Sir Francis Burdett, Bart. 14*th May*, 1823.

"Dear Sir,

"I cannot help troubling you with a few lines at this time, which I hope you will excuse. God knows whether I may have another opportunity to offer my grateful acknowledgement for your annual kindness to me, for these five years now closed. I have now, on the 3rd of last March, entered on the 77th year of my journey of life, for which I have great reason to be grateful to a gracious God, who has preserved and protected me during

[31] i.e. Rev. William Frend.

so long a period, and blessed me with so many kind friends, and in some perilous circumstances too. Even this 29th of May, 1794, is memorable as the anniversary of my being sent to the *Tower;* some of my valued friends who are no more, having been sent before me to that *Fortress*, all on a charge of High Treason, by a Privy Council of erring men; so that I am now thirty-four years older than they intended that I should be.

"I beg now to state, for your information, the amount of the different sums which I have drawn for yearly, from my kind friend *Mr. Friend*, who was good enough to take the troublesome office of Treasurer, but has now transferred it to my friend, *Mr. Place*, for what reason I do not know. I fear that it may be I had drawn too much from the account, or for some other impropriety on my part; if it be so, I am very sorry for it. My frequent applications to him were always readily answered, without a hint of that sort.

"Received from Mr. Friend, at several times from the 1st of May, 1823, to May, 1824	£100	0	0
"Ditto, Ditto, 1st of May, 1824, to May, 1825	100	0	0
"Ditto, Ditto, May, 1825, to May, 1826	130	0	0
"Ditto, Ditto, May, 1826, to May, 1827	120	0	0
"Ditto, from Mr. Place, altered to the 1st of June, 1827, to June, 1828	109	12	0

"I have now, Dear Sir, to beg that you will be so good to accept my sincere best wishes that you may long enjoy excellent health, and that you may be able to advocate, with success, the great cause of Civil Liberty, and the happiness of your country and your fellow men, as you have hitherto done.

"THOMAS HARDY."

29*th May*, 1828.
To Sir Francis Burdett, Bart.

"DEAR SIR,

"I HOPE you are quite well. I congratulate you on the pleasing prospect before us, which I hope we shall before long fully enjoy, that great national blessing—a *Parliamentary Reform*, which your great talents, years ago, were often exerted to obtain. Although not then successful, yet your efforts were not lost, for you then sowed abundance of good seed, which has been springing up ever since, and which I hope will now produce a plentiful harvest for the benefit of your fellow countrymen. I am much pleased with the present Government; I believe they are sincere, and will be active in their exertions to promote that great object to its completion. I am pleased to see so many converts to the important cause of Parliamentary Reform; some from conviction of its justice, and others from necessity. I hope the Ministers will be well supported by all the *old* and *true* Reformers. Perhaps, you may smile when I tell you, that I am now, *for the first time*, in my humble measure, a supporter of Ministers. I greatly rejoice to see the great cause of Civil Liberty prospering, not only in this country, but all over Europe, and that I have lived so many years to witness it, having entered on the 80th year of my journey of life, the 3rd of this month of March. I hope you will excuse me for troubling you with this, and accept my best wishes that you may enjoy long life in health and happiness.

"THOMAS HARDY,

7th March, 1831. "30, *Queen's Row, Pimlico*."

Sir Francis Burdett, Bart. M.P.

To this correspondence with the most upright, most intrepid, and most persevering Statesman of our own country, may appositely succeed the following Letter from Hardy to Lafayette, with that great and eminently virtuous man's answer.

"DEAR AND RESPECTED SIR,

"ALTHOUGH I have not had the happiness to see you, yet you are no stranger to me, for I have followed you in all your preregrinations with my good wishes, high approbation, and esteem, for your unwearied exertions to promote the happiness of your fellow men. Ever since the beginning of the American Revolution, I remember well your laudable efforts, together with that extraordinary man Washington, to gain that great object for which the brave Americans were contending—their emancipation from a foreign yoke, which they at last effected; and now they are a great and prosperous nation. I have great pleasure to remark, that you and I have been fellow labourers in the great cause of Civil Liberty, ever since that important period. We may now be permitted to rejoice together with the great body of the friends of liberty, that their honest efforts have not been lost. It was a maxim of the celebrated Reformer, Dr. John Jebb, that *no effort is lost*. Permit me now to congratulate you on the late glorious Revolution in France, in July last; it has no parallel in ancient or modern history. I also well remember the first Revolution in France, about forty years ago; and I am very happy when I recollect that I was instrumental in sending the *first* Congratulatory Address from this country, from *The London Corresponding Society*, to the *National Convention of France*, with which they appeared to be so well pleased, that it was read in the Convention, ordered to be printed, sent to the eighty-four Departments, and to be read at the head of the Armies of France. When the Paris newspapers, having that Address, came to London, it astonished and highly pleased the people; but not so the Government. When that useful and important Society, the fruit of whose labours the British nation are reaping at this day, unanimously voted that Address, they deputed four trusty friends to convey it in the safest and quickest way possible. Being the *Secretary*, and in fact the *founder* of the Society, I waited on *Monsieur Chaveline, privately*, to know whether he would convey it. He readily consented, and ordered the deputation to wait on him the next day, at 11 o'clock: they, of course, punctually attended, and read the Address to him, with which he was much pleased, and promised to send it speedily. The Address was signed the 27th of September, 1792, *Maurice Margarot*, Chairman, *Thomas Hardy*, Secretary. That period is worth referring to, were I in Paris, if any of the records of the Convention are now in existence.

"I cannot help mentioning to you how much I am pleased with the Revolution which has taken place in this country, for *revolution* it is. *The King, and his Ministers, are now turned Parliamentary Reformers!* They are guilty of the very same crime, if crime it be, with which Parliamentary Reformers, in the year 1794, were charged by the infamous Government of *Pitt, Dundas*, and *Grenville*, the greatest crime known in our laws—*High Treason*. Many were imprisoned, some were banished, and three were tried for it; but an English Jury had a very different opinion of the criminality of their conduct, and honourably *acquitted* them. I rejoice that it has pleased God to spare my life so long, being now in my 80th year, to witness this grand and beneficial change which has taken place in this country; and also great changes all over Europe. I ardently wish the oppressed people of every country may be relieved from their oppressors.

"Political knowledge is making a great and rapid progress; it is now diffused among all classes. The press—the printing press is performing wonders. It was a maxim of the great *Lord Bacon*, that *knowledge is power*. I fear that I have encroached upon your valuable time with my garrulity, if you will condescend to take time to read this long letter. I shall now conclude with my sincere best wishes, that you may enjoy long life, in health and happiness.

"THOMAS HARDY,

11*th April*, 1831. "30, *Queen's Row, Pimlico*."

Lafayette, France.

"My friend, Mr. Lewis, has been kind enough to say that he will convey this to you."

"*La Grange, July* 3*d*, 1831.

"My Dear Sir,

"Your much valued favour, April 11, has but this day been delivered to me. The wishes of the London Corresponding Society, for universal freedom, have been expressed in the beginning of the French Revolution; and now we can congratulate each other on the electric stroke of the French week of last July, and upon the happy spirit of Parliamentary Reform which is now prevailing in England. This mutual fellow-feeling must take place of the prejudices which aristocracy and despotism have so long kept up between nations. Be pleased to accept my acknowledgements for the sentiments you were so kind to express in my behalf, as well as the assurance of my good wishes and sincere regard.

"LAFAYETTE."

Thomas Hardy, Esq.

Up to the present day, his kind and benevolent friend—the friend of his country—the friend of mankind—with the other gentlemen alluded to in the above letters, have continued liberally to support him. He has ever strongly relied on Providence, and has not been deceived nor disappointed. He has now passed the middle of the 81st year of his age, and can look back on many of the actions of his life with approbation. Like all human creatures, he has, in many things, failed, and come short; but he commits himself with confident hope to the mercy of his Creator and his Redeemer, and awaits the period of his release from this state of mortality with patience and resignation.

James Watson

(1799-1874)

James Watson

On Monday, 23 January 1854, a "Public Tea" was held at the Literary Institution, John Street, Fitzroy Square, in honour of the retirement of the radical publisher James Watson. The gathering, described in the report as being "of all classes of opinions and politics", though most present had some connection with the freethought movement, listened to speeches by W. D. Saull, Thomas Cooper, Richard Moore, William Birch and Robert Le Blond, who presented a lengthy address to Watson, the preamble to which ran as follows: "We take the occasion of your retirement from the profession of Publisher to express the estimation entertained by your friends of your long and important services to the cause of Free Discussion. You, who have ever regarded publicism as consisting in work to be done, not in inflated talking thereof, will see, in the brevity of our Address, a sincere and definite appreciation, though clothed in few words. Since the days of Richard Carlile, into whose service you volunteered when imprisonment was the known and certain consequence of standing on the side of Free Inquiry, you have maintained the publication of the work of Thomas Paine, whose clear and penetrating genius gave an impulse in the old world and the new to political freedom. In maintaining a character of honour and integrity in withstanding the efforts of bigotry on the part of the Church and Crown to suppress Free Discussion, you have promoted it both by your conduct and your life. In acknowledging this, we put upon record the highest compliment in the power of your fellow-citizens to pay you. Distant friends, not able to be present on this occasion, share these sentiments, both in Great Britain and America, and join us in sincere wishes for the happiness both of yourself and Mrs. Watson." In reply Watson delivered an autobiographical speech, outlining his career from his childhood in Malton until the commencement of his association with G. J. Holyoake in 1846. The evening concluded with speeches from H. N. Barnett and Holyoake, who was taking over Watson's publishing business and paying him £350 for the goodwill.

A full report of the proceedings was published as a special "Supplement" to the *Reasoner*, Sunday, 5 February 1854. The *Reasoner* had been founded by Holyoake in 1846 for the purpose of promoting Owenism and freethought. After an unsuccessful attempt to combine religious and political material, the journal had devoted itself to theological matters, appealing to an audience of seriously minded working men and liberal clergymen. Its circulation had reached a peak of about 5,000 a week at the beginning of 1854; thereafter it declined and the journal ceased publication in 1861. The original idea for the *Reasoner* had come from Watson, who was its first publisher.[1] In 1853 he became President of the newly formed London Secular Society, and remained in office until he was replaced by Holyoake in 1855. On his retirement from publishing he moved with his wife to Norwood, near the Crystal Palace, intending to spend his old age visiting the exhibits and listening to concerts. He kept up an interest in politics, serving as treasurer of a defence committee set up to aid the two persecuted publishers of W. E. Adams's *Tyrannicide: is it justified?* in 1858,[2] and acting with William Linton, the engraver and republican and an old family friend, as joint organizer of the "Central Committee of the Friends of Poland" following the republican insurrection in Poland in January 1863.[3] His last public engagement was at the final gathering of the Owenites in London in 1871.[4] He died on 29 November 1874, following a long depressive illness. His wife later asked Linton to write a memoir of her husband. The subsequent *James Watson, A Memoir of the Days of the Fight for a Free Press in England and of the Agitation for the People's Charter* (1st edition New Haven, 1879; 2nd Manchester, 1880) incorporated most of Watson's speech,[5] and included a detailed pen-portrait of its subject: "In Personal appearance Watson was not remarkable: he would not have been spoken of as handsome, though he was well-made and well-featured, and of goodly stature,—his passport says—'height 5 feet, 8 inches', (I would have said taller), and 'light complexion, blue eyes and brown hair', square shouldered, and firmly but sparely made, certainly no tendency to corpulence. His head, square and well set; his features regular; till late in life close shaven. In the latter years he let his beard grow. In ordinary talk his manner was generally serious, earnest, always his matter weighty and sincere; the tone of his voice was pleasant, his words were correct and well-spoken; sometimes with those nearest to him, or when moved, recurring to the Yorkshire old country form, yet used, the quaker *thou* and *thee*, instead of *you*."[6]

[1] For the fortunes of the *Reasoner* and Watson's association with it, see Edward Royle, *Victorian Infidels* (Manchester, 1974), pp. 92–3, 97, 216–8 and Appendix III.

[2] Royle, op. cit., p. 254.

[3] F. B. Smith, *Radical Artisan* (Manchester, 1973), p. 138.

[4] J. F. C. Harrison, *Robert Owen and the Owenites in Britain and America* (London, 1969), pp. 253–4.

[5] Watson's speech, either in its original form or as it appeared in Linton's memoir, also formed the basis of the biographical sketch of Watson in W. E. Adams's *Memoirs of a Social Atom* (London, 1903), vol. 1, pp. 186–8. In 1866 Adams, anxious that "few men of my acquaintance could furnish the world with so graphic a narrative of the agitations in which he had taken part", tried unsuccessfully to persuade Watson to write a full-length autobiography (vol. 1, pp. xvi–xvii).

[6] W. J. Linton, *James Watson* (Manchester, 1880), p. 87.

Background Reading

G. J. Holyoake, *Sixty Years an Agitator's Life*, 2 vols. (London, 1900); W. J. Linton, *Memories* (London, 1895); W. J. Linton, *James Watson* (2nd ed. Manchester, 1880), reprinted in V. E. Neuburg, ed., *Literacy and Society* (London, 1971); William Lovett, *The Life and Struggles of William Lovett* (London, 1876); J. F. C. Harrison, *Robert Owen and the Owenites in Britain and America* (London, 1969); Patricia Hollis, *The Pauper Press* (Oxford, 1970); Edward Royle, *Victorian Infidels* (Manchester, 1974); Edward Royle, ed., *The Radical Tradition from Paine to Bradlaugh* (London, 1976); E. P. Thompson, *The Making of the English Working Class* (London, 1963); W. H. Wickwar, *The Struggle for the Freedom of the Press* (London, 1928).

James Watson

Reminiscences of James Watson

My Friends,—Few persons at their outset in life had less right to expect the warm reception you have given me to-night than the humble individual now before you.

Born of poor parents, in an obscure town (Malton, in Yorkshire) in the year 1799; our family consisted of my mother, my sister, and myself, my father having died when I wanted about a fortnight of a year old; so that I had but one parent to do the duty of two, and, I am proud to say, that duty was performed with all a mother's kindness and devotion. My mother, although poor, was intelligent, as a proof of which I may state that she was a teacher in one of the Sunday-schools of the town. To my mother I owe my taste for reading, and what school education I received. I could read well, write indifferently, and had a very imperfect knowledge of arithmetic. At twelve years of age a clergyman, in whose family my mother had lived before her marriage, and who paid for the last three or four quarters of my schooling, induced my mother to bind me to him, as an apprentice, for seven years, to learn field labour, work in the garden, clean horses, milk cows, and wait at table; occupations not very favourable to mental development. At that time there were no cheap books, no cheap newspapers or periodicals, no Mechanics' Institutions to facilitate the acquisition of knowledge. The government was then in the hands of the clergy and aristocracy, the people, ignorant and debased, taking no part in politics, except once in seven years, when the elections were scenes of degradation and corruption. During my stay with the clergyman my mother again became a servant in the family, and well do I remember reading by the kitchen fire, during the long winter nights. My favourite books were two folio volumes, with illustrations—one a history of Europe, the other a history of England. My interest in those books was intense, and many times have I thought, whilst poring over them, 'shall I ever see any of the places here described?' and I *have* seen many of those places since, although my position then seemed so unfavourable. At the end of six years my master's wife died, and he retired into Nottinghamshire, which caused my indentures to be cancelled. After this I lived with my mother and sister; but, not liking to be a burthen on them, myself and a companion, similarly situated, resolved to quit our native town, and seek employment (and some relatives) in Leeds. We succeeded in finding both.

I found employment at a drysalter's as warehouseman, and had the charge of a saddle-horse.

It was in the autumn of 1818 that I first became acquainted with politics and theology. Passing along Briggate one evening, I saw at the corner of Union Court a bill, which stated that the Radical Reformers held their meetings in a room in that court. Curiosity prompted me to go and hear what was going on. I found them reading Wooler's *Black Dwarf*, Carlile's *Republican*, and Cobbett's *Register*. I remembered my mother being in the habit of reading Cobbett's *Register*, and saying she 'wondered people spoke so much against it; she saw nothing bad in it, but she saw a great many good things in it.' After hearing it read in the meeting room, I was of my mother's opinion.

In that room I first became acquainted with one who became my friend and constant companion—his name was William Driver. His name and my own were spoken of together amongst our friends in the same manner as, afterwards, my name was mentioned with that of my friend Hetherington. From this time until 1822 I was actively engaged with Mr. Brayshaw, Joseph Hartley, Robert Byerley (my wife's father), Humphrey Boyle, Mr. Gill, and a number of other friends, in collecting subscriptions for Mr. Carlile, spreading the liberal and freethinking literature, and, by meetings and discussions, endeavouring to obtain the right of free discussion. In 1821, the government renewed the prosecutions for blasphemy, and Mr. Carlile (then in Dorchester gaol under a three years' sentence) appealed to the friends in the country to serve in the shop. Humphrey Boyle was the first volunteer from Leeds. He was arrested, tried, and sentenced to eighteen months' imprisonment. On the 18th September, 1822, I arrived in London as the second Leeds volunteer. I served in the shop at 5, Water Lane, Fleet Street, until Christmas, when I spent a week with Mr. Carlile in Dorchester gaol. At that time, Mrs. Carlile, and Mr. Carlile's sister, were his fellow-prisoners. We talked over many plans and business arrangements.

At this time the plan of selling the books by a sort of clockwork, so that the seller was not seen, was in practice.[1] Notwithstanding that precaution, Wm. Tunbridge was arrested, tried, and sentenced to two years' imprisonment, and fined £100. In January, 1823, Mr. Carlile took a shop in the Strand, No. 201. Mrs. Carlile, having completed her two years' imprisonment, resided in the rooms above the shop. Towards the end of February I was arrested for selling a copy of Palmer's 'Principles of Nature,'[2] taken to Bow Street, and, being unable to procure bail in London, was sent to Clerkenwell

[1] Inside Carlile's shop was a large screen with a printed dial, on which was written the names of all the publications for sale. When the purchaser turned the hand on the dial to the required work and deposited his money, the shopman, hidden behind the screen, dropped it down before him as if by clockwork.

[2] The sentence Carlile served between 1819 and 1825 was originally imposed for selling Palmer's deistical pamphlet.

prison, where I remained six weeks. Two of my Leeds friends, Joseph Hartley and Robert Byerley, then became bail for me. My trial took place on the 23rd April, at Hicks's Hall, Clerkenwell Green, before Mr. Const and a bench of magistrates. I conducted my own defence. Reports had been circulated that the persons who had been taken from Mr. Carlile's shop were but tools in the hands of others, and incapable of defending themselves—which was not true, as Boyle and others of the shopmen *had* defended themselves.

In my defence, I endeavoured to prove from the Bible that Palmer was justified in what he had written, when I was interrupted by the judge, and told that 'I might quote from the Bible, but not comment upon it.' I was convicted, and sentenced to twelve months' imprisonment in Coldbath Fields prison, and to find bail for my good behaviour for two years.

I had for fellow-prisoners Wm. Tunbridge and Mrs. S. Wright. Mr. Tunbridge and I had a room to ourselves. During these twelve months I read with deep interest and much profit Gibbon's 'Decline and Fall of the Roman Empire,' Hume's 'History of England,' and many other standard works—amongst others, Mosheim's 'Ecclesiastical History.' The reading of that book would have made me a freethinker if I had not been one before. I endeavoured to make the best use of the opportunity for study and investigation, and the more I read and learnt the more I felt my own deficiency. So the twelve months' confinement was not lost upon me. Mr. Tunbridge did not share my studies. The evenings I usually spent with another fellow prisoner (Mr. Humphrey), an intelligent man, who possessed a good collection of books. For three or four hours after dark we read to each other, after which, until bedtime, we conversed or played a game at cribbage. We found the governor (Mr. Vickery, an old Bow Street officer) a kind-hearted man, more disposed to multiply our comforts than to restrict them. And thus our prison life passed as pleasantly and profitably as was possible under the circumstances. I was liberated on the 24th April, 1824, and shortly after visited Malton, to convince my mother and friends that imprisonment had not made me a worse son or a bad citizen. In May, 1824, the government renewed the prosecutions of Mr. Carlile's assistants, by arresting, trying, and convicting Wm. Campion, John Clarke, T. R. Perry, R. Hassell, and several others, some of whom were sentenced to *three years'* imprisonment.

After visiting Leeds, and the friends there, I returned to London. I applied for employment at a number of places, but found my having been in prison, and shopman to Mr. Carlile, a formidable difficulty, and I incurred in consequence considerable privation. I had, however, a townsman and schoolfellow in London, whose bed and purse were always at my service; that friend, I have the pleasure to say, is now present.

In August of this year, Mr. Boyle, who had managed Mr. Carlile's business sometime, withdrew from it, and I was applied to by Mr. Carlile to supply his place. I conducted the business from that time until Mr. Carlile's liberation from Dorchester gaol, in November, 1825.

In November, 1824, Mr. Carlile's shop (No. 84, Fleet Street) had a narrow escape from fire, the houses on both sides being burnt to the ground.

At the end of 1825, I learnt the art of a compositor, in the office in which Mr. Carlile's *Republican* was printed. Whilst there, I was attacked by cholera, which terminated in typhus and brain fever. I owe my life to the late Julian Hibbert. He took me from my lodgings to his own house at Kentish Town, nursed me, and doctored me for eight weeks, and made a man of me again. After my recovery Mr. Hibbert got a printing press put up in his house, and employed me in composing, *under his directions*, two volumes, one in Greek, the other Greek and English. I was thus employed, from the latter part of 1826, to the end of March, 1828. In 1825 I was first introduced to the advocates of Mr. Owen's New Views of Society, by my friend Mr. Thomas Hooper, and to the end of 1829 I was actively engaged, with others, in forming societies for political and religious liberty, co-operative associations, &c., &c.[3] In April, 1828, I undertook the agency of the Co-operative Store, at 36, Red Lion Square, and I remained in that employment until Christmas, 1829.

In the beginning of 1830 I visited Leeds, Halifax, Dewsbury, Bradford, Huddersfield, Todmorden, Wakefield, and other places, to advocate the establishment of co-operative associations. In May, I took the house 33, Windmill Street, Finsbury Square, and *there* commenced the business of bookseller. During the excitement occasioned by the French Revolution in July, I took an active part in the numerous enthusiastic meetings following that event.

In 1831 I became a printer and publisher. My friend, Mr. Julian Hibbert, gave me his press and types. The first use I made of them was to print 'Volney's Lectures on History,' which I composed and printed with my own hands. At this time I became a member of the National Union of the Working Classes.[4] [For the information of those unacquainted with the struggle for unstamped newspapers, a word or two may here be necessary. At this time, 1831, the price of the newspaper stamp was fourpence for each paper. The object of Mr. Hetherington, Mr. Carpenter, Mr. Cleave, and others, was to get that tax of fourpence abolished. To effect this, the *Poor Man's Guardian*, and other papers of a similar kind, circulating amongst the working classes, introduced *news* into their columns. To suppress the sale of these publications was the aim of the government. After sending 600 persons to prison, they were compelled to reduce the price of the stamp from fourpence to one penny, its present price. To get rid of this penny is the

[3] Chief among these was the British Association for Promoting Cooperative Knowledge, founded in May 1829 by a large group of London radicals including Watson, Lovett, Hetherington, Cleave, Carpenter and Gast. Alongside its propaganda activities, the Association set up its own exchange bazaar. (See J. F. C. Harrison, *Robert Owen and the Owenites in Britain and America*, London, 1969, pp. 199–203; William Lovett, *The Life and Struggles of William Lovett*, London, 1967, pp. 34–5 and chap. 2 *passim*.)

[4] Watson was a leading and militant member of the N.U.W.C. He used to bring one of the lances designed by Colonel Macerone for street warfare to his class meeting to aid his members' education, and also kept one on display in his shop. (Patricia Hollis, *The Pauper Press*, Oxford, 1970, p. 41.)

object of the 'Society for the Abolition of the Taxes on Knowledge,' now meeting at 20, Great Coram Street, Brunswick Square, of which Mr. Collet is the active and untiring secretary.][5]

In this year Mr. Hetherington suffered his first six months' imprisonment in Clerkenwell prison for publishing the *Poor Man's Guardian.*

In 1832, the excitement of the people on the subject of the Reform Bill was at its height.

The cholera being very bad all over the country, the government, to please the Agnewites,[6] ordered a 'general fast.' The members of the National Union, to mark their contempt for such an order, determined to have a procession through the streets of London, and afterwards to have a general feast. In April I was arrested, with Messrs. Lovett and Benbow, for advising and leading the procession. We were liberated on bail, tried on the 16th of May, each conducting his own defence, and all acquitted. Towards the end of this year Mr. Hetherington was sentenced to his second six months' confinement, in Clerkenwell prison, for the *Poor Man's Guardian.*

In February, 1833, I was summoned to Bow Street for selling the *Poor Man's Guardian.* I justified my conduct before the magistrates in selling unstamped newspapers. They considered me as bad as my friend Hetherington, and sentenced me to six months in the same Clerkenwell prison.[7] I was liberated on the 29th July, and attended the same day a meeting to commemorate the third anniversary of the French Revolution, in which Mr. Julian Hibbert, the Rev. Robert Taylor, Mr. Hetherington, and others, took part. At the end of this year I was engaged with Mr. Saull, Mr. Prout, Mr. Franks, and Mr. Mordan in fitting up the Hall of Science, in the City Road, as a lecture room for Rowland Detrosier. In January, 1834, occurred the lamented death of Mr. Julian Hibbert. In his will he again gave me a marked token of his regard, by a legacy of 450 guineas. With this sum I enlarged my printing operations. My legacy was soon absorbed in printing 'Mirabaud's System of Nature', Frances Wright's 'Popular Lectures,' Volney's 'Ruins,' Paine's works, &c. In addition to the legacy, I incurred a debt of 500*l*, in printing and publishing those works. In April I attended the great meeting of the Trades' Unions in Copenhagen Fields, in favour of the Dorchester labourers.[8]

On the 3rd of June I was married.[9] Before the month was over I was again summoned to Bow Street, but preferred a short trip to Jersey, where I stayed

[5] Insertion by the editor of the *Reasoner*.

[6] The followers of Sir Andrew Agnew, M.P., the leading Sabbatarian of the period. The main instigator of the fast, which was held on 21 March 1832, was actually Spencer Perceval, M.P., eldest son of the assassinated prime minister.

[7] Despite his imprisonment, he continued to act as publisher of *The Working Man's Friend*, a weekly journal edited by his friend John Cleave, 22 Dec. 1832–3 Aug. 1833.

[8] Here Watson's career runs close to Dunning's. As part of the protest campaign he republished the *Address to Trade Unions* by "A Journeyman Bootmaker" (1827).

[9] His bride was Ellen Byerley, who took an active part in her husband's publishing affairs throughout their married life. They had no children.

three weeks. On the 7th of August the officers again seized me, and I was taken to Clerkenwell for my second six months' confinement. I was liberated on the 21st of January, 1835, and from that time to the present have remained unmolested. 1836, 7, 8, I was engaged with others, in the formation of Working Men's Associations, and assisted to prepare the document called the 'People's Charter.'[10] In 1839 the meeting of the Chartist delegates in national convention. In 1840 took place the trials of John Cleave and Henry Hetherington, for blasphemy. They were convicted and imprisoned. My friend Hetherington honoured me by dedicating his trial to me, and I have been more proud of his testimony and friendship than of anything I ever received. From 1841 to 1846 my bookselling and publishing is so well known to most of my hearers that I need not trespass further on their time.

From 1846 to 1853, my connection with Mr. Holyoake and the *Reasoner* is patent to you all.[11] You are also aware of his new undertaking and our recent changes, and I trust that the responsibilities he had incurred will be shared and sustained by your generous support. I am proud to have assisted in preparing a 'clear stage and no favour' for the Newmans and the Martineaus, who are now coming forward to aid the progress of freethought. I hope to see the same freedom extended to our brethren of France and Germany, and throughout the continent; and, more than all, to see the illustrious triumvir, Mazzini, carried back in triumph to the Eternal City.

I have trespassed at great length on your forbearance; but, in what I have said, I have had but one object in view—to show my fellow-workmen that the humblest amongst them may render effectual aid to the cause of progress, if he brings to the task honest determination and unfaltering perseverance. With regard to the question of retirement, I may say that a person who has led the active life I have done cannot relapse into idle indifference. If I leave London it will be to join my friend Linton, and to help him in his republican propaganda; and from an attachment of many years' standing, I can truly say that a more devoted and disinterested servant of the people's cause does not exist.—Permit me to thank you most cordially for your kind attention, and for this testimony of your regard.

[10] Watson was a founder member of the London Working Men's Association in June 1836, and was one of the six working men who formed a committee with six M.Ps. in June 1837 to draft the "People's Charter", which was eventually published in May 1838.

[11] Alongside his secularist activity with Holyoake, Watson was still involved in national and international politics. In 1847 he became a committee member of the newly formed People's International League, the first popular association in Britain to take a central interest in foreign affairs, and following the revolution in France in February 1848, organized with William Linton the first meeting in Britain to support the Provisional Government. Also with Linton he organized the London Charter Union in March 1848 in opposition to the O'Connor dominated National Charter Association. (He had split from O'Connor as early as 1840.) Watson was chairman of the Union, which sought closer links with middle-class reformers and had interchangeable membership with the People's Charter Union led by Thomas Cooper and C. D. Collet. The L.C.U. failed to attract a permanent following in the capital, and faded away in the summer of 1849. Thereafter Watson took little further interest in the campaign for parliamentary reform.

Thomas Dunning
(1813-1894)

Thomas Dunning

Alone of the five autobiographies in this volume, Thomas Dunning's remained in a manuscript form until long after his death. He had begun to write out his memories in his late seventies whilst still working full-time in his newsagent's business. Early in 1894, with his health failing, he decided to retire, and perhaps hoped to be able to finish his memoirs which had reached the mid-1840s. Unfortunately he fell seriously ill at the beginning of April, and died on the 24th, leaving his manuscript incomplete.[1] It remained in private hands until 1947 when it was discovered by Dr. W. H. Chaloner, who edited and published it in vol. LIX of the *Transactions of the Lancashire and Cheshire Antiquarian Society*.[2] The following text is taken from Dr. Chaloner's edition, as are the majority of the accompanying notes.

The narrative ends in about 1846, when Dunning was still only thirty-three. He was by then well established as a newsagent, and later branched out into book and music selling. Although he does not seem to have played any further part in national political movements, he continued to take a combative interest in the affairs of local charities, and as late as 1871 we find him writing a number of articles to the *Whitchurch Herald* on the subject of Wright's Trustees.[3] In the mid-'seventies he was also involved in transacting emigration business from Nantwich. He gradually gained a reputation as a historian of Nantwich and Chester, building up his own local history library and contributing a series of letters to the *Chester Record* between 1857 and 1868 under the *nom de plume* of "The Angler of the Weaver". He was a subscriber to James Hall's *History of the Town and Parish of Nantwich* in 1883, but as a comment on the extent to which working class radicalism was still not considered to be proper history, even at a local level, it is interesting to note that Hall's work, which was and has remained the standard history of the town, makes no reference whatever to the shoemakers' trial or to Chartism.

[1] The *Crewe Guardian* and *Crewe Chronicle* carried lengthy obituaries of Dunning in their editions of 28 April 1894.

[2] Chaloner's text is taken from an original manuscript in Dunning's handwriting, with certain passages, indicated by square brackets, interpolated from a second copy of the manuscript in the handwriting of the late E. A. Lloyd.

[3] Quoted in James Hall, *A History of the Town and Parish of Nantwich* (1972 edn.,), p. 270.

Background Reading

James Hall, *A History of the Town and Parish of Nantwich* (1883, 1972); Charles Shaw, *When I Was a Child, by an Old Potter* (London, 1903); G. D. H. Cole, *Attempts at a General Union* (London, 1953); W. H. Oliver, "The Consolidated Trades' Union of 1834", *Economic History Review*, 1964; S. and B. Webb, *The History of Trade Unionism* (rev. ed. London, 1920).

Thomas Dunning

Reminiscences of Thomas Dunning

I was born in the city of Chester on the twenty-eighth day of January, one thousand eight hundred and thirteen, at the first house in the passage leading from Abbey Street to the Cathedral Cloisters.[1] My mother's maiden name was Leah Millington, daughter of Mr. Thomas Millington, the principal chorister in the cathedral, and who for forty-nine years sang and gave out the anthems there, the house in which I was born being held by him from the Dean and Chapter as a freehold for his life. At the time of my birth my mother was living with her father as his housekeeper, she having the privilege of lodging and attending to patients sent to her by Dr. Rowlands of Abbey Street. My father was a native of Wilton; he was valet to the Hon. C. W. Wynn, M.P., brother of Sir Watkin, my mother being Mrs. Wynn's maid, and, while visiting Mrs. Wynn's father, Sir Foster Cunliffe, at his residence, Acton Park, Wrexham, they were married at Wrexham Church in 1810.

Although my father had excellent opportunities of entering into business at Chester, he preferred continuing in service.[2] Therefore, after the birth of their first child, which died in its infancy, my mother entered the service of Mrs. Ireland Blackburn of Hale Hall, as her maid, and she left that situation to be confined of me, at her father's, in January, 1813, residing with him as his housekeeper from that time until 1820. At that time my father was living with Colonel Smyth, Little Linford Hall, near Newport Pagnell, Buckinghamshire, and he wished us to reside near to him; we therefore left Chester for Newport, travelling by stage-coach as outside passengers, in the cold month of January, 1820, and as we neared our destination, the church bells of the towns that we passed through were tolling for the death of King George III. On our arrival at Newport we found a comfortable house ready for us. I was sent to the Church, or National, school, on Bell's system, to learn but very little. The boys who could read moderately well were appointed to teach the younger or lower classes. I was one of these and I had very little time allowed me for either writing or arithmetic, and none for grammar or

[1] Thomas Dunning, born on 28 January, was baptized in Chester Cathedral on 26 February 1813, as the son of Charles and Leah Dunning. The house in the Abbey precincts has been demolished.

[2] In the Cathedral baptismal register Dunning's father is described as a chairmaker.

geography. Our schoolmaster, Mr. Johnson, was the parish clerk, and he had to see to the bells being chimed for prayers on Wednesdays and Fridays; he sent the biggest boys to perform the chiming business, I being amongst them. All the scholars had to attend church on Wednesdays, Fridays and Sundays and gabble over the responses.[3]

Newport is fifty miles from London on the great road from London to Chester and Holyhead, and a great number of stage-coaches, gentlemen's carriages, four- and six-horse luggage waggons, fly vans, etc., including the Chester and Holyhead mail-coach passed through Newport daily to and from London, changing horses at the hotel and the inns. Newport in former times was of dangerous approach, by reason of the overflowing of the Ouse. It stands between that river and the Lovet near their junction, and though there are fine bridges over both rivers, it still suffers much from floods, during which several streets are rendered impassable to pedestrians, the water at full flood rising as high as the bedroom windows of the cottages and as it lowers carts are sent round containing provisions for the imprisoned inhabitants, who take them in from their second-storey windows. I remember that on several occasions the Chester mail was delayed several hours, not venturing to cross the rapid stream at the end of the bridge. On half-holidays we schoolboys amused ourselves with playing at "coach and horses". We harnessed ourselves with ropes, six in a team, a driver being elected who considered himself highly honoured by the appointment, and in this manner we visited all the villages for miles around, to the great terror of the quiet boys thereof. I had a place in the procession in honour of the coronation of King George IV in 1821. The mimic coronation ceremony was carried out with great pomp in our large school, the champion entering on horseback, throwing down his challenge gauntlet, etc., etc.

My brother Charles was born at Newport on the third of November, 1821, and was christened in the parish church.[4] The Ouse was well stocked with fish, for with my humble tackle I could catch a dish of perch, etc., any evening after schooltime. About two miles from the town there was the wood of Gayhurst, the most extensive that I ever saw, the ridings being a mile through; plenty of nutting for us. Gayhurst Hall, a fine old house built during the reign of Queen Elizabeth, and once the property and residence of Sir Everard Digby, who was arrested there, tried and executed for his participation in the Papist plot (Guy Fawkes and Co.). Large numbers of nightingales reside in this neighbourhood and give their delightful evening concerts. During portions of the year my father was at Linford and came

[3] The Newport Pagnell National School had been established in 1816, with Richard Johnson as schoolmaster, a young man "of very moral and religious habits, and of competent acquirements in writing and arithmetic . . . admitted at the Central National School for instruction in the Madras system". (Rev. John Fisher, *Proceedings of the District Committee of the Deanery of Newport Pagnell*, 1816, p. 26 and title-page.)

[4] Dunning's brother Charles was baptized on 1 February 1822. (Newport Pagnell Par. Reg.)

home frequently. At other times he was far away at Dallam Tower, Westmorland, the seat of Mr. Wilson, Mrs. Smyth's father. In 1824 Colonel Smyth and his family left Little Linford Hall altogether and went to reside at Hastings. My father went with them, leaving us 120 miles away from him, nearly as far as we were at Chester from Newport. My mother therefore determined on returning to Chester, and to be near her relations and old friends. We bid adieu to Newport in the bitter frosty weather of January, 1825, travelling by coach and fly van to Leicester, and as my mother wished to visit relatives at Warrington on our way to Chester, we had to take our passage from Leicester to Nottingham by a large four-horse fly waggon amid frost and snow. During the evening we stopped to bait at an inn adjoining a flour-mill, and when the horses were taken from the waggon, Mr. Waggon thought it well to run down the slope into the mill dam, and after much labour with the help of the horses of the neighbourhood, the waggon was brought up into the road. On entering the inn we found a kindhearted Yorkshireman who was warming a tankard of ale; when warmed he poured some gin into it and invited my mother to partake of it. I also got a share; it suited my palate and warmed my stomach, and I have relished gin and ale from that time to the present better than any other alcoholic drink. In due (very slow) time we reached Nottingham, where I had time to walk the principal streets and the market square. From Nottingham we again had to travel by waggon to Sheffield, and thence to Manchester over the hills. We left the waggon at Manchester, proceeding to Warrington by stage-coach, where we stayed a few days with relatives. I found my way to Chester on foot, mother and Charles following on coach.

During our absence at Newport my grandfather had died, and my uncle John and his son and daughter, who had been living with grandfather, were still in the old house where I was born. The following notice of my grandfather's death appeared in the Chester papers:

> "On Monday last in this City, after a protracted illness, borne with much patience, Mr. Thos. Millington, aged 78 years; he was a man respected by everyone who had the pleasure of his acquaintance. Mr. M. being a native of Lancashire, he at a very early age being particularly fond of Music, and possessing a good bass voice, soon became engaged with a Society in that County for the encouragement of native talent.—In the year 1775 the Dean and Chapter of this Diocese, hearing of his abilities as an amateur, were induced to solicit him to accept of a situation as a singer in our cathedral, to which he acceded, and from that time up to the present, during a period of 49 years, he has passed in their service, with fidelity and attention."[5]

[5] *Chester Chronicle*, Friday, 5 March 1824. The Cathedral register has the following entry on 4 January 1776: "Thomas Millington, elected conduct". (*The Registers of Chester Cathedral*, 1687–1812, Par. Reg. Society, 1904, p. 34.)

EPITAPH

To the memory of Mr. Thomas Millington, for many years a chorister in Chester Cathedral

Beneath this stone where discord never reigns
Repose harmonious Millington's remains,
Whose sacred song within this city's choir
From youth to age did heavenly thoughts inspire.
A chorister was he of decent skill
In So, La, Fa and ornamental trill.
At giving out an anthem 'twas confest
Beyond a doubt, old Millington was best,
And when to Heaven his trembling voice he raised,
'Twas plain he feared the Being Whom he praised.
His aspect grave, and clean and modest grace
Adorned his functions, and became the place,
A pattern he to all the choral race.
At home, his surpliced dignity laid by,
With sober industry his trade he'd ply,
And as he sung and toiled and toiling sung,
The well-marked time upon his lapstone rung.
But all is passed; no more his ancient voice
On earth shall be uplifted to rejoice,
For death's cold hand has closed the sense refined,
The scientific ear, that sound combined.
He died, his spirit seeming to aspire
To quit an earthly for a heavenly choir."

Chester Courant.

My mother took a house in Brook Street, and furnished it, thinking that she could make a living by letting lodgings. In this she did not succeed and in a short time gave it up, and became housekeeper to Richard Hill, Esq., Flookersbrook, my brother Charles being placed in lodgings with an old friend of my mother's. Sir John G. Egerton died May 25th, 1825, and was interred at Little Budworth. I was then about 12½ years old, and being a born Egerton, was determined to go to Sir John's funeral. Without telling my mother I found my way on foot over the forest to Oulton Park, where I found great preparations made for the accommodation of visitors to the funeral. From the Park entrance gates to the Hall quantities of hay were thrown down for the horses, and posts erected to which the horses could be tied.[6] Tables covered with eatables were placed here and there, together with casks of beer. I followed the respectable people into the Hall, up the stairs into the lying-in-state room, then down into a large room where

[6] This statement is corroborated by the account of the funeral in the *Chester Chronicle* of Friday, 10 June 1825: "... a plentiful supply of fodder and water was provided for the horses."

refreshments were laid out. Being told to sit down and eat, I did so, and then climbed a tree under which the funeral procession had to pass. It was headed by the band of the Cheshire Militia (Sir John's election band) playing a Dead March. Next came the Freemasons of the county, Sir John being the Grand Master, then the tenantry, followed by the hearse and carriages. The largest funeral I ever witnessed.[7]

I had to turn out before I was thirteen to earn a few shillings and a bit of food, first with Dr. Bromfield, Newgate Street, assisting in the stable, cleaning knives, shoes, waiting at table, and in the surgery, taking out medicines, etc. I was next with Dr. Griffiths, Pepper Street, for a short time and employed in a similar manner as before. During the year 1826 I entered the service of James Sedgwick, Esq., Hoole Hall, near Chester, as page in livery, under a cross old butler, a rigid disciplinarian, but a good trainer of servants. In addition to performing footman's duties, I had to ride to Chester for the letter bag every morning, receiving my bag at eight o'clock on the arrival of the Holyhead Mail for London. I remained at Hoole Hall some four years and left there intending to go to sea. On leaving Mr. Sedgwick gave me the following written character.[8] I then went to Liverpool and applied at Brown & Co.'s shipping offices to be taken as an apprentice on board their East India ships, which they agreed to, at the same time informing me that when ashore I should have to provide my own food and lodgings out of my very small wages, and as I had no home, this matter required some consideration.

I must now return to my father's movements. Colonel Smyth and family left Hastings for Westmorland, and my father left their service. He came into Cheshire and entered the service of the Rev. Robert Hill, of the Hough, near Nantwich, the father of Mr. Hill with whom my mother lived. After living at the Hough but a short time he got into disgrace through a misunderstanding with Mr. Hill's grandson, and he left there and came to Chester. He

[7] Sir John Grey Egerton, born in 1766, died in London on 24 May, and was buried on 8 June 1825. Politically he was a supporter of Pitt and represented the city of Chester in Parliament from 1807 until 1818. The importance of his funeral as a social event in the life of the county may be gauged from the fact that it occupied three out of the 24 columns of the *Chester Chronicle* of 10 June. The unprecedented number of 17 out of the 19 county lodges of freemasons took part in the funeral procession. It was estimated that 10–12,000 spectators were present, placing a severe strain on the transport facilities of the area: "For several days preceding the funeral not a single conveyance was to be had in this City,—every Coach, Landau, Chaise and Gig in Chester were engaged; Waggons and Carts were also in requisition, and the Canal Boat was hired by a very large party to take them as far as Beeston Locks, after which they would have to walk over five miles." (*Chester Chronicle*, 10 June 1825; see also issues of 27 May and 3 June.)

[8] Hoole Hall, near Chester. 31 October 1829. "The bearer Thomas Dunning has lived with me better than three years, and I believe him to be strictly honest, sober, good tempered and steady in his conduct. He does not leave me for any act of misconduct for I would willingly have kept him in my employ and I lament so promising and respectable a Boy should be determined to become a sailor. I can likewise recommend Thos. Dunning for good abilities and quickness in learning everything he undertakes and I shall be always glad to hear of his doing well. (Signed) James Sedgwick."

found mother had placed her linen and other articles of household use in the care of her brother, John, at the old house in Abbey Street, and by degrees he took them all away, sold them and lived on the proceeds, never attempting to procure a situation. Occasionally he met me on the road as I was riding to Chester for the letter bags and wished me to give him money, of which he knew I had but very little. I gave him all I could. He lodged at a public house in Northgate Street, and the neighbourhood was alarmed one morning by his being found insensible in a field near Bache pool. He recovered and left Chester and a few days afterwards was found dead in a farm out-building at Overton, near Frodsham. I accompanied my uncle Thomas and a few friends to his funeral at Overton.[9] I was a lad in his early teens left to fight my way in life without a father or a home, my poor dear mother being in service and had to support my brother Charles in lodgings at an old friend's in Brook Street. Both he and mother lived in my line of road to Chester and I called on them every morning. My mother continued in Mr. Hill's service some little time after the death of my father, and left there to go to Nantwich for the purpose of assisting a friend of her youth, Mrs. Williams, daughter of Mr. Tinker, formerly of the Globe Inn, Kelsall, in opening the Black Lion Inn, Welsh Row, which had become her property.

After being at the Black Lion some little time, mother formed an acquaintance with Mr. John Heath, a pretty well-to-do shoe manufacturer, and married him in 1828. I did not leave Hoole Hall until some months after her marriage. When, after engaging to go to sea, I went to Nantwich to bid mother adieu, she did not wish me to be a sailor. I was now amongst her husband's shoemaking family, and having a slight knowledge of that trade, my uncles being bootmakers at Chester, I was persuaded to stay at Nantwich and try the awl and end, instead of the larboard and starboard business.[10] My stepfather's trade consisted of the strong, serviceable kinds of men's and women's goods suitable for the working people of Lancashire. This class of work I learned to make in a short time, but wishing to master the best class of ladies' boots and shoes, I left my mother's and went to lodge with Mrs. Cooke, Hospital Street, and her sons Samuel and Benjamin, who were excellent workmen, and I paid them for instructing and assisting me to finish best goods suitable for the first-rate shop in the town, Mr. Barker's. In a short time I was able, without assistance, to make the best classes of

[9] Charles Dunning was buried at Frodsham on 14 July 1828, aged 42 years (Frodsham Par. Reg.). At the time of his death he was resident at Kingsley.

[10] At this time Nantwich was a market town of about 5,000 inhabitants. The shoemaking industry was long established, but still mostly confined to domestic workshops. In 1825 three master shoemakers, John Davenport, William Davenport and Thomas Barker, "being capitalists, opened small factories . . . and employed more labour" (James Hall, *History of the Town and Parish of Nantwich*, 1883, pp. 247, 270). These factories, or "colleges", increased the scale of production, but machines were not introduced until 1856–59, and then only in the teeth of fierce union opposition. When Dunning started work, wages were low, "few earned more than 9*s*. per week, though working from twelve to sixteen hours per day" (*ibid.*, p. 270).

ladies' boots, etc., for any of our employers. And finding that there were but very few men in the town able to make channel pumps, I obtained instruction in that branch of the trade and worked at it for some years.

During the early portion of my shoemaking career the agitation for the Reform Bill of 1832 was at its height, and I and my fellow-workmen did all in our power to forward the movement. The *Weekly Dispatch* newspaper was the leading reform (and republican) organ of the time, and the Rev. James Hawkes, our Unitarian minister, the brave advocate of reforms in Church and State, as well as local, joined I and my shopmates in subscribing to the *Dispatch*, price 8½d., the stamp duty being 4d.[11] It was too expensive for *one* ill-paid crispin to purchase weekly, the wages for making the best ladies' military heeled boots being 1s. 10d. per pair, flat heels 1s. 8d., seconds, etc., much lower.

Shortly after the passing of the Reform Bill, the trades societies generally, the shoemakers amongst the rest, amalgamated. At this time there was a shoemakers' society in Nantwich numbering some 500 members (five hundred) and we joined the Amalgamated. After paying entrance fees our society had about forty pounds to spare, and not knowing what better to do with it we engaged Mr. Thomas Jones to paint for us a banner emblematical of our trade, with the motto, "May the manufactures of the sons of Crispin be trod upon by all the world", at a cost of twenty-five pounds. We also purchased a full set of secret order regalia, surplices, trimmed aprons, etc., and a crown and robes for King Crispin, and on the following 25th October, St. Crispin's Day (1833), we organized a grand procession—King Crispin on horseback attired in royal regalia, crown, flowing robes, etc., attended by train-bearers in appropriate costumes. The officers were attired in vestments suitable to their rank, and carrying the Dispensation, the Bible, a large pair of globes, and also beautiful specimens of ladies' and gents' boots and shoes, and a many prize fancy boots, etc. Our banner was generally admired and did great credit to the artist, Mr. Jones, herald painter, Nantwich. Nearly five hundred joined in the procession, each one wearing a white apron neatly trimmed. The rear was brought up by a shopmate in full tramping order, his kit packed on his back and walking-stick in hand.[12]

[11] S. Maccoby says of this newspaper: "... the greatest power in Ultra-Radical journalism was the *Weekly Dispatch* with political columns which specialized in highly-spiced attacks upon Bishops, Peers, Parsons, the Pension List, and hoc genus omne, and with news columns which were never so popular as when tricking out luscious Court accounts of the drunkenness or sexual misbehaviour of the wealthy. Even at the 8½*d.* price ruling before the Stamp Duty reduction of 1836, it had acquired a monster circulation of 30,000." (*English Radicalism 1832–1852*, London, 1955, p. 415.)

[12] It seems probable that in the course of 1833, the Nantwich shoemakers' society linked itself with a rudimentary national organization of operative shoemakers ("the Amalgamated"). This national union of Operative Cordwainers, with its head office or "Grand Lodge" in London, became one of the constituents of Robert Owen's famous Grand National Consolidated Trades Union of 1833–34 (S. and B. Webb, *History of Trade Unionism*, 2nd ed., 1920, pp. 133–51, and esp. p. 150 n. 3). Or the Nantwich society may have joined the Manchester Order of Cordwainers (G. D. H. Cole, *Attempts at General Union*, London, 1953, pp. 69–144 *passim*).

We had sent a deputation to our Rector, the Rev. R. H. Gretton, with a request that he would perform a service and preach to us. However, as ours was a secret order he declined doing so, unless he could see our rules. We assured him that we were not a political society, but we declined giving him the rules, etc., and he refused to allow us the use of himself and church for the occasion. We knew that the Wesleyans were opposed to our trade societies, and therefore considered it useless to solicit them for chapel and sermon. Our good Unitarian minister, the Rev. James Hawkes, hearing of the Rector's refusal to preach for us, immediately offered us his services, which offer we thankfully accepted. Therefore, after parading the town, the procession moved to the Unitarian chapel, Hospital Street. This was the largest and most interesting procession ever witnessed at Nantwich.[13]

Not long after our joining the Amalgamated, the Whig Government became alarmed at the spread of trades unionism, it having reached even to the ill-paid labourers of Dorsetshire, and finding that these societies took an oath of fidelity after the manner of freemasons and other secret orders, warrants were issued against six of the officers of the Dorsetshire Labourers' Union, on a charge of felony, for having administered illegal oaths, contrary to the provisions of the Act 53rd of George III, which allowed such oaths to be taken by the Freemasons only. These six unionists were tried at the Dorsetshire Assizes before Mr. Justice Williams, and witnesses having been found who had joined the society, and who swore that the oath had been administered to them by the defendants, they were found guilty and sentenced to six years' transportation each and sent to Van Diemen's Land. They were intelligent workingmen who had assisted in the agitation for the Reform Bill of 1832 which established the persecuting Whigs in power. "Save us from our friends!"[14]

Just at the time that the Dorsetshire unionists were convicted, the men in the employ of Mr. Richard Walker, shoe manufacturer, Beam Street, were on strike, the dispute being connected with the society, Mr. William Lowe,

[13] The Rev. James Hawkes was the Unitarian minister and school-master at Nantwich from 1823 until his death in 1846 (Hall, op. cit., p. 391). The Rev. R. H. Gretton was rector of Nantwich from 1819 until his death in 1846, with a short break in 1844–45.

[14] Dunning makes several mistakes at this point. The Dorsetshire labourers were sentenced to seven years' transportation under 37 Geo. III cap. 123 (the Mutiny Act) and 39 Geo. III cap. 79 (the Corresponding Societies Act). The Mutiny Act, originally passed to discourage the efforts of "divers wicked and evil-disposed persons" who had "attempted to seduce persons serving in His Majesty's forces by sea and land and others of His Majesty's subjects from their duty and allegiance and to incite them to acts of mutiny and sedition" by administering illegal oaths, was later used against trade unions. The Act applied to cases in which illegal oaths were administered binding a person "to disturb the public peace". The Corresponding Societies Act suppressed certain named corresponding societies, "every other society now established or hereafter to be established" which was bound together by illegal oaths, societies the names of whose members and officials were kept from the members of the society at large, and any society organized in branches. The freemasons' lodges secured exemption from the operation of the Corresponding Societies Act (see sect. v–vii) under certain conditions, but none from the Mutiny Act.

solicitor, magistrates' clerk and friend of Mr. Walker's, on reading a report of the Dorsetshire trials, advised Mr. Walker to prosecute all the members of the Nantwich Society that he could procure evidence against, to prove that they had administered an oath to members on their initiation. Mr. Walker had in his employ a half-witted young man named William Cappur, a son of a gamekeeper in the service of James Hammond, Esq., of Wistaston Hall, a Tory of the first water. Cappur was brought from his home at Wistaston and lodged at Mr. Lowe's, Dysart Buildings, and he there gave the names of all he could recollect who assisted at his initiation into the Society, the oath of fidelity having been administered to him.

We were soon made aware of Cappur's arrival at Mr. Lowe's and were in no doubt as to the purport of his visit. The shoemaking portion of the town was soon in a state of excitement, the officers of the Society expecting to be arrested immediately. I then lodged with Mrs. Cooke, Hospital Street. Two of her sons, Benjamin and Samuel, also lived with her; one of them was treasurer, and the other tramping president, of the Society, and they expected every moment to be arrested. I assisted at the initiation of Cappur, one of the officers being absent. While several of us were talking the matter over in my lodgings, our chief Constable, Mr. Pritchard, entered the house of Matthew Bayley, who lived nearly opposite to us, and who was an officer in the Society.[15] We therefore felt confident as to the purport of the constable's visit. I, contrary to the advice of my nervous shopmates, went across to Bayley's and found the constable sitting with Bayley and his apprentices, who were all at work. I did not pretend to see Pritchard at first, but asked Bayley to lend me a pair of lasts of a certain size. He told me to look amongst his heap in the corner and select a suitable pair, which I did (as an excuse). On turning round to thank him I saw Mr. P.

"Hullo!" says I, "why surely, Mr. P., you are not going to learn how to make shoes at your time of life, after your long military services?", etc. "You be hanged, you Radical young rascal!" Pritchard replied. "You're a disgrace to your Chester relatives, who are all of them good, loyal Churchmen". After wishing that he might soon become a good workman, and join our Society, I jogged home to acquaint my friends with the result of my visit. But to my surprise I found the cage was empty; my birds had all flown away. Not thinking it safe to await my return they started on tramp to Manchester, leaving their books and cash as treasurer and tramping president for me to make the best I could of, according to circumstances. I soon found that a goodly number of the officers and others who were likely to be sworn

[15] When the Cheshire Police Act of 1829 (10 Geo. IV cap. xcvii) set up the rudiments of the first paid county constabulary in the United Kingdom, Robert Pritchard was appointed the first paid full-time petty constable for the township of Nantwich under a Mr. Becket, the special, or deputy, High Constable for the Hundred. Becket's position was equivalent to that of a modern divisional superintendent of police. The Mr. Mellor mentioned by Dunning later in the narrative and described as "our town constable" was Pritchard's junior colleague, presumably still appointed in the pre-1829 manner (Hall, op. cit., p. 68).

to by Cappur had left the town in a hurry. As I did not happen to be afflicted with this skedaddle epidemic, I resolved to remain at my post, and, should arrests be made, to do all in my power to defend the prisoners.

We were not kept very long in suspense, for during the evening Matthew Bayley and Richard Blagg were arrested on warrants charging them with administering illegal oaths, and were lodged in the lock-ups, Snow Hill. The news of their arrest spread through the town like wildfire, causing great excitement, as nearly every working man's family was more or less connected with the shoe trade. A few of us held a private meeting in a workroom immediately after the arrests, to decide on the best course to be taken in this emergency, when it was resolved to place the defence in the hands of Mr. Jones, solicitor, the Hough.[16] Chester Assizes had just commenced, and many of those present believing that Mr. Jones was at Chester, it was proposed that I should go there that night on foot, and retain him. I moved that as we had no proof that he was at Chester, a deputation should be sent to the Hough, as it was very possible he was at home. This was agreed to, and William Robinson and I were deputed to wait upon Mr. Jones, and off we went to the Hough instanter. We found Mr. Jones at home, explained the matter to him, and requested him to attend the magistrates' meeting next morning. This he declined doing, as he believed his presence there would tend to aggravate the case against the prisoners, the magistrates having had an ill-feeling towards him ever since he brought the poachers back from transportation.[17] He advised that we should in some way instruct the prisoners to "hear, see, and say nothing". We returned quickly and

[16] Thomas Wyndham Jones, attorney-at-law and a Cheshire antiquary of some distinction, died in 1867 at the age of 71. He was admitted a member of the Law Society in Michaelmas Term 1823 and, after renting a house and land at the Hough from the Rev. Robert Hill in 1823–24, began to practise in the Nantwich area, where he soon gained the reputation of being "an able, sound real property, as well as general, lawyer". From 1848 until 1858 he resided at Churche's Mansion, Hospital Street, Nantwich. On his death the *Law Times* said: "His unflinching zeal in the interests of his clients frequently placed him in antagonism with the magistracy, but it is a well-known fact that that body not infrequently during calmer moments publicly appealed to him for his opinion when practising before them in special sessions" (*Law Times*, 20 July 1867, p. 183; see also Land Tax Returns for Hough (1824–32) in the County Record Office, Chester; Hall, op. cit., pp. 124–5, 394, 472–4).

[17] Hall gives the following succinct account of this incident: "... On 17th Dec. 1828, a number of Nantwich shoemakers and others of the town and neighbourhood were implicated in a great poaching affray on the Darnhall estate, causing much excitement in the town ... the ringleaders were apprehended and imprisoned in the 'Round House' on Snow Hill. They were tried at Chester; six or seven were sentenced to fourteen years' transportation, and the rest to short terms of imprisonment. Through a technical flaw in this indictment, the same not specifying whether the offence was committed after twelve noon, or twelve at night,—a discovery made by the astute lawyer, T. W. Jones Esq., of Hough,—they were liberated after some months' imprisonment on board the 'Justicia' convict hulk at Woolwich." The apprehension of the poachers aroused great public feeling in the town and led to serious riots every time they were brought before the local magistrates. Eventually soldiers had to be sent from Chester and the scuffle which took place when the prisoners were being conveyed away chained together in carts and waggons led to a reading of the Riot Act (Hall, op. cit., pp. 240–1).

communicated the result of our mission to a few shopmates who were anxiously awaiting our return. As we could do nothing more that night, we separated, I promising to communicate Mr. Jones' advice to Bayley and Blagg, if possible, previous to their being taken before the magistrates the following morning. Expecting that the friends of the prisoners would take breakfast to the lock-ups, I wrote Mr. Jones' instructions on two slips of paper, one of which I left with Mrs. Bayley to give to her husband with his breakfast; and the other I wrapped in paper and placed it inside a buttered roll which Mrs. Blagg took for her son's breakfast. This latter one reached Blagg without detection, but Mrs. Bayley was not allowed to see her husband, the gaoler handing in the breakfast. The town was all alive betime, and the eight constables of the division were called in and on duty early. They were stationed near Mr. Lowe's magistrates' office, a private public court in those days. The said Mr. William Lowe seeing me pass through the constables several times during the morning on my business as aide-de-camp to Mr. Jones, he thought well to warn me "not to make myself too active on behalf of the prisoners." I thanked him for his advice, but not in a very humble manner. My principal reason for passing the officers so frequently was that if Pritchard held a warrant for my apprehension, I thought he would arrest me at once, and that if club members knew I was in limbo they would immediately appoint some one to take my place.

At ten o'clock the two prisoners were taken to the magistrates' room at Lowe's office, escorted by the constables, the streets being crowded with sympathisers. On their leaving the court, Mr. Pritchard allowed me to push through the crowd and walk with them to the lock-ups. They told me that they were committed for trial, but whether at the Assizes (which were then being held) or for the Quarter Sessions they could not tell. William Cappur was the only witness. The pressure of the crowd and the excitement of the men prevented me from obtaining any further information from them.

Blagg was quite illiterate. Bayley could read and write a little, but he was a lightminded, dancing, public house man, therefore I had a brace of very awkward clients to deal with. As it was necessary for us to know whether the men were committed for the Sessions or the Assizes, we applied at once to Mr. Lowe, magistrates' clerk, for a copy of the commitment. He refused our application and advised us to go to Chester and obtain it from the prison officials. I immediately went to the Hough and informed Mr. Jones of the morning's proceedings. He said that as the magistrates and their clerk were our enemies we should have to go to Chester Castle and apply to the porter of the lodge for a copy of the commitment. On my way home I met several of our members who had come on the road to tell me that Bayley and Blagg had been taken to Chester during my absence at the Hough. This being the case, there was no time to be lost, and I hurried on to reach the town in time for the Chester mail-coach, which passed through every afternoon at four o'clock. The mail was close on my heels and while it was changing horses at the Crown I got ready and was on my way to Chester in a twinkling. On our way from Tarvin we met a large number of pedestrians, both male and female, who had been at Chester to witness the execution of Samuel Thorley for the murder of his sweetheart at Northwich.[18]

On my arrival at Chester I went to the Castle and found the proper official to give me the required information. He told me that the two prisoners in question were committed for trial at the next Assizes and he promised to have a copy of their commitment ready for me in good time next morning. My mind was set at rest on gaining this information, knowing that we had several months in which we could prepare a defence, etc., before the next Assizes. I next waited on Mr. Jones's Chester legal agent, and he accompanied me to the Castle. We had an interview with the two prisoners, who had just donned their felon's uniform. We gained from them all the information they could give us as to the proceedings before the magistrates, we promised to obtain their release on bail if possible. I spent the evening with members of the Chester Shoemakers' Society at their club-house and reported to them our trade troubles. The next morning at the appointed time I attended at the Castle and was furnished with the required documents. I walked home in good spirits, waited on the club officers and then walked on to the Hough, and gave Mr. Jones the particulars of my Chester mission, together with the papers from the Castle. We then had some conversation respecting the procuring of bail for the two prisoners. He explained that there were only two ways of obtaining it, either by writ of *habeas corpus* or by writ of *certiorari*. The first of these I considered would incur an expense far beyond our means, as the men, together with the parties offering themselves as sureties, would have to appear at the Court of King's Bench, London, barristers' retainers, court fees, gaolers' expenses, etc., while *certiorari* required only affidavits from the prisoners declaring themselves to be poor men, and unable to bear the expenses of *habeas corpus*, these affidavits to be placed before the Judges in King's Bench by a barrister who would be instructed to explain and argue the case. The legal charges for this kind of proceeding being estimated at £25 at least, our Society decided on adopting this latter course, and we advanced Mr. Jones the cash he required with which to commence the application for bail. Mr. Jones having prepared the way by serving notices respecting bail on both the Nantwich and the Chester magistrates, I went to Chester on a day appointed with drafts of the affidavits and accompanied by Mr. Jones's Chester agent, went to the Castle to meet the magistrates.

On our way thither Mr. Agent told me that our application would be unsuccessful, as the judges did not believe in the poverty of trades unions and their pleading *in forma pauperis*. I replied that there were several leading

[18] This event took place on Monday morning, 7 April 1834, and the reference enables the Nantwich arrests to be dated (*Chester Courant*, Tuesday, 8 April 1834; *Chester Chronicle*, Friday, 11 April 1834).

families in Chester who kept carriages, but could not afford to keep horses and they had to apply to livery stables for them *in forma pauperis*. He gave me credit for my argument, wished us success, but shook his head. We met the magistrates, the prisoners were brought up, and the affidavits read to them and sworn to. As I have said, Blagg was quite illiterate, and Bayley was too talkative on matters that he did not understand; however, the magistrates kindly passed it over and signed the affidavits. I then walked to Nantwich and on to the Hough, and furnished Mr. Jones with affidavits, etc. Bail was duly applied for at the Court of King's Bench and granted by the Judges. We next had to seek for friends willing to become sureties, and succeeded in finding substantial parties. I was kindly instructed to engage conveyances and drive the sureties to Chester. The magistrates attended by special notice at the Castle for the purpose of admitting the prisoners to bail, Mr. Jones's agent being present. After going through the usual legal forms and the sureties being considered satisfactory, our two friends were liberated, and I had the pleasure of driving them home.

On reaching Highwayside, six miles from Nantwich, we met a number of people who had walked that far to give the first welcome home to the felons. As we drove slowly along, the hand-shakers kept increasing every mile and on reaching the town the crowd was so great that it was difficult to drive through it; so much so that our town constable, Mr. Mellor, a good old Church and King Tory, forced his way through to me and threatened what he would do if I did not drive on quickly and break up the crowd. I invited him to take my place and try his hand at driving through a mass of people such as had never before been seen in the streets of Nantwich. My passengers disembarked all well without accident. I then walked to the Hough and reported progress to Mr. Jones, who gave me credit for the correct manner in which I had carried out his instructions both at home and at Chester and he desired that no one else but me should be sent to him on this subject, as he and I perfectly understood each other respecting the case.

I must now hark back a little. A few days after our men were committed for trial Cappur was liberated from Mr. Lowe's and he went home to Wistaston. Early on the morning after his arrival there I paid him a visit and succeeded in getting from him the names of all the men he had informed of, as having taken part in his initiation; he had quite forgotten me. He gave me the names of all that he had informed of without any hesitation, at the same time expressing his sorrow for what he had done. Mr. R. Walker had persuaded him to give the names to Mr. Lowe. His parents were also much grieved at what he had done. He now recollected that I assisted in making him a member, but did not think of me when he gave the names to Mr. Lowe. The greater number of the men Cappur had named had left the town, and on my return from Wistaston those of them who remained made their exits quickly. In the course of my conversation with Cappur I asked him if he would like to leave the neighbourhood until the affair had blown over. He said he should be glad to go if he knew where to get work. I said if he would like to go to Manchester I would undertake to procure him both work and lodgings and also some assistance until he got settled. He was delighted with the offer and so were his parents. I had no authority to make the offer, but feeling sure that my committee would ratify it, I struck the iron while it was hot by telling him that Richard Wilkinson, a shopmate whom he knew, was going to Manchester the next morning by A. Cooke's coach, and if he would walk a mile on the road Wilkinson would pick him up and pay his fare and make him alright at Manchester. This being agreed to, I toddled home and reported to the committee what I had done, and what I had promised to do, all of which was approved of, and it was settled if Wilkinson would undertake the mission he should be furnished with the needful. I knew that Wilkinson was well acquainted with shoemaking Manchester and that he could be depended on. I went to his residence, explained the matter to him, and he agreed to go the following morning and carry out our instructions. He was furnished with cash to meet all necessary expenses and left the town quietly. He took up Cappur on the road, and left him at Manchester in lodgings with Unionist shoemakers who promised to take care of him and keep the secret.

After remaining at Manchester some time it was thought better to remove him to a safer locality, for as many Nantwich shoe manufacturers attended the Manchester Shoe Mart every week, together with a number of Nantwich journeymen shoemakers working at Manchester, it was feared his whereabouts might be discovered. We therefore determined on sending him to Dublin, and Wilkinson accompanied him from Manchester to Dublin, where he left him lodging and working with trusty men. Cappur was a very inferior workman and we had to send cash to assist in his maintenance. Our Post Office was at the Lamb Hotel, and we had reasons for suspecting that an espionage was kept over it. Mr. Lowe and his Tory friends took their evening glasses there and were very intimate with the host, Mr. Copestick, and his female relatives who had the care or management of the Post Office as well as of the bar. We therefore thought it dangerous to post letters containing cash here for Dublin, so I volunteered to walk to Chester and post them whenever required at my own expense. I walked down on Sunday mornings early, reached Chester at breakfast time, had a look round the old city, a chat with uncles and cousins and walked home in the evening.

In due time the Assizes came on.[19] I went with Bayley, Blagg and their sureties to Chester. The sureties surrendered their men to the prison authorities and returned home. Mr. Jones did not go to Chester, but left me the honour of staying at Chester and of walking to the Hough in a hurry should Cappur put in an appearance. The Criminal Court was occupied the whole

[19] The Assizes opened on Saturday, 2 August before the Rt. Hon. Justice Vaughan (*Chester Courant*, Tuesday, 5 August 1834). The district Attorney General, J. Hill, was the public prosecutor.

week, ours being the last case called on, the crier of the Court repeating several times, "William Cappur, come forward, or your recognizances will be forfeited", but William did not appear. Constable Pritchard then entered the witness-box and on oath said "he believed that the unionists had sent Cappur out of the way, but that he should be able to find him before the next Assizes". The trial was therefore adjourned until the next Assizes and the prisoners liberated without a renewal of bail.[20] A few days after Cappur went to Manchester a third man, who had not left the town, Robert Edwards, was arrested on the same charge and lodged in the lock-ups on Snow Hill. He was taken before the magistrates and remanded, no Cappur forthcoming. I visited him in prison, lent him a flute to amuse himself with, and told him that Mr. Jones advised him not to allow himself to be bound over to appear when called on, as they could not keep him over a fortnight. Our Rector-magistrate, the Rev. R. H. Gretton, being informed of my advice to Edwards, ordered the gaoler not to allow me in the lock-ups again. Edwards was, however, liberated without bond.

During the interval between the Assizes, Cappur was taken seriously ill of measles. Only four of us were in possession of his address, and we felt very uneasy lest he should die. I went to Chester and posted cash to support him during his illness. Fortunately he recovered; had he died, his relatives might have suspected that he had been foully dealt with and this would have led to criminal proceedings being taken against us, which would have been very unpleasant to me in particular. The Assizes came duly on and I, with Bayley and Blagg, attended them, and as before were kept waiting there the whole

[20] By combining the laconic entries in the Cheshire Assizes minute books (P.R.O. Assizes 61 vol. iv) with the account given in the *Chester Courant* of Tuesday, 12 August 1834 (printed in full below), it is possible to check the accuracy of Dunning's account. One can also realize the extent of the danger in which Dunning and his associates stood when the Judge himself was quite sure of the reason for the non-appearance of the chief witness for the prosecution. The case of Blagg and Bayley came up for hearing on Tuesday, 5 August. They were not indicted, the affidavits were filed and motion was made to continue their recognizances. No copy of the indictment could be traced in the Public Record Office. The following appeared in the *Courant* under the heading "Nantwich Unionists":—"Mr Dunn made an application somewhat similar to the last (i.e. that the prisoners might be released from their recognizances). The facts of the case are simply that two men named Matthew Bailey and Richd. Blagg were committed to Chester Castle some few months since on a charge of being members of an unlawful combination, at Nantwich and administering illegal oaths. Soon after their admittal they were admitted to bail, and now appeared to make their trial, but in consequence of the absence of William Capper, the principal witness, no indictment could be preferred. The Attorney-General, having put in the affidavits of Robert Pritchard, constable of Nantwich, and Richard Walker, the prosecutor, in which they deposed that Capper was the principal witness against the defendants; that every exertion had been made to find him without effect, and that they believed his absence was caused by the defendants or some friend on their behalf; he made application that their bail be respited until the next assizes. Mr. Dunn opposed the application; but the learned Judge said that such prosecutions were instituted for the benefit of the public; the public prosecutor had done all that it was possible to do to find the witness, who, there could be no doubt was kept away by some party having a common interest with the defendants, and therefore they must be held to bail to appear at the next assizes.—Capper's recognizances were ordered to be estreated."

week, Cappur being the last witness called on by the clerk of the court. As he was not forthcoming, and as Supt. Pritchard did not mount the box and swear that he could find him in a given time, the prisoners were discharged, free men, to their great joy, and to the satisfaction of the Nantwich people generally.[21] It was a great relief to me, for during these lengthy proceedings I could scarcely find time to earn a scanty living. But my work was not yet over. Our cash box was getting empty, and it had to be replenished. Mr. Jones's law bill amounted to about £80 (eighty pounds), travelling, etc., expenses of sureties to bail the prisoners, and also to the Assizes, expenses attendant on the sending of Cappur to Manchester and Dublin, and assisting him while there, assistance to the families of men who left the town through fear of arrest and these men had to be sent for home and some travelling expenses allowed them. These payments amounted to a large sum, and our income gradually diminished, the prosecution causing members to fall off rapidly, and the Amalgamated soon resolved itself into a Cordwainers' Club, as it was before joining the Union.[22] However, we managed to pay all our debts. The cowards on their return home amused themselves by finding fault with all that had been done during their absence, expenses too great, etc. This disgusted the men who had borne the burden and the heat of the day, many of whom took little or no interest in the Society afterwards.

And thus ended the prosecution of trades unionists by the Reform Government!

Cappur did not return from Ireland until some year or two after the law proceedings had terminated, and he expressed himself quite ignorant as to where he had been, or what he had been doing during his long absence. Shortly after he left home, Squire Hammond of Wistaston Hall discharged his father, believing he knew where his son was hidden; but he was totally ignorant of his son's whereabouts. During the time I was engaged in these law proceedings in addition to working at shoemaking, I was practising on the flute and clarinet, and became a member of our military and string bands.[23] I played for the procession and festivities at Nantwich on the occasions of the accession and coronation of our Queen Victoria.

Shortly after our trades union excitement had ended, the agitation for the People's Charter commenced, and a good number of the Nantwich working men joined the movement. During the year 1838 Feargus O'Connor, Esq., commenced the publication of a newspaper at Leeds entitled *The Northern*

[21] The Assizes minute books reveal that during the Spring Assizes of 1835 (3–11 April) the prosecution was abandoned, that Blagg and Bayley were released from their recognizances and that the Attorney General undertook to enter a "nolle prosequi" on the indictments.

[22] This provides additional evidence that the "Amalgamated" refers to the national organization of the Operative Cordwainers inside Owen's Grand National Consolidated Trades Union (see Webb, op. cit., p. 150, n. 3).

[23] Dunning must have been a versatile musician, for he later became a member of the Nantwich Wood Band as a violin player. At his death he was described as a "music dealer" as well as a bookseller and newsagent (*Crewe Chronicle*, 28 April 1894).

Star, as the organ of the Chartist Party. It was a registered newspaper bearing the penny stamp, free by post. I and a dozen or more of my Radical associates wished to subscribe to the *Star*, and I being secretary to our young Chartist association, was requested to order of Mr. Griffiths, bookseller, the only newsagent in the town at the time, the required number of *Stars*. I requested Mr. G. to supply me with fifteen copies of the *Northern Star* weekly, and for which I offered to pay him a quarter of a year in advance. He declined taking the order in a most contemptuous manner, with "Oh! Ah! a Radical paper, I believe. I am a stamp officer and will not order it, etc." Mr. Griffiths had been recently imported from Bath and London, a very proud man, High Churchman, Tory and Freemason. On Mr. Griffiths' refusal to order the *Star* I wrote to the publisher of that paper, requesting him to say whether, under the circumstances, he would supply me direct from the office. Mr. Ardill, the clerk, replied that he should be glad to send any quantity I might require at wholesale price. I immediately sent order and cash, and from that moment, thanks to Mr. Tory Griffiths, I became a newsagent. I was then working and lodging with William Robinson on the Snow Hill; our Chartist committee meetings were held in his workshop, and the subscribers to the *Star* came there for their papers. At that time newspapers bore a penny stamp, therefore my news-parcels came free by post. Early in 1839 our association joined the Staffordshire Potteries district, and, by the payment of a small weekly subscription to it, we had the privilege of lecturers being sent to us for open-air meetings. The first of these was held on Snow Hill on Monday, April 8th, 1839. I, together with Robinson, my brother Charles, and three or four others of my brother bandsmen (the remainder of the band being Tory Churchmen), played before the lecturer, Mr. John Richards, and a large muster of working people, from the Swan Inn, Pillory Street, to the place of meeting.[24] There was a large and attentive audience, and Mr. Richards explained the principles of the People's Charter to the satisfaction of all present. Thus ended our first open-air Chartist meeting.[25]

We afterwards held open-air meetings in Wood Street in the evening, once or twice a week, and also on Sunday evenings, all (addressed by) local speakers and readers of articles and speeches from the *Star*, including the Rev. J. R. Stephens' sermons against the New Poor Law. On Sunday evenings hymns were sung and Mr. William Cooper delivered a Chartist sermon. Weekly meetings were held in our workshop; there were no political beer-and-billiards club houses in Chartist days. My landlord, W. Robinson,

[24] For the missionary activities of "old John Richards", a prominent Potteries Chartist and a delegate to the National Charter Convention of People's Parliament in 1839, see Mark Hovell, *The Chartist Movement*, 1918, pp. 130–1. He spoke at Sandbach and Congleton in March 1839. See also the account of his activities during the Plug Plot riots of 1842 in the Potteries given by Thomas Cooper in *Life of Thomas Cooper by himself*, 1872, pp. 191–2.

[25] For an account of the meeting see the *Northern Star*, 4 May 1839, in which the people of Nantwich are described as suffering from low wages and high prices.

was a tenant of James Hammond, Esq., Wistaston Hall, the man who discharged Cappur's father, and his steward, Mr. Hector, called on Robinson and told him if he kept lodgers like me his rent would be raised. However, despite this threat, I continued in my lodgings, and our meetings were held there as before. I was appointed delegate to a Chartist District Meeting held at Hanley in July, 1838, during the week in which the Birmingham Bull Ring riots took place. I met with a many determined "physical force" men at the meeting [also Mr. Capper, who, together with Mr. Richards, our lecturer, Thomas Cooper and others, were imprisoned at Stafford for the Hanley riots and fires in 1842.][26] While at Hanley I visited Mr. Salt's coffeehouse and arms depôt. Mr. Salt had a large stock of guns, pistols, swords, bayonets, pike-heads, etc., the motto of the Pottery Chartists being, "Peacefully if we can, forcibly if we must". I was presented with two china tobacco pots, which I carried home, one for self, the other for my landlord. Mine is still in existence. I was informed that a considerable quantity of arms had been sold in the Potteries, Thompson, gunmaker, of Birmingham, having supplied them to agents "on sale". Amongst the Hanley speakers who visited us was Mr. Ellis; he was tried at Stafford for being present at the Hanley riots and sentenced to twenty-years' transportation, and I have never heard of his return. He was an able politician and a fine speaker. The people of Hanley believed him to be innocent. He was a terror to the Whigs and Tories and they were only too happy to get him out of their way.[27]

The years 1839 and '40 were years of persecution and imprisonment for the poor Chartists, our Reform Government appearing to vie with their Tory predecessors in endeavouring most cruelly to crush out the agitation for universal suffrage, etc. During the agitation for the Reform Bill of 1832, Lord John Russell, in his great speech at Liverpool, said, "I shall never rest satisfied until taxation and representation are co-extensive". The bill once passed, he turned round on the unrepresented and told them that the Reform Bill was a final measure. And this expression gained him the title of "Finality Jack". I have the names, etc., of 93 Chartists who were undergoing various terms of imprisonment at the end of 1840, including Frost, Williams and Jones,[28] and 17 others at Monmouth, at Chester 12, including William Benbow of Middlewich, Liverpool 32, including the Rev. W. V. Jackson,

[26] The portion of the text in square brackets is not in the MS. in Dunning's handwriting and is interpolated from the second copy of the MS. written out by E. A. Lloyd, a close friend of Dunning's.

[27] Joseph Capper, Thomas Cooper, William Ellis, and John Richards were tried at Stafford Assizes in 1843 on charges of sedition and conspiracy. Ellis received a sentence of twenty-one years' transportation, Capper and Cooper sentences of two years' imprisonment, while Richards had to serve a year's term (Hovell, op. cit., p. 266; *Annual Register*, 1843, ii, pp. 161–3; *Life of Thomas Cooper by himself*, pp. 173–270 *passim*).

[28] On 3 and 4 February 1840 the Nantwich Chartist William Cooper attended a delegate meeting in Manchester to discuss obtaining a pardon for the three men. He reported that a three-hour meeting had been held in Nantwich about the matter. (*Northern Star*, 8 February 1840.)

Bronterre O'Brien, J. R. Richardson and Christopher Doyle (the latter one lectured at Nantwich several times), York 23, nearly the whole of them for delivering seditious speeches.

Dr. P. M. McDouall and the Rev. J. R. Stephens were tried at the Chester Assizes held August, 1839. I walked to Chester for the purpose of being present at these trials. The indictment in each case was misdemeanour, McDouall for having attended an unlawful meeting held at Hyde on the 22nd of April, 1839, and with having used seditious and inflammatory language, tending to raise discontent in the minds of her Majesty's subjects, and bring the laws of the realm and the ministers of the Crown into contempt. McDouall was tried before Baron Gurney on Friday the 16th day of August, 1839. It was generally expected that the Attorney General, Sir John Campbell, would attend as counsel for the prosecution, but as he was retained in an important civil case tried on the same day in the Nisi Prius Court, Mr. Hill, District Attorney General, prosecuted. During the trial I stood with my arms resting on the dock, close behind the defendant. McDouall conducted his own case and cross-examined witnesses very ably and addressed the jury for some 4½ hours in his defence. During his peroration Sir John Jervis, who sat below the dock, appeared spellbound with the doctor's eloquence. At the close of his speech there was a good cheer in court for him. During the trial the Grand Jury entered the court with a true bill against McDouall and others for conspiracy. This bill was withdrawn, it was said, through the instrumentality of Sir John Jervis, one of the counsel retained against McDouall and others. On the departure of the Grand Jury, McDouall said humorously to the jury, "Gentlemen, you may possibly have heard of Captain Scott, a celebrated American marksman. Well, once he levelled his gun at an old raccoon. 'Hullo! are you Captain Scott?' said the raccoon, 'don't fire, I'll come down and give in. You're sure to hit me.' So with me, gentlemen, I may as well give in. I'm sure to be hit". McDouall was found guilty and sentenced to one year's imprisonment, and was bound over to keep the peace for five years, himself in £500 and two sureties £200 each.[29]

Thompson, the gunmaker, Higgins and others were tried in the same court for seditious conspiracy and sentenced to various terms of imprisonment. During these trials the barristers' table was covered with arms of various kinds, guns, swords, pikes, etc., which had been found in the possession of the defendants, offering on sale. This exhibition of arms in

[29] According to the *Annual Register* McDouall, "the principal chartist leader of Lancashire", addressed the jury "in a speech of considerable talent." He denied that the meeting at Hyde was an illegal one. No violence had been used, "the people having merely met together for the purpose of considering the expediency of adopting the people's charter." He denied using the language attributed to him by the witnesses. In reply the district Attorney-General contended that the charge had not only been proved by the witnesses called, but also confirmed by statements which McDouall had that day made (1839, ii, pp. 148–50). The two sureties were in £100 each.

court, it was believed, was for the purpose of influencing the jury to convict.[30] On my way to the Assizes I met on the road between Tarvin and Chester pickets of the Cheshire Yeomanry on the lookout for the expected mob from Lancashire and Staffordshire coming to rescue the Chartist prisoners. During the Assizes a quantity of gunpowder, etc., was brought through Chester and lodged in the magazine at the Castle. It was generally understood these explosives had been consigned to a Chartist agent, and had been seized in transit. This report must have been circulated to influence both juries and the citizens generally, for it was proved the gunpowder, etc., was a purely commercial transaction.[31] In addition to the Cheshire Yeomanry being on duty at Chester during the Assizes, a large number of special constables were sworn in to protect and assist the authorities in the event of a rescue of the political prisoners being attempted.

The Rev. J. R. Stephens was tried in the Nisi Prius Court, Sir John

[30] On 14 August 1839, George Thompson, gunmaker, of Birmingham, Timothy Higgins, of Ashton, James Mitchell, beerseller, of Stockport, and Charles Davies, of Stockport, were indicted and later sentenced to eighteen months' imprisonment each. The *Annual Register* commented:—"The evidence, which was quite conclusive, went to show that they had in their possession considerable quantities of fire-arms, with the intent to aid the violent designs of the chartists." An inflammatory poster was found in Higgins's possession, part of which read: "Are your arms ready? Have you plenty of powder and shot? Have you screwed up your courage to the sticking pitch? . . . remember that your safety depends on the strength of your own right arm . . . Nothing can convince tyrants of their folly, but gunpowder and steel; so put your trust in God, my boys, and keep your powder dry. Be patient a day or two, but be ready at a moment's warning; no man knows what to-morrow may bring forth. Be ready, then, to nourish the tree of liberty with the blood of tyrants." These "physical force" sentiments ended with an amusing piece of doggerel:—"In tyrant's blood baptize your sons,/ And every villain slaughter./By pike and sword your freedom try to gain,/Or make one bloody Moscow of Old England's plain." The jury took five minutes only to consider their verdict of guilty against all the prisoners (1839, ii, pp. 144–5).

[31] The account given of this incident in the *Annual Register* differs from Dunning's:—"Apprehensions were . . . entertained of serious disturbances at Chester. Five hundred special constables were sworn in, and the garrison held in readiness to suppress rioting, but none occurred: and the worthy citizens were beginning to feel at ease, when intelligence was received of the seizure of a large quantity of arms at the little port of Ellesmere near Chester. It appeared that since the disturbances, the boats from Birmingham had landed there 272 heavy packing-cases, which were warehoused a few days. They had no directions upon them, nor marks, with the exception of the letter B; and by some means or another it came to be known that they contained arms; and on opening the cases, it was found that each contained twenty guns and bayonets, with flints fixed ready for use. As it was not known to the carriers to whom they belonged . . . Mr. Case, a magistrate of the neighbourhood . . . immediately ordered them to be re-shipped and sent to the port of Chester, for greater security. On their arrival at Chester, the carriers refused to receive them, but sent information to the clerk of the peace; who consulted the authorities, and it was deemed advisable that the same should be seized. The infantry were accordingly despatched to the wharfs with waggons; and shortly afterwards the wholesale seizure was lodged in the armoury of Chester castle. It still remained a mystery as to whom they belonged, some persons having surmised, that they were secretly sent down by the government for the purpose of arming the middle classes, pursuant to the letter of recommendation of Lord John Russell to the lords-lieutenant of counties" (1839, ii, pp. 139–40). For the text of the Home Secretary's letter promising Government arms to the "principal inhabitants" of disturbed districts banded together in associations "for the protection of life and property" (May, 1839), see Parliamentary Papers, vol. XXXVIII (1839), p. 13.

Campbell, Attorney General, appearing for the prosecution. The indictment against Stephens was similar to the one against McDouall. A large sum had been collected and given to him for his defence. However, he chose to defend himself, and, in his cross examination of the witnesses for the prosecution, he proved the old adage that "The man who defends himself has a fool for his client" was correct in his case. For instance, a tradesman was under examination for the Crown, to prove the meeting in question was held, and that Mr. Stephens was the principal speaker at it, but the witness could not recollect that the speech contained anything of a seditious or physical force nature. Mr. Stephens not being inclined to let well alone, questioned witness as to other speeches he had heard him make, and whether in any of them he had heard him recommend violence. After much pressing witness said that on one occasion he heard Mr. Stephens advise the people to bring long knives with them to the meetings, as they would serve to cut bacon or anything else with. Sir John Campbell took a note of this and requested the judge to allow the witness to be recalled, and under Sir John's re-examination the witness was made to say a many things Mr. Stephens had not bargained for. Mr. Stephens addressed the jury at great length some six and a half hours, quoting from his sermons and speeches, that he had never advised force, that he was not a Chartist but an anti-New Poor Law advocate, and that the meeting he was charged with attending was, as he understood it an anti-Poor Law meeting. Sir John Campbell then addressed the jury for the Crown. He said that, after hearing the speech of Mr. Stephens, the jury must be satisfied he was a man of great ability, and not likely to have been mistaken as to the kind of meeting he was attending. They had been told that in the procession to the place of meeting a number of flags and banners were carried, the inscriptions on them being "Universal Suffrage", "Vote by Ballot", "Annual Parliaments", "No Property Qualification" and other mottoes made use of by the Chartists, but not a word about the Poor Law was to be seen on the banners, etc. Mr. Stephens commenced his address with, "Knights, bannermen and you, my little powder monkeys" (pointing to the young piecers from the cotton mills). "This," said Sir John, "this was indeed teaching the young idea how to shoot!" This rhetorical hit caused general laughter, in which Mr. Stephens joined. After a short retirement the jury returned a verdict of "Guilty", and Mr. S. was sentenced to eighteen months imprisonment. I was in the court during the trial and heard every word of it.[32] The Chartists had subscribed liberally towards the defence of Mr. S., but he having on his trial denied all connection with Chartism, Chartists felt no further sympathy for him; in fact

[32] Stephens was charged with attending an unlawful assembly on the night of 14 November 1838, at a place called the Cotton Tree, a mile and a half from Hyde, and inciting those present to a disturbance of the public peace. Many who attended the meeting carried arms, some of which were discharged at the end of a speech in which Stephens said that "he had been to the barracks, seen the soldiers, and the soldiers would not act against the people" (*Annual Register*, 1839, ii, p. 147). Hovell says of Stephens's defence at the trial:—

many felt pleased he got a heavier sentence than Dr. McDouall, who defended his Chartist principles in a speech second only to that of Robert Emmett. The day following the trials I went to Liverpool, and on my return to Chester in the evening I called at the Bull's Head Tavern, Northgate Street, an old inn frequented by many persons connected with the Cathedral, and amongst the assembled company I found a party of special constables who had just received their wages for defending the city against the Chartists who didn't come to take the city and rescue the prisoners. These specials were ordering in jugs of ale and drinking the health of Dr. McDouall, whose speech in defence had converted them to Chartism.

On the 29th of September, 1839, I was married to Elizabeth Latham of Nantwich, at Chester, in the parish church of St. Oswald's (the Cathedral).[33] We drove to Chester (no railways then) and arrived just in time to hear our banns read out third time of asking, and in some twenty minutes after we two were made one. I was born in a house at the top of the refectory steps (the old Abbey kitchen), and I was christened at the font in the nave, and married in St. Oswald's church under the Cathedral roof, now forming a portion of the nave. It being Sunday, all the church bells in Chester rang for our wedding gratis. My uncle, Thomas Millington, and my cousin, Eliza Millington, were the witnesses to our marriage.

We were promised a house in Welsh Row, but were disappointed in it and had to take one in Love Lane, the only one available at the time, and quite out of the way for a newsagent. However, I made the best of it. I posted my *Northern Star* contents bill on a stable adjoining, and I filled my window with Chartist and other radical pamphlets, etc., of the day; and so attractive were they, that our Rector, the Rev. R. H. Gretton, warned me he, having heard that I was selling seditious and free-thought publications, intended to have my window strictly watched, and, if he found that I was exposing for sale books or pamphlets of that character, he would see that I was prosecuted. Despite his threat I continued exhibiting my Radical wares.[34]

"... It was a very bad defence. In spite of the fact that he had been arrested for attending an exceedingly riotous Chartist meeting, he devoted his speech to a long denunciation of Carlile, Paine, Bentham, and Radicalism generally ... Stephens cut a really bad figure, and with his trial and imprisonment he disappeared from the Chartist world" (op. cit., p. 171). The sole adequate modern account of Stephens's career is by J. T. Ward, "Revolutionary Tory: the life of Joseph Rayne Stephens of Ashton-under-Lyne (1805–1879)", *Trans. Lancs. and Ches. Antiq. Soc.*, vol. 68, 1958, pp. 93–116.

[33] His wife died in 1888.

[34] Gretton's attempts to suppress Chartist activity do not seem to have been very successful. In February 1840 he attempted to ban an open-air meeting in Nantwich, but it went ahead in spite of him, and was attended by 1,000–2,000 people. Dunning was one of the speakers. (*Northern Star*, 15 Feb. 1840.) At the end of March 1840 he was a sponsor of a meeting called by middle class Anglicans and Wesleyans in Nantwich to enforce strict observance of the Sabbath. The meeting was invaded by the local Chartists, led by Dunning, who launched a series of verbal attacks on the Sabbatarians from the floor of the meeting which eventually broke up in disorder before any resolutions could be proposed (*Northern Star*, 28 March 1840).

At this time Mr. William Pearce, the butler with whom I had lived at Hoole Hall, came to lodge with me. He had been living for several years as butler with Mrs. Scarisbrick at Golborn Park, Newton-le-Willows, and while there I had paid him several visits. On one occasion I cleaned all the plate, which had been deposited in Warrington Bank for fifteen months during the absence of Mrs. S., and on her return home I assisted in waiting on a large party of the aristocracy and gentry of the district. Mrs. S., being without an under-butler, wished to engage me. I foolishly enough declined her offer in favour of miserably-paid shoemaking. Shortly after this Mrs. S. died, and I went to Golborn to assist Mr. Pearce at the sale of the wines (more particularly as I had assisted in packing them in the bins and entered them in the cellar-book on their arrival at Golborn Park from Scarisbrick Hall). Mr. Pearce did not stay with me many months. The change from a mansion to a shoemaker's cottage did not agree with him. He left me and went to Chester, and invested his savings with a solicitor who allowed him an annuity. He died soon afterwards.

The house in Welsh Row was again promised me, and during 1840 I gave notice to leave Love Lane, but was once more disappointed, and I took a house in Oat Market, it being more central. In the course of six months the promised house in Welsh Row was ready for me. It belonged to Mr. James Cooke, a thoroughly Liberal Unitarian-Baptist ex-minister. In Welsh Row I had a better frontage for exhibiting advertisements of publications supporting the Chartist etc., movements. I continued the sole agent for the *Northern Star* and secretary to the Nantwich branch of the Chartist Association. The agitation was now at its height, and we held open-air meetings in Wood Street on evenings during the week, and on Sunday evenings we sang Chartist hymns, and Mr. William Cooper delivered political sermons from scriptural texts. The police officers were more or less generally in attendance at our meetings, and had Mr. Superintendent Laxton been a political policeman, he might have caused arrests to be made for the making use of seditious language. However, as he knew us all to be peaceable citizens, he allowed us to read speeches from the *Star*, sing, and talk as we pleased.[35] We obtained in Nantwich about one thousand bona fide signatures to the great national petition for the People's Charter.[36] I wrote to our county members, Sir P. Egerton and Mr. Tollemache, requesting them to support the prayer of the petition. Sir P. Egerton replied very kindly, promising to vote for its introduction, but reserving his opinion as to its details. Mr. Tollemache, on the other hand, refused to vote for its introduction, saying he should oppose the measure altogether, as the suffrage

[35] Charles Laxton (d. 1882) was special, or deputy, High Constable for Nantwich Hundred from February 1841 until 1857, when he became superintendent of police for the Nantwich division under the County Constabulary Act of 1856 (Hall, op. cit., p. 251).

[36] Nantwich also supplied at least 600 signatures to the 1842 petition (*Northern Star*, 30 April, 1842).

would prove a great injury to the working classes. He wrote me a severe lecture on my democracy. I gave these letters to Mr. Jones, solicitor, to place in his collection of autographs.

During the riotous proceedings in the Potteries a troop of the Shropshire Yeomanry marched into Nantwich to prevent the Staffordshire Radicals laying siege to the old town.[37] Our Rector was so alarmed that he had his windows defended with iron bars. Many of the Yeomanry attended our out-door meetings and seemed highly interested in them. I was secretary to the Nantwich Chartist branch and took the working part in it from the commencement to the end of the agitation.

By some means I was pushed to the front in our movements for local reforms, viz. rates for lighting, paving, etc., church rates, Beam Heath mismanagement, etc. In 1842 a rate was made at the vestry meeting for lighting, etc. I and a few others refused to pay this rate after £70 had been collected. Six of us were summoned for non-payment. This was the first and last summons that I ever was served with.[38] I went to the Hough and stated the case to Mr. Jones. He considered that my grounds for refusing to pay were well-founded and advised me to defend myself in preference to his coming as my advocate. At that time the magistrates held their court in Mr. Lowe's office privately. I requested the magistrates to allow the admission of a few ratepayers in addition to the parties summoned. This was granted, provided the room was not overcrowded and this was the first time the magistrates' room at Lowe's office was opened to the public. The petty sessions were held at the Lamb Hotel, when the public were admitted. Our Rector, the Rev. R. H. Gretton, and Mr. Broughton were on the bench. My first objection to the rate was, the notice given for calling the Vestry meeting was informal. Mr. R. C. Edleston, vestry clerk, was my opponent; he could not find a copy of the notice. The bench considered the production of the notice was highly necessary and wished to know if I would go on without it. I agreed to do so. My next objection was, the rate was seconded at the meeting without it having been proposed. The bench could not understand this and wished me to explain. I said it was certainly proposed by Ralph Cappur, Esq., who was not a ratepayer and therefore nobody in point of law. Mr. Charles Welch, the rate-collector, being present, was requested to look at his collecting-book. When, after much hesitation, he admitted Mr. George Cappur was the ratepayer for the firm, the bench considered this to be fatal to the case. However, I decided to go on with it, and Mr. Edleston and I

[37] This refers to the Plug Plot rioting which began in Hanley after Thomas Cooper's Crown Bank meeting of 15 August 1842 (Hovell, op. cit., pp. 261–2; Charles Shaw, *When I Was a Child*, London, 1903, pp. 155–70).

[38] This document is preserved at the end of Thomas Dunning's MS. It bears the date 9 February and called upon the constables to summon him to appear personally at Lowe's office on 11 February 1843 in connection with the non-payment of a sum of 2*s*. 8*d*. levied to defray the cost of lighting the township of Nantwich with gas for the year ending August 1842.

argued the matter for nearly three hours, the bench requesting me to read each clause of the Act and to give my opinion on them, Mr. Edleston, of course, taking an opposite view of the Act. The bench, however, took my view of it and dismissed the case. Mr. Edleston sent a statement of the case to Mr. Tidd Pratt for his opinion. Mr. T. P.'s reply was favourable as to the legality of the rate, and six other persons were summoned for the non-payment of it. On the dismissal of my summons Mr. Jones sent for me to meet him at the Leopard Inn. I reported to him all that had transpired in court. He gave me credit for my defence, treated me to a glass with him and promised, should any further proceedings be taken against me and my goods be distrained, he would proceed against the magistrates without any expense to me or to my non-paying friends. I attended the petty sessions held at the Lamb Hotel to hear the case against the six fresh-catched ones. Mr. Edleston read Mr. Tidd Pratt's opinion and, seeing me pay great attention to him, he said to me, "I see you are here. What do you think of this barrister's opinion?" I replied, "You ought to have summoned the same parties as before. Had *they* sent the case for Mr. T. P's. opinion, it would have been a different one to yours, I feel sure." "Well, then," said Mr. Edleston, "you are at liberty to state to the bench your objections to it". I accepted the offer and used the same arguments as before and concluded by telling the bench that, if my goods were distrained for the rate, I was advised by Mr. Jones, solicitor, to enter an action against the magistrates. The bench, after a consultation, dismissed the case, and the rate was never collected.

The agitation for the abolition of church rates had now commenced in good earnest. Our veteran reformer, the Rev. James Hawkes, took the lead in it.[39] He was the Unitarian minister, and a many of his congregation, together with several Primitive Methodists and a few Independents, attended vestry meetings and proposed, perhaps, a penny rate, as an amendment to the 3d. or 4d. rate required by the churchwardens and this led to a poll on several occasions the amendments always being the winners. The Small Tenements Act was now passed, and the tenants whose rates were paid by the landlord were eligible to vote. Presently they were prevented from voting, it having been decided that the landlords were to have the votes in proportion to their property. This led to litigation, and Dr. Kenealy was retained to appear before our magistrates on the subject. However, the opinion of the judges as to the meaning of the Act settled the question, and we were allowed to vote again. I wrote to Mr. John Bright asking his opinion, as, when the bill was before the House, he asked the law officers whether the payment of rates by the landlords would disqualify the small tenement

[39] Hall says of this period: "During his (the Rev. R. H. Gretton's) incumbency dissent increased much in the town. The system of Church Rates was so strongly opposed in noisy vestry meetings that on 3rd Dec. 1844, he resigned his living." He was reinstituted, however, on 10 April 1845, and remained rector until his death in 1846 (Hall, op. cit., p. 306).

holders. He replied, he had quite forgot putting the question, but when the new reform bill was passed . . . Thank you for nothing, Mr. J. B.!

On one occasion a penny church rate was proposed in opposition to a much higher one. A poll took place, and I proposed to my Wood Street and neighbouring voters that we should all go to the poll together in the middle of the afternoon, thinking the well-do-do Church folk and tradesmen would poll at that time, after the small fry had cleared away. Between 70 and 80 of us assembled at three o'clock and marched two and two to the church buildings. We took possession of the narrow staircase and had just concluded polling at four o'clock, when the poll was closed, leaving the well-to-do out in the cold. The majority for the penny rate was 70 odd, about the number of our tally. I could give many amusing anecdotes relating to the church rate opposition, and which, if health and leisure permit, I intend doing.

The management, or mismanagement, of the Beam Heath estate—when I first came to Nantwich my attention was drawn to this Beam Heath question. Everybody was continually talking about it and suspecting the Trustees of wrongdoings. Occasionally very small meetings were held on the Barony to discuss the subject, the Trustees were denounced, but no resolutions were ever moved, or deputations appointed to wait on the Trustees. In those days of Church and Tory rule none of the working classes dare "bell the cat". The trusteeships of the charities, almshouses, Beam Heath, etc., were in the hands of the Church party, and if persons who talked loudly about the abuses were asked to assist in reforming them, they would probably reply that some of their relatives were in almshouses, or in receipt of some other of the charities, and they would rather not interfere. And so the charities made cowards of a great many of the bred and born Nantwichians. I and others of a new generation got married and became ratepayers. We could then attend vestry meetings and assist in the election of Beam Heath Trustees.[40] The Act of 4 Geo. IV, (cap. xii) session of 1823, enacted that the following 32 gentlemen be appointed Trustees—"James Bayley, John Barker, Thomas Bebbington the younger, William Betteley, George Cappur, Washington Cliffe, James Cooper, Thomas Copestick, John Downes, Thomas Deriemer, John Eardley, William Garnett, clerk, John Jasper Garnett, Edward Kent, John Latham, clerk, John Latham, Richard Leversage, John

[40] The Beam Heath trustees administer to this day land in the neighbouring agricultural township of Alvaston which has been the property of "all the men of the whole commonalty of the vill" of Nantwich since before the year 1130. At the time of Dunning's activities this land amounted to two-thirds of the area of Alvaston. The powers and duties of the trustees are still regulated by two private Acts of Parliament (43 Geo. III. cap. cxxiii of 11 July 1803 "for inclosing and improving a certain tract of common or waste land, called Beam Heath" and a more important amending measure, 4 Geo. IV. cap. xii of 30 May 1823). The latter provides that when the surplus of income from the land amounts to £500 the same shall be distributed in equal shares among the inhabitant householders of Nantwich who have either been born in the town, or paid rates for seven years or else served a seven years' apprenticeship in the town. Widows of householders so qualified are also eligible. In 1879 the recipients numbered about 1,250 and received 22*s*. per head. Payments are made annually (Hall, op. cit., pp. 404–11).

Minshull, William Massey, Charles Mare, James Parrott, James Plevin, John Pratchett, Benjamin Rodenhurst, Joseph Sherrett, William Sprout, Thomas Steele, Crowdson Tunstall, William Tomlinson the elder, Henry Tomlinson, Daniel Tomlinson and John Withenshaw and he and they are hereby appointed Trustees for executing this act". It also enacted that when and so often as any vacancy shall occur amongst the said Trustees (from causes enumerated) such vacancy shall be made known publicly. Such vacancy shall be supplied at the next general vestry meeting for town business, or by the justices of the peace at any general quarter sessions for the county. At the time I was entitled to vote at vestry meetings (1840), there were only some 6 or 7 Trustees left, and they opposed all attempts to increase their number. However, during the next few years we succeeded in electing a few Dissenters, viz. Mr. W. Johnson, Mr. Wood, Mr. Gregson and another or two and so soon as I had completed my seven years' tenancy and had become entitled to leys, etc., I commenced a movement, single handed, for the correction of certain abuses that had crept into the management of the estate, the first of them being the distribution of the surplus monies. It was enacted that "when and so often as the surplus of the income arising by virtue of this Act shall amount to the sum of five hundred pounds, and not before, after paying of expenses, debts and salaries already incurred, the same shall, with all convenient dispatch, be distributed by the said Trustees amongst such inhabitant householders of Nantwich, as under or by virtue of this Act, shall be entitled to the benefit of leys, in equal shares, share and share alike". For many years the provisions of the Act relating to the £500 had been overlooked, and one pound every two years had been distributed by a Mr. Walley, Trustees' agent, and he paid it away without having a cheque book to prove who were the persons he had paid it to, the public balance-sheet merely stating, "paid to so many claimants so many pounds". My object was to have the money distributed every year, or whenever there was a surplus of £500, according to the Act. I met with no encouragement from my liberal-talking friends. I therefore undertook the task single-handed. I wrote a series of resolutions relating to the management of the estate on sheets of paper, and then waited on my working men acquaintances in Wood Street and neighbourhood, requesting them to attend a meeting to be held at the Swan Inn, Welsh Row, the room having been lent to me for holding the meeting in by Mrs. Latham. The resolutions, if carried, were to be presented to[41] the Trustees at their next meeting. Feeling sure of the resolutions being carried, I wrote out an address, with resolutions, etc., on a sheet of foolscap, ready for presentation, before the meeting was held.

I paid the bell-man to give the meeting a good announcement, and at the time appointed, 6 o'clock, the room was filled. As arranged, I was chairman, as only I knew the long and short of the matter. I explained my reasons for calling the meeting, and the resolutions were all carried unanimously. I and

[41] At this point Dunning's handwriting ceases.

John Hobson were appointed as the deputation to the Trustees. I signed the result of the meeting as chairman, and we reached the Trustees soon after they met, much to their surprise. I read the memorial with resolutions of the meeting to them, when the leading Liberal tradesman and Trustee, Mr. Edward Harrison, grocer, whom I had every reason to expect would be friendly to our movement, turned out to be the mar-plot. He said to me, "Thomas, with respect to the £500 being in our hands, you cannot prove that we have that amount." I replied, "No, sir, I cannot, but if you will allow us your books for a short time, we will retain an accountant to go through them." He said, "The books must not leave our hands. We cannot always get the rents in to the day". I said we were not so unreasonable as to expect the distribution of the money before the Trustees had it in their hands, but hoped they would let us have it paid as early as convenient, etc. We then took our leave of them and returned to the Swan to give a report of our mission, the meeting having kept together until our return. In the course of a few weeks after the meeting Mr. Thomas Johnson[42] was appointed distributor, vice Walley, pitched overboard. He appeared with a cheque book in hand and 12/6 each to the entitled recipients on the year, instead of 10/– as formerly, although the Trustees had recently been expending a considerable amount in the planting of trees and other improvements on the estate. For several years after this movement the dividends gradually increased, the land being now let by auction and higher rents obtained, and from 10/– per annum the dividends rose to . . .[43]

Dunning MS.—

The additions to the foregoing, were copied by me from a rough draft in Mr. Dunning's own handwriting.

E. A. L(loyd).

Lloyd MS.—

[Unfortunately these reminiscences end very abruptly, Mr. Dunning not having time to finish them. They were written at odd times, often interrupted by the entrance of a customer and other causes. He was in the act of retiring into private life when the illness from which he was suffering ended fatally. He died on the 24th of April, 1894. He was respected by all who knew him, those who knew him best respecting him most.

E. A. Lloyd.]

[42] Thomas Johnson had already been appointed Assistant Overseer of the Poor for the township of Nantwich by a poll of ratepayers on 12–13 August 1846, and confirmed in the office 25 August 1846 by the Rev. Thomas Brooke, J.P., of Wistaston, and the Rev. Edward Hinchcliffe, J.P., of Barthomley. (Certificate of appointment in possession of Mr. H. T. Johnson of Nantwich.)

[43] As the oldest surviving minute book in the possession of the Beam Heath trustees only goes back to 7 January 1873, it is impossible to date these occurrences exactly, but Dunning states that they took place "so soon as I had completed my seven years' tenancy". This would mean the period immediately following 1846. Accounts of Dunning's death and funeral are to be found in the *Crewe Chronicle* of 28 April and 5 May 1894 and the *Crewe Guardian* of 28 April 1894.

John James Bezer
(1816-?)

John James Bezer

The anonymous *Autobiography of one of the Chartist Rebels of 1848* appeared in serial form in twelve issues of the *Christian Socialist* between 6 September and 13 December 1851.[1] In pursuit of their mission to re-assert the dominion of Christianity over all forms of man's activity, and in particular the economic and political activity of the working class, the Christian Socialist movement had founded the Society for Promoting Working Men's Associations which in turn launched the *Christian Socialist* as a successor to the defunct *Politics for the People*. The journal's specific object was "to diffuse the principles of co-operation as the practical application of Christianity to the purposes of trade and industry", although its editor and principal leader writer, J. M. Ludlow, set out to deal with the whole field of economic, social and religious affairs. The first issue, printed by the Working Printers' Association, appeared on 2 November 1850, containing eight pages, price 1*d.*, and its circulation gradually rose from an initial 1,500 to about 3,000. For a while it exerted considerable influence within the co-operative movement, but towards the end of 1851 tensions grew among its promoters, particularly between Ludlow and Kingsley; it began to run into financial difficulties, despite a change in format, and the last issue appeared on 27 December 1851, to be succeeded by the *Journal of Association* in the new year.[2]

The author of the autobiography was John James Bezer, the publisher of the second and final volume of the journal.[3] The tenth chapter of the auto-

[1] Ch. I, issue no. 45, 6 Sept., p. 157; II, no. 46, 13 Sept., p. 173; III, no. 47, 20 Sept., p. 190; IV, no. 49, 4 Oct., p. 222; V, no. 51, 18 Oct., p. 253; VI, no. 52, 25 Oct., p. 269; VII, no. 53, 1 Nov., p. 286, and no. 54, 8 Nov., p. 301; VIII, no. 55, 15 Nov., p. 317; IX, no. 56, 22 Nov., p. 333; X, no. 57, 29 Nov., p. 348, and no. 59, 13 Dec., p. 381.

[2] See Charles Raven, *Christian Socialism 1848–1854* (London, 1920, 1968), pp. 154–62 and *passim*; Torben Christiansen, *Origin and History of Christian Socialism 1848–1854* (Aahrus, 1962), pp. 151–61; N. C. Masterman, *John Malcolm Ludlow* (Cambridge, 1963), pp. 102–4, 124–6.

[3] Apart from the congruence of the careers of the 'Rebel' and Bezer (also known as Beezer), the main evidence of authorship is to be found in an article in the *Christian Socialist*, 5 Dec. 1851, signed by "The Chartist Rebel", which discusses the mounting financial problems of the paper. The article begins in the form of a mock dialogue between the "Rebel" and the journal's publisher, "an intimate friend of mine, sir". As the article proceeds the attempt at maintaining the fiction of the separate personalities is increasingly abandoned. Bezer contributed a two-part poem entitled "The Prisoner's Prayer (Written in one of the Condemned Cells of Newgate)" under his own name to the first volume of the journal, and adjacent to each chapter of the autobiography there appeared a large advertisement for Bezer's shop.

biography ends, like its predecessors, with the words "to be continued", and it is clear from various references in the text that he intended to go on at least until what he calls the "Newgate Affair"—his arrest in the government clampdown in June 1848 and subsequent trial and two-year prison sentence for sedition—but was prevented from doing so by the demise of the *Christian Socialist* two weeks later. He was released from prison in April 1850, and opened a radical bookshop at 183 Fleet Street, a few yards from Hardy's old home at 161. He continued to play an active part in the declining Chartist movement, and in the winter elections of 1851, whilst the "Autobiography" was being published, gained a seat on the nine-man executive of the National Charter Association. The executive was at that time rent with dissension over personalities and policies. Bezer sided with Ernest Jones in his opposition to the move led by another executive member, G. J. Holyoake, to seek closer co-operation with middle class reformers, and he resigned from the executive in April 1852 when Holyoake seemed to be gaining the upper hand. Later in the year he gave up the struggle and emigrated to Australia.[4]

There was a significant divergence between the views of Bezer and those of the journal's sponsors. His attitude towards religion, in particular his attack on the aridity and hypocrisy of the dissenting churches, reinforced the campaign of the Christian Socialists, but his resolute defence of Chartism ran directly counter to one of the group's main objectives, to wean the working class co-operators away from the increasingly socialist Chartist movement. The title of the autobiography, and the comments on "April 10th, 1848" in the opening chapter, suggest that Bezer was specifically attacking the image of Chartism and Chartists transmitted by Charles Kingsley, a leading member of the group and a frequent contributor to the journal under the pen-name of "Parson Lot". 10 April 1848 was the date of the demonstration on Kennington Common called to present the third Chartist petition. Prior to the event the Government whipped up the fears of the London middle class, enrolled 150,000 special constables, entrusted the aged Duke of Wellington with the defence of the capital, and created the scenario for a final confrontation between the forces of law, order and property and those of anarchy and violence. When the event passed off peacefully, it was hailed as the definitive proof of the ineffectiveness and irresponsibility of working class protest and the strength of middle class institutions. The Government's version of the event was reinforced by Kingsley's fictitious working man's autobiography *Alton Locke*, which appeared in August 1850. In the work, the Chartist Alton Locke is brought to his senses by his experiences on 10 April, and concludes that as a result of the event, "Chartism is a laughing-stock as well as an abomination".[5] It was this interpretation that Bezer set out to attack, and it is a tribute to either the tolerance or the disunity of the

[4] See R. G. Gammage, *History of the Chartist Movement 1837–1854* (2nd ed., Newcastle, 1894), pp. 338, 353, 380, 384, 402; J. T. Ward, *Chartism* (London, 1973), chs. 8 and 9.
[5] Cassell, 1967 edn., p. 366.

Christian Socialists that the work was included in their journal. In the end, however, Kingsley's voice proved more effective. In 1905, Bezer's old Chartist antagonist, G. J. Holyoake, commented, "The 10th of April, 1848, has for more than half a century held a place in public memory. The extraordinary hallucination concerning it has become historic and passes as authentic. Canon Charles Kingsley was the chief illusionist in this matter. . . ."[6]

Background Reading

R. G. Gammage, *History of the Chartist Movement 1837–1854* (2nd ed., Newcastle, 1894, reprinted London, 1969); Charles Kingsley, *Alton Locke, Tailor and Poet. An Autobiography* (London, 1850; Cassell edn., London, 1967); Henry Mayhew, *London Labour and the London Poor*, 4 vols. (London, 1861); William Lovett, *The Life and Struggles of William Lovett* (London, 1876); Iorwerth Prothero, "Chartism in London", *Past and Present*, 44, 1969; Charles E. Raven, *Christian Socialism 1848–1854* (London, 1920, 1968); Dorothy Thompson, *The Early Chartists* (London, 1971); J. T. Ward, *Chartism* (London, 1973).

[6] G. J. Holyoake, *Bygones Worth Remembering* (London, 1905), vol. 1, p. 74. See also, Ward, op. cit., pp. 206–9; M. Hovell, *The Chartist Movement* (2nd ed., Manchester, 1925), pp. 290–2; John Saville, "R. G. Gammage and the Chartist Movement", introduction to Cass 1969 reprint of Gammage, op. cit.

The Autobiography of One of the Chartist Rebels of 1848

"And every one that was in distress, and every one that was in debt, and every one that was discontented, gathered themselves unto him."[1]

1 Samuel, xxii, *v.* 3.

THE PAST.

"Let those who have in Fortune's lap
Been softly nursed, repine
At days of childhood past and gone,—
Their sorrows are not mine.

Let those whose boyish days were free
From every ill and care,
Regret their flight, in pensive mood,—
Their grief I cannot share.

Let those whose youth in pleasant years,
Untroubled, swift, went by;
With aching heart sigh for the past,—
With them I cannot sigh.

Let those whom now, in manhood's prime,
No cares of peace bereave,
Lament the rapid pace of time,—
With them I cannot grieve.

The retrospect of childhood's years,
To me no pleasure brings;
Nor are my thoughts of boyish days
The thoughts of pleasant things.

[1] The sentence is actually from verse 2 and is part of the account of David's retreat to the cave Adullam.

My youth was crossed, nor on my prime
Does better fortune shine;
Then why should such a luckless wight
O'er the dull past repine?

No! speed thee time—speed on, speed on!
Thy haste I would not slack;
Still less, believe me, honest friend,
I wish to see thee back.

Speed on—speed on then, to thy goal,
And still with swifter wing!
From me thou can'st take nought away,
Whatever thou mayst bring."

1

THE BIRTH

["A Chartist Rebel permitted to write in the *Christian Socialist!* I'll not take in another num."—"Hold, 'Tory Bill,' say nothing rashly." "What *do* poor people want? Isn't there a prison for those who *do* grumble, and a workhouse for those who *don't*, with a Bible and Prayer-book in both places; and a Protestant (we'll have no Popery there)—a Protestant Chaplain to explain the texts properly, in order that they may know their duty to their superiors, and learn meekly to bow to all those placed in authority over them. *Can* the rich do more?"—"Yes. They can 'do unto others as they would be done unto.' They can 'sell (hard saying) *all* they have and follow Christ.' They can glorify God, and 'let his will be done on earth, as it is done in heaven.' They can confess (out of church as well as in it) 'that they have done that which they ought not to have done'—own that 'the earth is the Lord's, and the fulness thereof.' Shake hands with the poor, and

'Brothers be for a' that.' "

"Is there anything remarkable then in your life?"

"No, not very; except, perhaps, the Newgate affair—it is the life of millions in this 'happy land,' 'the admiration of the world, and the *envy* of surrounding nations'—where glorious Commerce has reached such perfection that everything, even the blood, and sweat, and lives, of white slaves, is bought cheap and sold dear,—so dear that the average lives of the poor in some towns amount to about seventeen years."

"Oh, I see it all now! You had *nought* to *lose* in 1848, and so your motto was, 'Down with everything, and up with nothing but anarchy, confusion, and civil war.' Thank God, however, and the *Special Constables*, the 10th of April showed"—

"Showed what?—that class had arisen against class, where there ought to be no classes; that the lower orders had to wait a little longer; that there was a great gulf fixed between the poor and the rich which nothing but practical—mark! practical Christian Socialism can remove."

"Pooh, pooh—there *must* be always poor—the Lord ordained it—it is His will;—besides, the rich are very charitable—very; good Dukes of Cambridges[2] everywhere; and this is a fine country after all—full of soup-kitchens and straw-yards for the *deserving* poor; but they are *never* satisfied."—]

Between the hours of eleven and twelve on the morning of Saturday, 24th August, 1816, in Hope-street, Spitalfields,[3] stood a little barber's shop, serving for parlour, kitchen and bedroom as well.

"They tells me as how you shaves here for a *penny*," said a patron of competition, who had been operated upon aforetime at the shop over the way for three halfpence.

"Yes, sir, I does," was the bland reply.

The man, after being barberously used,—paid, was thanked, and the penny—the *first* that day—placed on the mantle-shelf by the proprietor of the establishment with a sigh; in five minutes after, the Chartist Rebel was born in that self-same shop, with that solitary penny between the *three* of us, and the *brokers* in the place for six weeks' rent at 4*s*. per week! Strange to tell, mother and father were *both* confined on the same day—the former with a surplus population of one, the reward of twenty years' matrimonial love,—the latter with a drunken man in a dirty little watch-house, at the corner of Spitalfields' Church, the reward of knocking down the broker's man,—father considering in a moment of passion, that he was a surplus population of one in such an eventful hour as that. "All's well however that *ends* well." Father was *up* and *out* again in a few hours, (as well as could be expected, as the ladies say), five shillings were borrowed from a cousin in White's Row,

[2] The first Duke of Cambridge, the seventh son of George III, was an indefatigable supporter of public charities, serving, until his death in 1850, as President of at least six hospitals, and as patron or vice-patron of more than a score of other charitable instiutions.

[3] Bezer could scarcely have been born at a less auspicious time or place. Spitalfields, the centre of the East London silk-weaving industry which employed about 50,000 persons at this time, was in the throes of a long decline, set in motion by competition from Lancashire cotton. In 1795 John Thelwall claimed that the industry was almost derelict: "The little summer-house and the Monday's recreations are no more; and you will find the poor weavers and their families crowded together in vile, filthy and unwholesome chambers, destitute of the most common comforts, and even of the common necessaries of life." (*Tribune*, XXIX, 23 September 1795, quoted in E. P. Thompson, op. cit., p. 157.) Even within the context of the long decline, 1816 was a period of particular misery. A contemporary observer described Spitalfields as "a grand drain for the distress of the Capital—a kind of metropolitan workhouse, to which all that is wretched resorts" (T. F. Buxton, *Speech . . . on . . . the Distress of Spitalfields*, 1816, p. 7), and according to the "Report of the Spitalfields Association" of that year, two-thirds of the workforce were unemployed (p. 18). The chances of survival for the infant were slim; Buxton noted that "at this time multitudes of children are swept into an untimely grave by disorders of which abstinence was the only cause, and for which food would be the only cure" (p. 17). See also G. Stedman Jones, *Outcast London* (Oxford, 1970), p. 101; *Add. MS. 34245B*, fos. 3 20, report of Richard Cray.

and never paid, I believe, (but I can plead the Statute of Limitations; besides I was a *minor* then), and better still, the landlord forgave us the rent, saying it was all through me. Thus was I worth to my parents, the first day I made a noise in the world, the sum of 1*l.* 4*s.* sterling. So it proved "good tidings of comfort and joy" after all. My *ungrateful* parents have often told me that I was worth more to them on that day than I have been worth to them ever since.

I can assure my readers that the fact of the goods and chattels being seized upon made no effect on me,—nay, it would have made none even if I had been seized upon myself; so that mammy had been seized with me I should not have minded, the little I wanted I had, and if I could have sung, I should have chanted

"I am content—I do not care,
Wag as it will the world for me."

Six months after my birth, my left eye left me for ever,—the small pox, the cause.[4] For two months I was totally blind, and very bad, the "faculty" giving me over for dead more than once. The "faculty" were wrong; I recovered, minus an eye, and often have I been nearly run over through having a "single eye" towards the road; and often have I knocked against a dead wall, and hugged it as if I really loved the dark side of a question. Ah, I've had many a blow through giving *half* a look at a thing! How many times since I became a costermonger has a policeman hallooed in my ear, "Come! move hon there, vill yer! now go hon, move yer hoff!" while I've actually thought he was on duty in some kitchen with the servant girl, taking care of the house as the master and mistress were out. It was not however so; there he has stood in all his beauty, a Sir Robert Peel's monument—a real one, alive,—and sometimes have I seen him *kicking*.

2

THE SUNDAY SCHOOL

"Then he got eddication,
Just *fit for his station*,
For yer knows we all on us a *summet* must larn."

Mister Benjamin Block.

Right, "Ben," but *what?* Shall it tend to good or ill? A most important question, that not only infinitely concerns the neglected victims of a bad or insufficient education, but society at large; evil training, sir, is like the measles—catching! he who commits a bad action has generally learned to do so, and then he *learns* another, and so the disease goes on.

[4] He was known among his fellow Chartists as "Monops".

My education was very meagre; I learnt more in Newgate than at my Sunday school, but let me not anticipate.

Among the many days I shall probably for life remember, is the 21st of December, 1821, when breeched for the first time, and twopence in my bran-new pocket, I proudly marched to Raven Row Sunday School and had my name entered. From that hour, until the hour I finally left, which, with the exception of two intervenings of short duration, lasted nearly fifteen years, I can truly say I loved my school,—no crying when Sunday came round.

"I loved that blessed day
The best of all the seven."

I yearned for it;—whether it was because my home was not as it ought to have been, (a painful subject I shall feel bound to say something about in due order,) or because association has ever seemed dear to me, or because I desired to show myself off as an apt scholar, or because I really wanted to learn, or all these causes combined—most certainly I was ever the first to get in to school, and the last to go out.[5]

I ought to have learned a great deal, say you, in fifteen years; well, in the opinion of some, I did, for notwithstanding the disadvantages I laboured under both at home and at school, and there only being six hours a week for me, I rapidly rose from class to class; at seven years old I was in the "testament class"—at eight, in the highest—shortly after, "head boy"—soon after that, "monitor"—at eleven, teacher—and long before I left, head teacher;—and yet, what had I learned? to read well, and that was all. Three years ago I knew nothing of arithmetic, and could scarcely write my own name.

I have just spoken of the *disadvantages* at school—I shall doubtless displease some of my readers in what I am going to say, but when I commenced this history, I determined that it should be a *genuine* one, and that I would put down my thoughts without reserve. Now, that school did not even learn me to read; six hours a week, certainly not *one* hour of useful knowledge; plenty of cant, and what my teachers used to call *explaining* difficult texts in the Bible, but little, very little else.

I am not going to enter into any theological discussion, but I *am* going to tell the discipline, routine, and teaching of an average London Dissenting Sunday School of a quarter of a century ago.

'Tis nine o'clock, Sabbath-day morning, the girls and the boys, old and young, are promiscuously mingling together on the door steps; about a quarter past, the teachers begin to arrive, and the doors are opened—a rush up stairs, and a little order restored by the superintendent going round with

[5] For a similar treatment of Sunday School as a haven from a hostile home and work environment, see "An Old Potter" (Charles Shaw, b. 1832), *When I was A Child* (London, 1903).

the early attendance reward tickets, taking at least another quarter of an hour,—then a hymn sung, very likely the following:

"Not more than *others* I deserve,
Yet God hath given *me* more."

And worse still—

"For *I* have food, while *others* starve,
And beg from door to door."

Now, I would rather believe in no God at all, than in such a one as is described in this verse. What! praise the Great Supreme Being, who is no respecter of persons, for giving *me* plenty to eat, and causing others at least as good as I, to starve though surrounded with plenty;—rank blasphemy! it is such teaching as this, that keeps up our monster social evils, from generation to generation, the young mind is taught to attribute that to God, which only "Man's inhumanity to man" has brought about. However, I used to sing it most lustily, though sometimes hungry myself,—and so did my fellow scholars, whether hungry or full deponent is not able to say. Well then, after the singing, an extempore prayer by one of the teachers in turn—a prayer, the language and meaning of which few children could, or desired to understand. At last, about ten, the classes are arranged only to be disarranged at half-past, that being chapel time. Afternoon at two, the same manner of "teaching the young idea how to shoot," till near three,—the classes are arranged again, and the teacher (probably *not* the one who taught in the morning) commences to teach, and what does he teach? It is an A B C class, say, composed of twelve tiny little boys, number one says in a drawling dying tone, "*hay*," number two, "be-e," and so on, till some one makes a blunder, and then he's sent last, his blunder *sometimes* sharpening the wits of the rest, but more frequently causing jealousy and in some instances, (I have known them myself,) lasting hatred. Even this secular education, bad as it was, did not last above half an hour. The teacher would tell us to shut up our books, and talk to us about hell-fire, and eternal brimstone, and how wicked we was, and if we didn't believe all he said to us, we should be burnt for ever and ever, which of course made us feel very comfortable till four,—then another hymn, and an address delivered from the desk to all the children, the orator dwelling on some theological dogma, giving his own peculiar views in an exceedingly peculiar manner—a prayer—a rush out, and all was ended for a week.

I ask, is such education as this worth having? is it suitable? is it that sort of "milk for babes," calculated to nourish and strengthen, and elevate the growing man, who *will* grow for better or for worse. You inquire, perhaps, "Would I advocate a purely secular education?" I cannot say I would. I would inculcate the being of a God—a God of justice—of love—of mercy; more—I would impress on the young mind, that this world of ours was a probationary state, that they that *done* evil were punished here and hereafter, and they that *done* good, their reward was with them, and future glory in another and better world than this; but beyond this, I would no further go; all else I would leave entirely with the parents, and their respective ministers, every creed standing on its own foundation, without help or hindrance from the state.

3

MY FATHER AND MY HOME

"A crust of bread, a bed of straw, and rags."

HOOD.

Father kept a barber's shop, trade was brisk, and times much better than they are now, so that when he really *did* attend to his business, he cleared a good round sum weekly. Mother also earned at cotton winding (before machinery, or rather the monopoly of machinery altered it,) nine or ten shillings weekly;—yet there we were, miserably poor, and the quotation at the head of this chapter was literally my experience for years during my childhood, except a few short months that I remained with my aunt, who, though well off, treated me shamefully, and I ran home again, that being the lesser evil.

Father was a drunkard, a great spendthrift, an awful reprobate. Home was often like a hell; and "Quarter days"—the days father received a small pension from Government for losing an eye in the Naval Service—were the days mother and I always dreaded most; instead of receiving little extra comforts, we received extra big thumps, for the drink maddened him. The spirit of the departed will pardon, and, I verily believe, will rejoice at my speaking thus plainly, not only because it is the truth, but in order to show, as I shall show, the power of Christian principles as exemplified in the after life of him who was as a "brand plucked from the burning."

Father had been an old "man-o'-wars man," and the many floggings he had received while serving his country, had left their marks on his back thirty years afterwards; they had done more,—they had left their marks on his soul. They had unmanned him; can you wonder at that? Brutally used, he became a brute—an almost natural consequence; and yet there are men to be found even to this day, advocates of the lacerating the flesh and hardening the hearts of their fellow creatures simultaneously.

The loss of a considerable sum of money by my father while at sea through the chicanery of his sister, tended, I doubt not, to increase his love for drink. Church or chapel was never thought of by him from his youth till he was upwards of fifty years of age; then—but I will give the facts without comment.

The late Mr. Isaacs, of Gloster Chapel, Hackney, used to lecture on Tuesday evenings, at the time I am speaking of, at Staining Lane Chapel,

City.[6] This gentleman was a favourite minister with my mother, and she was constantly begging father to go and hear him, without avail; she would always get ridiculed for her pains, till Tuesday evening, November 15, 1823, I think,—on that night he offered himself to go if mother would treat him to some gin. She did, and we all three went; father scoffing and swearing, and mother, I doubt not, inwardly praying on our journey. The service had commenced; indeed, the text—the 40th Psalm, 1st verse ("I waited patiently for the Lord, and he inclined unto me and heard my cry")—was just being read as we entered. Presently I noticed, child as I was, the altered looks of father, and as the minister seemed to increase in energy and zeal, father literally trembled again, so much so that several of the congregation noticed it. At length the service ended, and directly we got out, father said, "Mary, my dear,"—the first kind words I had heard him utter for years—"Mary, my dear, let us go home. God have mercy upon me, a miserable sinner." Not a word else, to my recollection, escaped him that night. We all kept awake, for the scene appeared to my young mind terrible. The agony of father was indescribable for several days. At last, without any visitor coming to him, but solely through reading the Bible, hope dawned upon him, and from that time till he died, above eight years, he was a changed man—no more drunkenness or immorality. At the expense of being laughed at, and called a canter, as I know I shall be by some who read this, I cannot refrain from giving a few lines from a hymn he never seemed tired of singing, because they exactly pourtray his altered character and feelings:—

"These eyes that once abused their sight
Now lift to Thee their watery light
And weep a silent flood."

* * *

"These ears that once could entertain
The midnight oath, the lustful strain,
Around the festal board,—
Now deaf to all the enchanting noise,
Avoid the throng, detest the joys,
And press to hear Thy word."

The consequences, however, of this remarkable change in my father did not better our pecuniary circumstances. This may appear strange, but it is easily explained. My father's conscientious convictions would not allow him to open his shop on Sundays, and as it was a very poor neighbourhood,

[6] Staining Lane Chapel is described as "a small inconvenient building, of an oblong form, with three galleries of unequal dimension" (Walter Wilson, *History . . . of Dissenting Churches . . . in London*, vol. 3, 1810, p. 128). "Mr Isaacs" is actually Benjamin Isaac, who was minister at Gloucester Street Chapel, Hackney, until his death in 1850. According to his obituary, he "never seemed more happy in his work than when inviting the thoughtless and perishing by the wayside and in the open air". (*Congregational Year Book*, 1850, pp. 98f.)

Sunday was better than all the week beside to him. His customers rapidly fell off because he was not such "a jolly good fellow" as he was wont to be. All called him mad, the *publicans* especially condemning him as a matter of course; his constitution, too, was so much injured by drink, that the sudden change to strict sobriety seemed utterly to prostrate him, and he was always ill. Mother's work also got slack and worse paid. Still they persevered, and still things got worse, and though "a dry morsel with quietness" was a glorious improvement on the past, they could not at last meet the expenses of the veriest necessities of life. The climax to all was, that the Government pension was stopped altogether, in consequence of father petitioning for an increase, the authorities offering him the hospital. Our little home, which though humble, had become precious to us, was broken up, the persecuted saint went to Greenwich College, and mother and I became out-door paupers to a parish in the City that father claimed through his apprenticeship. "All these things were against us," except that they made a lasting impression on my youthful mind, and I stuck to my Sunday school and to my faith with all the fervour and enthusiasm God had given me.

4
MY FIRST EMPLOYMENT

The parish allowed us four shillings weekly, and with that miserable stipend, and about two shillings more for cotton winding, we managed to pay rent and buy bread till the near approach of Easter in the next year; *then* we bought buns—not for the purpose of eating, (though we *did* eat them after all), but for the purpose of selling again. Three shillings and one little basket were borrowed for this important occasion:—mother put two shillings' worth of buns in the basket, and one shilling's worth in the tea-tray for me, and off we trudged different ways. Mother had given me my round, but then it was much nearer home and Sunday school than I cared about, and worse still, it was a leading thoroughfare. Did I want people to see me? No.—"if people couldn't buy buns without seeing the seller, it *was* strange," so with aching heart, and scalding tears, and scarlet face, I walked up and down the most by-streets, and *whispered* so low that nobody could hear me,

"Hot cross buns!
One a penny, two a penny, *hot* cross buns,"

till, all the gods of Homer will bear me witness, they were as *cold* as the corpse of a Laplander; still I called them *hot* from seven till twelve, and took the magnificent sum of Twopence! . . . Philosophers talk of never giving up,—I think it was Charles II. who said, after reading the following epitaph on a tombstone,

"This man never knew fear!"

"Then he never snuffed a candle with his fingers,"—and I say to any philosopher of *nine years old*,—cry hot cross buns for the first time, for five hours, till you are as cold as they are, and hungry enough to eat the "stock," and then if you don't talk of giving up, you are a noble little fellow. I went home—folks had laughed at me, had rejoiced when I wept, but only two persons had bought,—I went home, I say, determined most dutifully to present mother with the remains of my merchandise, thinking, of course, she had sold out, and would be ready to sell mine too, when lo! my venerable and courageous parent had sold none at all; having met a person she had known years before when she was better off, her courage failed, and she came home again almost directly, and had been looking for me all round the neighbourhood. To tell you the real truth, reader, I was right glad of this, spite of our desperate circumstances—it prevented her finding fault with me; so after we had had our soiree of tea and buns, mother moved, and I seconded, a resolution, to the effect that we would never go out with buns any more, hot or cold. But then what *was* to be done? "I'll get a place," said I. "You, boy! so young and so ailing?" "I will;" and so I did the very next Monday.—May God forgive my tyrant master for the acute sufferings I then endured. . . .

"If you please, Sir, do you want a boy? My name is ——; mother winds cotton for *you*, sir; father is in Greenwich College, and we are in great distress—almost starving, sir,; I'll be very willing to do anything." "Why, you're so little! What's your age?" "Past nine, sir, and I'm *very* strong!" "What wages do you want?" "Anything you please, sir." (The *healthy* competition was all one side.) "Well, come to-morrow morning, six o-clock, and if you suit I'll give you three shillings a-week; but bring all your victuals with you—we have no time for you to go home to your meals." Thus was I duly installed at a Warehouseman's in Newgate Street.[7]

Black slavery is black enough, I doubt not, and white slavery is a very horrid thing in all its ramifications, for it has many—the factory children, and so on;—there is pity, however, manifested towards these unfortunates, and sometimes help, but who ever thought of errand-boy slavery? "Willing to do anything." Yes, and *any*thing I did,—wait in the cold and sleet for half-an-hour each morning at master's street door—clean a box full of knives and forks, a host of boots and shoes in a damp freezing cellar—gulp down my breakfast, consisting of a hunk of bread, *perhaps* buttered, and a bason of water bewitched, called tea, in the cold warehouse—*run* to Whitechapel with a load they called a parcel—back again—"John, make haste to Piccadilly with *this*"—back again—"John, your mistress wants you to rub up the fire-irons and candlesticks, and clean the house windows"—"John, look

[7] Bezer was here following what was to be the most common pattern of employment for boys in London during the century. According to returns made to the House of Commons in 1899, of boys leaving London schools, 40 per cent became errand boys and vanboys, and 14 per cent became shop boys. See Stedman Jones, op. cit., p. 69.

sharp, and have your dinner, you're wanted to go over the water with a lot of things," (dinner! God help me! a penny saveloy when it was *not* in the dog days, and a "penn'orth of baked plain" when it *was*, or bread alone at the latter end of the week)—trail along with my bag full of "orders" along Blackfriars, Walworth, London Road, City, and back to Newgate Street—"John, look alive, —— of Islington Green, wants this parcel directly"—back again—"Now, John, all the 'orders' are ready for the West, so as soon as you've had your tea (tea!), you can start; you needn't come back here to-night,—bring the bag in the morning." Though master *said* my time was from six to eight, yet it was always half-past seven, sometimes later, ere I could start to the "West," which meant haberdashers shops up Holborn, Soho, Oxford Street, Regent Street, Piccadilly, over Westminster Bridge to two shops near the "Broadway," and *then*, eleven o'clock at the earliest, trudge home to Spitalfields, foot-sore and ready to faint from low diet and excessive toil, and this, too, for years without one day's intervention save Sundays, for my master was religious of course. Every night would I crawl home with my boots in my hand, putting them on again before I got in, trying to laugh it off while I sank on my hard bed saying, "never mind mother, I don't mind it, you know I'm getting bigger every day." Indeed 'tis hard

"To smile when one would wish to weep,
To speak when one would silent be,
To wake when one would wish to sleep,
And wake to agony."

Certainly I could have left my place, for this is a free country. What then, should I have got another? And if I had, that's not all—my master was my *mother's* master; and if I had discharged myself, he would have discharged her; he has told me so often—which of course is free trade—so I toiled on, for father was as it were dead to me, and mother always ailing, and I saw no alternative but the workhouse, that worst of all prisons so dreaded by the poor,—so I toiled on, I say, till I was about eleven years of age; then typhus fever laid me prostrate, and for weeks I was to all appearance dying. I was glad to hear that the parish doctor gave me up, and the farewell of my teachers and my fellow Sunday scholars I loved so well, and my poor dear father who crawled on crutches to see me, was, though affecting, happiness to me. I felt an ardent desire for death—but it was not to be. I at last recovered. Still was I thankful even for my illness, inasmuch as it gave me a respite from

"Iscariot Ingots Esquire,
That highly respectable man."

5

SIGNS OF REBELLION

My Master was continually inquiring after my health, though he gave not a sixpence towards improving it; but when I had sufficiently recovered, sent for me, and offered to take me back at 4*s.* a week instead of 3*s.*, and give my mother full work besides, if I complied with his request. I did so, and the day after heard that five boys had discharged themselves during my three months' illness. I had to go through the same routine—endure the same bullying—but mother *did* get more work, (though at 1*d.* a pound, the same as she got 4*d.* four years before, and 2*d.* for just before my illness, but then that was to make up, I dare say, for the extra 1*s.* he gave me). Well, Father *would* come out of the College; he rallied somewhat, and went "a barbering" round Bethnal-green, a sort of itinerant shaver. The parish stopped the supplies immediately; but Father cleared about 6*s.* or 7*s.*—Mother about 3*s.* 6*d.*, which, with my earnings, amounted to 13*s.* or 14*s.* per week;—provisions were dearer then than they are at the present time, yet as we were very economical, not only did we manage necessaries, but our home became gradually more comfortable. As winter, however, came on, Father's rheumatism—as bad an *ism* as a man can be plagued with,—I speak feelingly—laid him on his beam ends; and separation was again our fate. The "College" received him till he died. Mother, too, just at this time fell dangerously ill; and for many nights—hard as I worked in the day—I had no rest. God bless the poor! *they* saved her life when parish doctor, and parish overseer had passed her by, and said that the workhouse would take me, after they had buried Mother;—the poor neighbours—not the rich ones—played the part, as they always do, of good Samaritans, by rushing to the rescue, and nursing her in turns night and day for weeks, without fee, or thinking of fee. God bless the poor! Amen!

Master's tyranny became more and more insupportable. I will give the reader an instance. In the second week of Mother's illness, I was sent to Mile-end Road with a parcel, and as we then lived in High-street, Mile End New Town, close by, nature predominated over my fear of offending, and I came home; it was thought Mother would not live an hour. I stayed that hour, and yet she breathed—and I ran back with quick step but heavy heart. "What has made you so long, sir?" I told him the truth, and he *kicked* me! I never remember feeling so strong, either in mind or body, as I did at that degrading moment; I threw the day-book at him with all my might, and before he could recover his presence of mind, sprang on the counter, and was at his throat. I received some good hard knocks, which I returned,—if not with equal force,—with equal willingness, crying, "Oh, if my poor Father were here,"—"I'll tell Father"—"I'll go to the Lord Mayor"—"I'll tell everybody." The tustle didn't last long, and the result was that we gave each other warning; and I, nothing daunted, threatened to stand outside the street door, and create a crowd by telling every one as they passed all about it;—whilst he threatened, in his turn, to give me into custody for tearing his waistcoat and assaulting him, saying I should get into Newgate Closet before I died. The spirit of prophecy must have manifested itself in a remarkable manner at that moment to that great man. For, lo! as he said, so it came to pass, though many years afterwards. I will not however, give him *all* the praise. The "*signs* of rebellion" were just then rather clear. I was, to all intents and purposes, a "physical force rebel," and I doubt not that "the coming event cast its shadow before" the mind's eye of the immortal W. that is to say, if the immortal W. *had* a mind.

The craven, on that day week, asked me to stay with him; I refused, except for a week longer; that same night, though, I "got the sack." It was past nine o'clock when I started for the West, and trailing up Holborn-hill with my bag full of orders nearly dragging the ground behind me, a policeman—a *new* policeman we called them then—stopped me: "You sir, what er ye got in there, a?" Now I was not in the best of humours just then; indeed, "Crushers" were never very popular with me;—so, (alluding to the policeman who had stolen a leg of mutton a while before, and which was all the talk), I answered promptly, looking at the gentleman as impudently as an embryo Chartist well could, "Legs o' mutton." "I'll leg o' mutton yer," says he; and off I was taken to the Station. The Superintendent behaved very kindly to me, sending the policeman back with me to Master's, with the complimentary message, that "M. —— ought to know better than send so young a boy at so late an hour, with such a load, round the West-end, and that the 'Force' had strict orders to stop any one with loads after nine o'clock, so I had better go in the morning." Master at once gave me my wages, and ordered me not to come again, telling me at the same time that when Mother got better, she need not apply to him for work. But what think you? the next day he sent for me again, and I staid with him two months longer, for 5*s*. a-week, which, with the parish allowance, that had dropped to 3*s*. was all that we had.

The Superintendent of my Sunday-school about this time offered me a place at 1*s*. a week and my victuals, and didn't I close in with the offer without hesitation! The word *victuals* decided me at once, for Mr. A. kept two Ham and Beef Shops, and the bare idea of becoming a "beef-eater" was so agreeable a novelty, that without a moment's warning to my Newgate-street master, I went to my new situation. I trust my vegetarian readers will pardon my backsliding; I had been compelled to luxuriate so long on vegetable *marrow*, that I confess it appeared no *marrow* to me, and I desired a change; besides, you know, I was led into temptation;—Ham and beef, after bread and potatoes! Oh! 'Twas a consummation devoutly to be wished!

I did not keep this good place, however, but about four months, and it was my own fault. The apprentice, who was also Master's nephew, was a wild animal of seventeen years old, and Mr. A. told me from the first, that I was to try and reclaim him. "John, talk to him, I know you can, and though he is five years older than you, your example will shame him into reformation." I *did* talk to him like a parson, at first, and acted as I talked; but alas, evil communications corrupt good manners. At last he influenced *me*, not I him; and though I cannot recollect committing any really immoral or dishonest act, I became very flighty and careless, and incurred the displeasure of my kind master, who at length discharged me, and served me right, for the following very *dirty* spree:—one day we had cooked an extra quantity of hams and rounds of beef, and *then* got into the coppers to swim, as the apprentice called it; he escaped without observation, but I staid enjoying myself, and floundering about in this novel bath for the people, till, who should come right into the cookery but mistress herself; it was all over with me; I implored for mercy but in vain. Master, with tears in his eyes,—he was a glorious soul—said that he wished he could discharge his nephew instead of me, but we must part; he gave me a most excellent character to my next place, a Chemist's, at the corner of Jewin-street, which I kept for near five years. What happened there to me, my Christian experience during those five years, the effects the agitation for the "Reform Bill" had on my mind, &c., shall form the subject of my next chapter. What I have already written, and what I shall write for a little time, is not very interesting to the readers of this journal, I dare say—it is merely one of "the simple annals of the poor;" but as John Nicholls has it "It may perhaps, appear ridiculous to fill so much paper with babblings of one's self; but when a person who has never known any one interest themselves in him, who has existed as a *cipher* in society, is kindly asked to tell his own story, how he will gossip!" Exactly so.

6

SACKCLOTH AND ASHES

I once clothed myself in sackcloth and ashes, *literally so;* and this is how it was,—attend, reader, while I explain, for, believe me, it *is* important. We had a library in our Sunday school; ah, we *just had such a library*,—"Drelincourt upon Death"[8] with the lying ghost story attached, that Defoe forged, (little thinking, good soul, that it would be made a Sunday school Old Bogie of); then "Allen's" I think, or "Aleyn's" "Alarm to the Unconverted,"[9] and many others too, nearly all of the same stamp. But two

[8] Charles Drelincourt's *Les Consolations de l'Ame Fidele, contre les frayeurs de la mort* appeared in English translation at the end of the seventeenth century and was constantly in print during the eighteenth and early nineteenth centuries.

[9] In fact Joseph Alleine, a seventeenth-century puritan who started one of the very first Sunday schools in London. His *An Alarme to Unconverted Sinners* was first published in 1673 and was republished at least seven times between 1807 and 1829.

bright stars in this black firmament we had—Nos. 85 and 86, I shall never forget the numbers, how many times have I read them—Bunyan's "Pilgrim's Progress," and Bunyan's "Holy War."—My own dear Bunyan! if it hadn't been for you, I should have gone mad, I think, before I was ten years old! Even as it was, the other books and teachings I was bored with, had such a terrible influence on me, that somehow or other, I was always nourishing the idea that "Giant Despair" had got hold of me, and that I should never get out of his "Doubting Castle." Yet I read, ay, and *fed* with such delight as I cannot *now* describe—though I think I could *then*. Glorious Bunyan, you too were a "Rebel," and I love you *doubly* for *that*. I read you in Newgate,—so I could, I understand, if I had been taken care of in Bedford jail,—your books are in the library of even your Bedford jail. Hurrah for progress! How true it is, that

"Even the wrong is *proved* to be wrong!"

I am digressing though;—let's see, we were talking of sackcloth and ashes. My teacher, at the time I was speaking of, was an earnest gloomy soul who, if he delighted in anything, delighted in minutely describing the wrath to come; and he *could do it* well. How have I cried while listening to him, and how *pleased* he'd be at my tears, as if sorrow and religion were inseparable. One Sunday afternoon he was particularly eloquent on the anger and *vengeance* of God, and as a climax, told us about the men of old who went in "sackcloth and ashes," and whose "tears were gathered up in the Lord's bottle" (D—— was always very grand and *figurative* at *expounding*). As I went home I felt dreadful, yet a beam of hope shone—oh, if I could only get the opportunity, nobody seeing me, of doing as the "*ancients*" did, I should be saved! So, begging of father and mother (I was not *nine years* old at the time) to let me stay in, while they went to chapel—I actually undressed myself to the skin, got out of the cupboard father's sawdust bag, wrapped myself in it, poured some ashes over my head, and stretched myself on the ground, imploring for mercy, with such mental agony and such loud cries that the people in the house heard me, and told my parents about it, though nobody even then knew the truth. Readers will doubtless laugh at this childish folly, —I marvel if some of them have not committed quite as fantastic tricks, if they would only own it! One fellow-scholar I told this to a few years ago, and who is now an *infidel* through such teaching, admitted that he had done precisely the same. *Yes, through such teaching*,—and I know several such cases, —children have been brought to compare themselves to the Manasseh and the "*Chief*" of sinners, till the *rebound* in after years has led them to suppose that they are no sinners at all, and now they laugh at everything sacred, because everything sacred was mauled about and distorted to suit the views (views!) of anybody who unfortunately "had a call." They were told to believe in a God of *vengeance*, and worse still, *partiality*, and so now they believe in *no* God;—they have been told that there were "children in hell not a span long," and rather than believe *that*, they have banished every idea of a future state altogether. It had nearly that effect on me. "High Calvinists," prepare to meet your God! your gloomy, blood-stained, fanatical, teachings, have been one of the principal causes of the spread of atheism among us. Oh, my dear fellow Sunday school teachers! we have done that which we ought not to have done—we have bent the twig the wrong way—it is we, not infidels, but *we* who have often "turned the truth of God into a lie", and made a creature of Him Who is the Creator, we have *crippled* the glorious image God had made, and *then*—horrible—*then* likened it to the image-maker.[10]

Of course I was "converted" as they call it—oh, to be sure!—and made head-boy of, because I was a "miserable sinner," and didn't I get promoted for it; and wasn't I monitor, and teacher—ay, *teacher* long before I was twelve years old,—and didn't I join the Church at sixteen, and was baptised, and called a "dear promising youth," one who was to be a "burning and a shining light," a minister in "God's own time," one of those "few champions for the truth" who would prove to all the world that nearly all the world was damned, and that the "elect precious" meant only our own precious selves? But now "I am an apostate," say you; am I? Judge not that ye be not judged. I am earnest in propagating that which I think to be truth *now*, and so I was *then*, but I did it ignorantly, and shall be forgiven.

One thing must not be omitted in these humble memoirs; and that is, to give my testimony against those persons who are so fond of saying, that religious people *are so* because it is their interest, and that their zeal is in accordance with their pay. I must admit that there are many white-washed walls, many hypocrites; I could lay bare facts relative to the conduct of both ministers and people, black enough, God knoweth. What then? Such statements would only cause additional pain to conscientious men of all creeds, and serve no good purpose either. Besides, if we are to attack persons for principles, there is an end to all argument,—yet is the outward walk of professors, the first, the primary thing the poor unlettered men look at—no logic is so powerful with us as *that*,—and if the outward walk be wrong, most of us jump to wrong conclusions. I deny, however, most emphatically, and with long experience on my side, I deny, that the motives of Christian people, as a *rule*, are impure. Those who look after and get the "loaves and fishes" form the exception, and this exception is principally confined (will the Editor allow this sentence to be inserted?) to the parsons—indeed, when *they have dined*, there are nothing near twelve baskets' full of fragments remaining, *they'll* take care of *that*. In the Christian world or in the outer, both among the Dissenters and in the Church, those get the most pay who do the least work. There were always collections, monthly, quarterly, and annually, besides

[10] This account bears some resemblance to the fictional childhood of Kingsley's "Alton Locke", who places a similar value on Bunyan and suffers similar guilt torments as a result of a Calvinist upbringing. See pp. 3–8 (Cassell edn.).

tea-meetings and other dodges, for the "dear minister" at the chapel I was a member of; and often have I gone hungry, and mother too, because we gave our very bread into the "plates" at the door, which the deacons on both sides thereof held so close to each other that they seemed to say, "No thoroughfare to Dissenters on the voluntary principle." Yet the "dear minister" didn't work a tenth part so hard as I did in the cause,—but then, mine was a "labour of love." Just as if preaching couldn't be a labour of love also; I see no reason why people couldn't make sermons and make tents too (especially as there's a surplus population of them—I mean parsons, not tents—just now) in 1851 as they did in 51. Perhaps, however, it's all through machinery. . . . At all events, I feel that I am now meddling with things too high for me, and that the bare suggestion is a kind of spiritual rebellion. You must pardon my egotism though, if I describe my Sabbath day's work:—'Tis a summer's Sunday morning. I rise at six o'clock, and get to Spital Square by seven, in order to commence the out-door services, which closed after eight; school just after nine, hard at it, arranging the classes (I was superintendent at this time), till chapel service, which I had to commence, being clerk—giving out the following hymn, perhaps,

> "Well the Redeemer's gone
> Before His Father's face,
> To *sprinkle o'er the burning throne!*
> *And turn the wrath to grace!!*"

(Reader, pause, and ask yourself solemnly the question, if this is a true, a reasonable, a *scriptural* picture of the unchangeable God, in Whom there is no variableness or shadow of turning, and Who is the same yesterday, to-day, and for ever.) Well, chapel would not be over till one, and at half-past, I'd be teaching a select singing-class; at two, school commenced again; at four, I would go out distributing tracts, if it wasn't my turn to deliver the address to the children, then at half-past four; this took me till evening service (often have I had my tea at Spitalfields' pump). Evening service closed, a prayer-meeting in a large room close by, at which I gave an address one Sunday, a fellow teacher composing the hymns suitable—he giving an address the next Sunday, and I composing the hymns that night for him, which, by-the-bye, as it was rather a novel thing, every hymn sung for upwards of a twelve-month being original, soon filled the place, and we could often boast of having a larger congregation than the minister of the chapel. I was never home till after ten at night. I did it without pecuniary reward, or dreaming of it, and this toil, for toil it was, though I did not think so then, lasted a considerable period.

7

A SLAP AT THE CHURCH

I have been requested by more than one valued friend to insert a few hymns and other compositions of my earlier years. There are several reasons for respectfully objecting, but two will very likely suffice. First, I can't, because but one is preserved; and secondly, I won't, because that one is not worth preserving. Indeed, if I am to go on jabbering at this rate, there'll be nobody to read the Rebel's Autobiography save the Rebel himself, and I want to get over that part relating to my religious experience as quickly as can well be, connecting it together at once, without referring again to the subject.—I have been a Churchman as well as a Dissenter, and the being a Churchman for a few months made me a Dissenter for ever. Mother was a Churchwoman according to Act of Parliament. The poor old body didn't perfectly comprehend the difference between a church that was established by law and a church that wasn't, and I have often thought that if others had been as dark in their understandings on the matter as she was, there would have been much less malice, hatred, and all uncharitableness among us. But no; we have "perfectly comprehended" how to differ, forgetting—some of us, I fear, wilfully—that it would be much easier to agree. A good old minister once said: "There is Calvinist-street, and Baptist-street, and Wesleyan-street, and Independent street, and Church-street, and Dissent-street, all leading to the High Road, if we are but sincere, and we needn't jostle each other, though the streets *are* narrow." That's it, *sincerity*—

"He can't be wrong whose life is in the right."

But then that's not orthodoxy.—Well, its *my* doxy, and I am writing *my* auto., if you please.—I protest against a great deal that is called Protestantism and Dissent from a great many Dissenters, yet must I have a "Slap at the Church."—This phrase is borrowed. When I was errand-boy at the Doctor's, the agitation for the Reform Bill, the whole Bill, and—botheration to it—nothing but the Bill, was all the go. I well remember the bellman going round Cripplegate, announcing the majority of *one*, and the excitement created round the neighbourhood. Among the many periodicals living on the agitation, was one yclept "A Slap at the Church,"—my master's favourite paper;[11] for master was a great radical—one who'd beat his wife and shout for reform with all the enthusiasm of a glorious freeman; like many radicals in the present day, who can prate against tyranny wholesale and for exportation, and yet *retail* it out with all their hearts and souls, whenever they have an opportunity. Well, this "Slap at the Church"

[11] An illustrated radical journal, edited by William Carpenter and John Cleave, which ran from 21 January to 12 May 1832. As its title suggests, it was principally preoccupied with abuses within the Anglican church. It claimed to have sold 7,000 of its first number and to have had a readership of 300,000. (Patricia Hollis, *The Pauper Press*, Oxford, 1970, p. 118; Joel Wiener, *A Descriptive Finding List of Unstamped British Periodicals 1830–1836*, London, 1970.)

I'd con over in my leisure moments. I don't recollect what it contained, except that it was of a very meagre and abusive description; but I *do* recollect that there was always on the frontispiece a superior wood engraving of an exceedingly elevated character, most likely a Bishop, who was sure to be represented as enormously stout. I never had the honour of seeing but one Bishop in my life, but I have been taught both by oral and written traditions to believe, that to be a Bishop you *must* be a fat man; and so rooted and grounded was I in this faith, that when a Bishop who *happened* to be remarkably thin passed through Newgate Prison, while I was examining for a few months the place, I wouldn't believe it *was* one. "He is indeed," said the Governor, "it is the Lord Bishop of ——." "Then, sir," said I, "the Whigs have been starving not only the People but the Priests, and there *will* be a row, for *they* won't stand it."

In a former chapter it has been told you, that mother and I were paupers. —Now mother, directly she got on the "books," was expected to attend her parish Church; I say *expected*, because that was the emphatic expression of the poor-law guardian, and all paupers know that when his worship the guardian *expects* a thing, he generally gets it. Moreover, there were some free seats *made on purpose for paupers*, so admirably constructed that most of the dearly-beloved rich brethren—separated of course by pews, in direct contradiction to the injunction of that uncouth Christian Socialist James—could see how their poorer brethren behaved themselves. An excellent arrangement,—else, there would have been nothing to look at but the clergyman, and nothing to hear but merely the gospel. If those seats hadn't been filled by a respectable number of non-respectable dependants on our free institutions, the awful spectacle of Fraternity would have been exhibited in all its revolutionary deformity in the very House of God—shocking! So, to obviate such infidelity as *that*, Twopenny Loaves—always of the same size—and Sixpence, were given away weekly to all who could claim the parish, and who couldn't claim a conscience. I was one of that number,—yes, for more than six months every Sunday morning, one of that number. "B——, why don't your son come with you? you know he's on our books." "I'll tell him, sir." *She* knew how hard it was to get me away from my dear Sunday school. At last the order came, ay, the *order*—do you doubt my word? do you tell me that this is England? I repeat, the *order;*—tyrants can play their game by more moves than one—the order, in the shape of the following protestant inquisitorial mandate, given by the Right Honourable the Guardian, in the year of our Lord, 1828, in the city of London as aforesaid. "Your boy *belongs to us* the same as yourself, and we shall *expect* him next Sunday; if he don't come, why, of course we can't *keep* two of you, that's all *I* got to say." So I went—was ushered into the presence of the Rector, and examined in the most pompous manner imaginable, "Do you know your Catechism?" "Yes, Sir;" (I meant the Assembly Catechism by Watts). "What is your name?" "My name, sir?" "Yes." ". . ." "Who gave you that name?" I hesitated:—the question was repeated with an extra frown, and I replied, "Uncle, sir; I think he wished me to be named aft—" "Tut, tut; how have you brought up this boy, Mrs. B.?" "If you please, sir," said mother in all proper humility, and with a profoundly reverent curtsey, "he goes to a Dissenting Sunday School." "Yes, sir," I added, as bold as a quaker just seized on, "I'm a Dissenter." "Dear, dear, a youth like him talk in this manner! You ought to know better, B——." "Can you read, boy?" "Yes, sir," (I could with truth have added—"a great deal better than you read the prayers to-day"). "Do you know the Lord's prayer?" "Yes, sir." "The Belief?" "I believe not, sir." "Well, you must learn all these things." And so I did; and I don't know that I'm any the worse for it; perhaps better; but I do think that the *effects* of learning them would have been different, had the wandering sheep been kindlier treated by the shepherd. *He* didn't put me in his bosom, or even carry me on his shoulder to the fold, but he dragged me there, and that was *one* of the reasons at least, that I wandered again. I was confirmed at Bow Church, (by the way, I have made a mistake—I have seen *two* Bishops; but upon my word, he who confirmed me, I don't know if he was fat or lean),—it was all a *task*. After Confirmation, I sat on the same bench with mother, till one practice, which above all others, to my mind, young as it was, appeared even then absolutely revolting, caused me to leave:—the vile paupers partook of the Sacrament *after* the respectable among the congregation! Yes; when *they* had supped off the sacred elements, the lower orders had the leavings—Spiritual Lazaruses, waiting for the crumbs falling from a Saviour's table, the "Common-people's" Saviour. A long way off, in the Southern States of America, black people take the Lord's Supper after the white people, and "talented lecturers," who can't bear black slavery (no more can I, or white slavery either) expatiate on this matter with "thrilling" eloquence, and amid loud cries of "shame, shame." Yet is this same damning insult to God and man perpetrated in our own Temples, and "talented lecturers" never think of crying "Woe, Woe." Never mind, my black and white brother slaves, The Eternal will set all to rights soon. The day is near, that great day—the books shall be opened, and the first shall be last, and the last first, Glory to God in the highest! This sure and certain hope, though, shouldn't deter us from speaking out on these matters. God hates wrong in all its forms, as much as we *ought* to hate it, and He will help them who help themselves. The "Board" took 6*d*. a-week off the allowance three weeks after I refused to go any more to Church—I don't know *why*, because they wouldn't tell us, and I'm not going to *insinuate* any thing; but such was the fact; and if it *was* because of that refusal, why I won't grumble; to be fined only 6*d*. a-week for conscience sake is very cheap as the market goes. Ask France.

You must not suppose that I have not been to a Church since—I have many times—the first day, the service appeared very cold and dead-like, but that perhaps was, because I was so used to Dissenting forms of worship;

for afterwards I gradually warmed towards it, and there is nothing in the Church service (which appears to me to be very Socialist), at all justifying such a scandalous separation of the Lord's people as I have just been describing. Indeed, Dissenter as I am, (though for reasons Dissenters little think of,) I do love the idea of a National Church, but then it must be National;—a Church for the people—the poor man's Church, till there are no poor. Don't let's whitewash the thing. "Well, what is to be done?" Done! you have to *do* very little; your great work is to *undo*—fall back upon primitive principles and primitive practices; let there be *one* action, and there will soon be but one Lord, one Faith, and one Baptism. Hunt after the foxes less and the people more, and you will not have to hunt after them long; think of the "labour aggression," and you need not fear the "Papal aggression." Come to the help of the Lord against the mighty, and the mighty shall fall, and the weak your *real* strength, shall gather themselves together and take shelter under your protecting wing; they have gone under other wings and found them hollow; take advantage of this circumstance. Many Dissenters have strayed farther from the good old way than you, and if they had the power would be much greater despots than you, with all your faults, have ever been. Take advantage of this circumstance, I say, in your favour; and let the Spirit and the Bride say "Come," and we will come. Fewer creeds and more deeds and we *will* come.

This is my Slap at the Church, given, I appeal to God, in all humble sincerity. There must be something done by somebody soon. Will you do it?

8

TRADE TRICKS AND SNOBBISM

My employer, the chemist, retired from business with, he admitted, a good round sum (the profits on physic are *rather* considerable), so I had to retire too, from *that* business, with half-a-crown he gave me—no doubt a fair share of the earnings *we* had accumulated during five years. Shortly after I got a place at Camberwell. The fact of its being so far from mother and school was unpleasant; but then, I had my victuals again—an important consideration —a good bed to lie on, for the first time in my life, and more enjoyed the pure air, to me, an unadulterated cockney, not so valuable but almost as yellow as a guinea, after seeing for so many years little else than mud; having an intimate acquaintance with tiles, but no knowledge of stiles; not remembering anything of fields, except of Spitalfields and Moorfields, which were no *more fields* than a horse-chestnut is like a chestnut horse. The change was like emigrating to another country—another world. I had lived previously for a long time in Whitecross Place, near Barbican.

It is said, God made everything. I don't believe it; He never made Whitecross Place, the entrance to which was the narrow way that leadeth unto stinks. A gutter passed through the middle of the court—a pretty looking gutter, from which the effluvia rose up, without ceasing, into our elegant second floor front; a room, or rather a cell (we paid 2*s.* 3*d.* rent weekly, for the blessed privilege of breathing in the accumulated filth below); a hole in which the bugs held a monster public meeting every night, determined to show what a co-operative movement could do. I say, God never made Whitecross Place. He is not the author of filthy lanes and death-breeding alleys. Landlords and profit-mongers make them, and then proclaim national fasts to stay the progress of the cholera. "Be not deceived, God is not mocked; whatsoever a man soweth that shall he also reap." Camberwell looked more like God's work, a great deal, and getting up as I did at daylight every morning, with my master, to help him to dig in his beautiful garden, made me so happy, and so healthy-looking during my five months' stay there, that my brother and sister Cockneyites scarcely knew me, when I returned to Dirtshire. I made a great mistake in leaving that place; not that the situation was over remunerative, or the master over kind. He kept a grocer's shop—that is to say he sold everything—a sort of co-operative store, of which he was the sole manager, and I the only member; doing all the cheating according to his order. I will not be too hard upon him, though he *did* make the half-penny bundles of wood smaller, by taking out the middle pieces for his own fire-side; though he *did* sell the same batter at three different prices, and performed other numerous innocent trade devices, by which he became a landlord, and builder of several houses, and was looked upon as a respectable man of some standing in society, too magnanimous to pick a pocket, and not hungry enough to steal a penny loaf. I will not be too hard upon him, I say, for he salved his conscience every night by reading prayers, and every week by going to chapel. Beside, he was not worse than his glorious descendants, the chicory dealers in Fenchurch Street, and certainly not worse than the system that engenders and maintains so much hypocrisy and wrong, nor worse than my former employers to wit. The first would cut his ribbons and nearly everything else two yards shorter than their warranted value, and then sell them at an "enormous sacrifice;" for ever "selling off," yet never sold; a bottomless pit of "bankrupt's stocks." Every article he sold he lost at least fifty per cent by; yet did he live well by his losses, keeping his servants, and his country house at Norwood. How was it done? That question puzzled me for a long while,—how anybody could live by their losses—till one day an Irishwoman selling murphies explained it beautifully. Says she, "Sir, by my *sowl* I loses by every tatie I sells." "How do ye manage to live, then, Biddy?" "Och, I sells so *many on 'em*, that's it." Ay *that's it*, and the *many* fifty per cents. W—— lost kept his head above water. He'd have certainly sunk, had he lost *one* fifty per cent., but he took good care of that. Well, even my ham and beef man could oil his stale saveloys day after day, and ticket them as fresh Germans; so with my friend, the chemist, whose antibilious pills (I have made some thousands of them, God forgive me), were the best in all the world—proved so by hundreds of testimonials in the possession of the philanthropic inventor, whose self-interest was the last thing he dreamed of. The care of the afflicted was this philosopher's sole aim, and the only reason of his "twenty years' ceaseless study of that dire and excruciating pain, the head-ache." I don't think he lost much by his pills, or he'd have said so, for he was a man of strict truth, and benevolence, withal; advice was given gratis, which advice invariably ended in pills; gluttony in pills was a cardinal virtue—the more you took the better—for *him.* So with the Calvinist grocer, whose high, or rather low, antinomian principles had taken such deep root, that he thought no more of lying and cheating to save three farthings, than the Whigs do to save their places. And so *used* had I been for many years to help in these swindling transactions, that no qualms of conscience caused me to leave Camberwell but this:—On the 16th day of April, 1833, I was helping the servant to shake a carpet, in the lane, when her attention was directed to a woman who had fallen on the ground a little way off. I ran with her to assist, and it was mother—poor mother! She had gone to Greenwich College, that being her regular day to see her husband, and *did* see him, but it was in the "dead house," and then walked from there to Camberwell, to pour out her grief with the only soul she could, but the sight of me had unnerved her, and she fainted away on the high-road. It appears father had fallen suddenly ill, and though both our directions were with the nurse, she had omitted to let us know, hence our friend, without shaking hands with either of us, stepped into the river—*the river.* His last words were, according to his attendant and fellow wardsmen,

> "Sweet fields beyond the swelling flood,
> Stand dressed in living green."

and so he swam over to the other side, without a murmur or a doubt. "Ah," says some very clever *reasoner*, "his brain was turned;" yes, thank God, it was —the right way. "May I die the death of the righteous, and my last end be like his."

> "A happy man, though on life's shoals,
> His bark was roughly driven;
> Yet still he braved the surge because
> His anchorage was in heaven."

We shall meet again. I would not lose that blessed faith for all the "*reasoners*" in the world. He was buried in the College ground, keeping death-company with those who had fought for their king, their country, and their grog. The warriors rest *there* in peace; when shall the hated name be altogether forgotten? Oh! for the hour when

> "*War shall die*, and man's progressive mind
> Soar as unfettered as our God designed?"

Oppression must cease first, though; let the Peace Society remember *that.*

Mother, who was never of a very strong mind, was this time nearly broken hearted, and she so earnestly begged of me to leave my place, and get one nearer *her*, that I did so, certainly against my own inclination, for the little surplus of money I had over and above my urgent necessities helped to comfort her. But I did leave it; and then began *again* a bitter struggle for bread. Week after week did I crave leave to toil; but, no; the curse which to me would have been a blessing, was denied, and destitution—the very poor know what I mean by that terrible word—was really felt by us. At last a cousin says to me:—"Why don't you learn the snobbing, Jack;[12] I'll teach you for nothing, and the first money that you earn you shall have." "Agreed." (I dare say some of my readers think that my father might have learned me to shave; I think so, too; but, for some reasons or other, he ever had a repugnance to it, and that's all I can say in explanation.) The first week of my "snobbing" we lived upon mother's pauper allowance, and the *last* two old chairs we sold for 1*s*. 9*d*. The second week I earned by "sewing" 1*s*. 10½*d*., and I lived on *that* with bread at 8*d*. a quartern loaf; a pound of which, and a "ha'porth" of treacle, was my day's allowance, with a halfpenny baked potato, and a suck at the pump, for my supper. Can any Vegetarian beat that? I had 4½d. left on Sunday, which I expended on threepen'orth of bread, a pen'orth of pea-soup, and my treacle. The next week I rose to 2*s*. 6*d*., and rose my extravagance in the same ratio, not saving a cent. The next week, 3*s*. 9*d*., a shilling of which I gave mother. *She* thought that I had had my victuals given me the last three weeks, but *I* deceived her, as she had often deceived me aforetime, by saying she had had a meal when she hadn't, in order that I might have it; so it was only tit for tat. Well, after that "George" gave me 5*s*. a-week, for a month, and then I worked again for myself, and earned about 6*s*. weekly, not increasing for a long time, because each new part of the mystery shown me necessarily backened me for a while. At last, in less than a year, I became a snob, but not a *shoemaker*; not a tradesman. No; it would be harder for me to learn to make a *good* shoe, than perhaps, if I had never learned how to make a bad one. Cousin was what is called a "Chambermaster,"—making up on his own account, "Bazil work;" and after buying leather, and all the etcetras, how much do you think he had for them? 1*s*. 4*d*., which was soon reduced to 1*s*. Mind, ladies, "spring heels," labour, materials, and all. Of course, the leather was of the worst description; the insoles only paper and oilcloth cuttings, from the dust yards, and the stitches —I can't *exactly* state their length, because we were never particular for an inch or so, but they were well black-balled over, to look tidy to the eye, and ticketed as ladies' shoes, of superior quality, only 1*s*. 9*d*.—the warehouseman and shopkeeper getting 9*d*. a pair between them, and the *maker* not above 3½*d*. Well may a friend of mine cry, "Cheap, cheap, cheap, means cheat, cheat, cheat."

[12] "Snobbing" was the dishonourable side of the shoemaking trade. "Snobs" were unskilled and non-unionized, and their increasing numbers were both a cause and a reflection of the declining status and prosperity of the London artisan shoemakers.

Cousin managed, by the help of his wife cutting out and binding, and one of his children sewing, to earn a pound, or perhaps a little more, weekly, but I never could rise above 10*s*., and this by dint of hard and close work, so much so, that in two years I was nearly blind, and the doctor ordered me to abandon it at once, on pain of losing my sight altogether.

9

LOVE, MARRIAGE, AND BEGGARY

While I was a "Snob" I fell, (they may well call it *falling*), in love, and I proved myself quite as much a snob in *that*, as in trying to make shoes. There were some marvellously pretty girls, teachers in Artillery-street Sunday School,—most of whom got mated while there, as a reward, I suppose they thought, for their labours; but I loved the ugliest of the lot, as my wife will testify, who was *not* the ugliest of the lot, as she also is willing to testify. Mary B——, at the time I was 18, was 25 years of age; *very* short, much pitted with the small pox, bandy, and remarkably bad tempered. Yet, how I loved her, no "Lyrics of Love" can tell; and the many poems I wrote, and took them myself to her in order to save postage, and get *one* smile, which was hard enough to get,—I can tell you, by reason of her plurality of frowns, are too sublime for this periodical.

I *could*, I think, write a whole chapter on love—all about "divine images" and "angelic forms,"—and how the sun shone when she smiled, and how all the stars looked dim when she didn't—for lovers can tell the weather by signs better than anybody else—but age, and reason, and the *one object* in writing this "auto," call on me to stay; nor should I have mentioned this circumstance at all, had not the fact of her jilting me three separate times (the false Bloomer!) been one of the principal causes of my leaving my first love—my Sunday School—and having led me thence by degrees to the very confines of atheism.

There were two young men in our school, called severally "David" and "Jonathan," from the fact of their being always together; and their hearts seemingly knitted together by long affection. We (for I was David) had joined the school together, got promoted together, distributed tracts together, joined the same church together, been baptised together, and—oh, tell it not in Gath!—kept company with the same woman together; but *that*, "David" didn't know, till one Sunday night, having missed her for a while, who should come into the Chapel but her own delicious self and—yes, *and* "Jonathan!" I was just going to give out a hymn, for which I immediately substituted another, commencing with

"How vain are all things here below,
How false, and yet how fair."

And I *did* sing it too, as spitefully as a disappointed one of five feet high well could. "Jonathan" carried off the prize. How she could have induced him—for it *was* she I'm sure—bothered me, but I attribute it to her tongue, which was of considerable length—most ladies' tongues are.

Well, nothing seemed to go right after Mary refused to be such a fool as to cast in her lot with a boy earning ten shillings a-week.—The Chapel looked gloomy and desolate, and I quarrelled with everything. Even the parson I rebelled against—serve him right, though, for he was very proud and overbearing to us teachers, refusing even to let the scholars meet to sing; so I and one of the deacons headed a little band of malcontents, and opened an opposition shop to preach the gospel of brotherhood in; that deacon is now the minister of a flourishing congregation in the Tower Hamlets. After a time I left him too, and became Clerk at a little Chapel, the minister of which used nearly every Sunday to say that nobody but himself preached the truth; and so must his small congregation have thought, for when he died, they all split up into individuals, refusing to listen to any other man.—What hard thoughts of God!

About this time I unfortunately got married, and I did very wrong. Without any clinging to the unnatural Malthusian doctrines, I own we did very wrong—both of us. Thank God I did not deceive her; she knew precisely my circumstances, and bitterly, very bitterly, have we suffered for our folly. When I married, I was porter at twelve shillings a-week, at a place where they bound books for the Bible Society;—every man, woman, and child working there, were terribly beat down in their wages. Good Christian people distribute Bibles to the poor at a very cheap rate, with the words "British and Foreign Bible Society" outside;—and inside it is written "Cursed is he that grindeth the faces of the poor." Outside and inside—the comparison is indeed odious,—oh the cursings I have heard in that place! not a soul throughout the establishment, that I knew of, even professed religious principles, except myself, and I got discharged for doing so.—I was singing a hymn quite in a low tone while working; one of the mistresses happened to hear me and imperiously ordered me to desist, though *songs* were often sung among the binders up-stairs. I replied, that I thought it strange I couldn't praise God while working among Bibles, and so was immediately sent about my business. This was but three months after my marriage, and get another place I couldn't. God knoweth I tried, as a drowning man would try to get to land, for our little home we had somehow scraped together—and which was much more comfortable than we have ever been able to get up since—was every week going—going—going, and our little child every week coming—coming—coming; and at last it came. That was a horrible day—the birth-day of my first boy! Wife, it was thought, would die; *and I knew why* die—from sheer staring want. No joy was in our nearly empty room, but all was desolate, and the very blackness of despair. "Why not apply to the parish?" Because ever since the day the guardian had told mother that he wouldn't "keep two of us," it ran in my head, and mother's too, that if I applied, her money would be stopped. It was a foolish idea, but we had nourished it for so many years that it became as it were a creed, and so rather than rob mother, as I thought, why, let us all die! The next morning, that we might not die, I went to aunt's at Old Ford—my rich aunt's, she that had gotten her brother's money,—and she shut the door in my face. From thence I went to Brixton. "What for?"—To sing, to beg, to cadge: I was thinking of omitting this portion of my life; but no, the truth shall be told—the whole truth. That was a hard day's work, that 7th day of February, 1838.[13] Fancy now; I, a hungry man, running before daylight (for I *did* run) all the way from Ray Street, Clerkenwell, to Old Ford, half-hoping, half-despairing, half-mad, to a rich relation I despised, and whom I had not seen for years, to ask her for a miserable five shillings, because I knew her miserly, ugly heart—the being refused with the brutal taunt, that it "served me right and my fool of a wife too". The crawling back homewards down-spirited and ready to perish, with no text in all God's word floating in my turning brain but Job's wife's advice, "Curse God, and die," "Curse God, and die." While wandering along Whitechapel Road, the sudden idea struck me that I would sing a hymn or two for bread and wife, and child—but I couldn't just there, known as I was all about the district. So on I went through the city, and passed over London Bridge, determined to begin at once, stepped into Thomas Street for that purpose, and then stepped out again; and thus I acted in several streets along the Borough. However, I *would* commence, *that* I would, when I got to the other side of the "Elephant and Castle." But no, courage failed again, and on I travelled.—I will not weary my reader as I was wearied, by recounting my repeated trials, and my as repeated failures, till I got right on to Brixton. Necessity, it is said, has no law, and I began to feel the truism by then; nobody knew me there surely, and if they *did*, here goes—"God moves"—begin again—"God moves in a"—out with it, and so I did, almost choking,

"God moves in a mysterious way
His wonders to perform."

Just before I had concluded singing the hymn, a penny piece was thrown out, and without waiting to thank the donor, or even to give any further specimen of my vocal abilities, I pocketed the affront and went and spent it in Gin! "Oh you impostor!"—it is a lie! "Oh you drunkard!"—another lie! I was

[13] There is some doubt about the dating of the final section of the autobiography. According to the narrative he joins the Chartist "Locality" meeting at "Lunt's Coffee House on the Green" just over a week later. However, at this date there was virtually no Chartist activity in the capital, and the Charter itself, to which he refers, was yet to be published. The Finsbury Locality of the National Charter Association was formed in about October 1840 and met at Lunt's Coffee House at Clerkenwell Green from about December 1840 to about June 1842, when Lunt's Coffee House moved to a new address and the Locality found a new meeting-place. This suggests that "1838" is misprinted or misremembered and should read either 1841 or 1842.

never drunk in my life, and I dare to say never an impostor. I own my first thoughts were for bread, but I felt too far gone for that, and an invisible spirit seemed to say, Have some gin, it will give you courage. And so it did, whether false or true; it answered my purpose, for I went on again with energy to the tune of "Church Street,"

"God moves in a mysterious way,"

and then, hymn after hymn, and street after street, without flagging, while the coppers came rattling down like manna from heaven. Whether it was my singing loudly—for I had a good strong voice at that time,—or my peculiar earnest manner, I know not, but, when I counted up my gains at about six o'clock, they amounted to six shillings, and, I think, fourpence. Heavy at heart, and yet much lighter than before, I laid out threepence in bread and cheese and beer, and began to march home, so tired, that in spite of my eagerness to see how things were, I did not reach it till late at night; and when I did, the first words that greeted me from her mother were, "Hush, for God's sake, Jane is dying;" and from my mother "Why, John, my boy, you look dying too—where have you been to?" "Oh I've been—don't bother me." And then a faint voice from the bed, "John,"—I ran to her side, and, says she, "where have you been to?" I whispered, "I've got a place, my dear, got to go to-morrow, a good place, too—cheer up." It was a lie! but a white one, and I believe it is not recorded against me in the book above. I then put the six shillings on the table, and sank into a chair exhausted. "Why, where did you get all that money?" said both mothers at once, "I've earned it," said I, "Well earned it—don't bother me." And so I had *earned* it, for that was a hard day's work both for body and mind, was that same 7th day of February, 1838. Quite as hard days, however, were yet in store—in the next chapter I will tell you all about it, and how and *why* I became a Rebel—a chapter I think of dedicating to my Lord John Russell, for he ought to know *why* men become Rebels.

10

HOW I BECAME A REBEL
DEDICATED TO MY LORD JOHN RUSSELL

The second morning of my begging experience, I took out sixpence, and afterwards was sorry for it, for somehow I *could not* begin my wretched toil, till all was expended, nor did I get rid of my last penny till towards evening. During all these hours—for I started early—I must have travelled many miles, round the north of London, all the time, just *going* to begin, but not commencing. When it was just dark, however, I summoned courage enough to strike up in a back street at Holloway,

"O God, our help in ages past,
Our hope for years to come."

No money:—then

"Grace, 'tis a charming sound."

But no money. Thinks I, I'll just sing my favourite "God moves," and then if nobody gives me anything, I'll just give up for to-day at any rate,—and nobody did, so home I went, and then saw doubly my folly, for Jane was still worse, and the money I had gotten the day before was nearly gone. My mother's pauper allowance was all mortgaged for victuals eaten nearly a week ago, from a chandler's shop; and her mother was as poor as ourselves, not having had a place as monthly nurse—the labour on which she depended—for many months; and her husband—Jane's father—had left them and gone no one knew where, ever since his child was five years' old. Well, on the third morning, after praying to God most heartily, that He would open a new path, and in the meantime, give me the courage of a Christian under these trying circumstances, (I note this fact, because I had not *really prayed* for some days, and because on that day I *did* seem to have more faith and courage), I went out, determined, as a punishment for my yesterday's weakness, to commence at once. And sure enough, in Wilderness Row—a thronged thoroughfare, and not a quarter of a mile from my residence—begin I did, and got a halfpenny while singing a hymn. Now, thought I, I've put my courage to the test, and paid penance into the bargain; but for fear I should be seen by those who know me, I'm off farther a-field. At Islington I fairly began my day's work, and had scoured it well by two o'clock, with four shillings save one farthing, (a poor old woman *would make* me take a farthing, with many apologies that she hadn't more, God bless her), as my reward. I ran home with this sum, with the intention of going out again after an hour's rest. But fortitude failed when the stern necessity had temporarily hidden itself—*there was enough for the day*, and I didn't like my new business well enough to work at it till we were all getting hungry. Besides, I began already to think that, by perseverance, I could get any day enough food and something to spare,—in other words, could live much more comfortably by begging than by hard work. Look at the *Tariff*, legislators,—2s. for draining one's very life-blood out by incessant laborious toil, from six in the morning till eight at night—3s. 11¾d. merely for *asking for it*, from nine till two P.M. Oh! if that idea had taken root, as it has taken root in thousands, spite of your treadmills and vagrant laws—what an accomplished beggar I'd have been by this time! This idea, however, was only a passing one with me, but mark—I got *bolder* every day. The next day was Saturday, and I, by dint of keeping my sense of shame in the background for ten hours, managed to scrape up either a few halfpence under or over 7*s*.—I don't recollect which—but I *do* remember having a Sunday's hot dinner on the following day. No remarkable proof of my powers of memory by the way, for when a man has to go without a dinner for weeks and months consecutively, and then happens to make a mistake and get one, a hundred chances to one but he remembers the "why and because";—dinner *time* comes regularly enough, but dinner and dinner time are not quite synonymous terms. I can't say that I much enjoyed my hot mutton and dumplings; for though wife had got somewhat better, she couldn't eat a bit, and the unceasing thinking of *how* I gained it, made me feel very uncomfortable;—not that I thought I had done wrong, nor do I think so now, but most certainly, a potatoe, with the knowledge that I had *sweated for it*, would have gone down much easier. On that day I sang too, but then it was in the dark at S—es Street Chapel, Bethnal Green. The congregation little thought when I gave out, with a deep sigh,

"God moves in a mysterious way,"

that I had sung it scores of times on the previous days in the streets! Ah! the heart only knoweth "its *own* bitterness," a wise arrangement. On Monday morning (pardon, reader, if I weary you by being so particular,—I am telling, as briefly as I can, of eight days of real agony, and the telling of it seems to relieve me even at this hour)—on Monday morning, after,—like a "giant refreshed" with two strong cups of tea and a bit of yesterday's mutton, I started off for Brixton again, with this idea,—that I'd go day after day the same round, once more, saving every farthing over necessities, for capital to buy things to sell again in the streets,—*that* was better than begging. Well, I got but 2s. 9d. all day—yes, I got something else—a threat to be sent to the "Mill" just handy. "That'll cure you of your singing about here, I'll *warrant*," said a gentleman to me—what a many spurious things people do *warrant* to be sure! Now that gentleman was no social doctor at all, though he might have been one of the many social *quacks*. Being sent to the "Mill" would *not* have cured me, or at least if it had cured me of *that* disease, it would have perhaps brought on a worse—thieving. Prisons are not *hospitals* for social disorders, I'll *warrant*, though they ought to be, I'll warrant.

Tuesday, had 1s. 7d. I was out many hours too, but very low-spirited. Just as I was going to commence, I met a person I had known from childhood—an old schoolfellow; we talked over the days that were gone, and when we parted, the reminiscence seemed like a cold weighty stone at my heart. He went on his way, not knowing of my day's task;—if he had, he would have helped me, I believe, with his last penny;—but then he was poor, and nothing seemed so recoiling to me as that any one should know what I did for my bread. I think it was on this day that I began singing in a street where some other beggar, with a woman and two children was imploring the inhabitants for relief. I didn't notice him at first, but he soon called me aside, and with a terrible oath said he'd kill me if I dared to oppose him. I tried to explain, but to little purpose, and we parted with the comfortable assurance from him "that I was either *jolly green* or a b——y rogue, and that if I didn't know that to come and cadge in a street where another cadger was *working*, was not against the *rule* in the "Siety," he'd make me know it by jumping my guts out." I think I hear the ejaculation, "*There* was a wretch past all redemption."—Nonsense; he might have been redeemed with very little trouble; there was at least the germ of something good in that man; ay, that *man*—his sentiment was manly after all; if you take away the chaff, and the rough way in which it was delivered, and *sift* it well, the wheat will appear, meaning simply this, "Don't enter into such public competition with your fellow-man, and thus rob him of his share—there's room enough for all, if you'll only give *all* fair play." The man was right, and so was the "Siety."

Wednesday. A very lucky day; 9*s.* and odd—including a half-crown a lady gave me. "Ma'am, this is a half-crown." "I'm aware of that," says she, as a tear started to her beautiful eye. "God bless you!" "And God bless you," I repeated, "Pray let me tell you *why* I am thus;"—but no,; with another most benevolent look, she vanished. I have often thought she knew me; whether or not, she did right, and she did wrong. She *happened* to do right by giving that half-crown to *me*, because I expended it properly, but she did wrong in not inquiring and ascertaining first. The people who give half-crowns away in the streets must have good hearts, but not very sound judgments; they err on the right side, but still they err. If benevolent people would give with judgment, not depending on any society, but on their own *personal observations*, they would do twenty times more good, and save half their money. In all my eight days' cadging experience, I was never asked a question; so I might have been an impostor all the while. Well, well, better give an impostor now and then money, by mistake, than miss the blessed opportunity of saving a poor starving wretch from dying, by withholding a penny, or even half-a-crown, if God has made you steward of a good many.

I put away, out of the 9*s.*, 5*s.*, with the determination to begin on Saturday with that trifle, if I couldn't get more, by the sale of memorandum books, and other stationery. On Thursday morning, going along Fleet Street, or the Strand, I saw, what I looked out for every day in my travels—a bill up in a window, for "A Man Wanted;" and I lost three parts of the day before I could get an answer. And the anxiety I felt—the war between hope and fear, all those hours—was very severe. "Call again in an hour;" then "another hour," and so on. At last the lottery turned up a blank. He couldn't take me, because I'd been out of work so long, "six months, and above; oh, dear no." Suppose I'd told him what I had been doing the previous week, it *would* have been an "O, dear, no," most heartily given. *That's it*, you see. Once an outcast, mind what you're at; if you are only hungry six hours, why they'll give you to eat, but if hungry six months, O, starve away, or beg, or steal, there's plenty of workhouses and jails for such obstinate burdens, and we pay rates, and very heavily too, to keep them out of our sight. God save the Queen!—I went on late that afternoon to Chelsea, sick at heart with hope delayed, and then—as it had been many times before—blasted—and took seventeen pence, the last money I got by singing in the streets.

The next day I became a Rebel, and this was how it was, "Lord John,"—all facts, without a comment. Going up Holborn on Friday morning, I met a man carrying a board with bills on it, having words to the following effect:—"Give no money to beggars,—food, work, and clothing, are given away to them by applying to the Mendicity Society, Red Lion Square."[14] What, food, work, clothing, given away! O! here's good news! Let them give me work though, and I'll find food and clothing myself.—"I say, governor," to the man with the board, "what's all that mean?" "What's all what mean?" said as comical a looking figure-head as any Great Exhibition directed by phrenologists could well produce. "That bill." "Vy, dos'ent yer know?" "No." "Vell you *is* raw, and no flies." Now what this distinguished agent of the Association meant by *raw*, I did not then comprehend, and what flies had to do with his reply is also a mystery which future enlightened generations must unravel; for he did'nt tell, and I did'nt ask him. I wanted just then to get at something else. "Do, my good fellow," said I, "pray do tell me if I really *can* get food, work, and clothing, and how." "Is yer a beggar?" "No—yes." "Now none of yer lies, 'cos if yer is'nt a beggar, the gemmen vont giv yer not nuffin." "I am, I am, my friend." "Vell then, you must get a ticket." "A ticket?" "Yes, or it's not no account I tells yer." "And how am I to get a ticket?" "Vy go to Russell Square, or any o' them air grand cribs, and axxe the first gemman you meets." "Shall I say you sent me?" "O no, yer fool; jist axxe, I tells yer, for a ticket for the Mendickety Siety, and they'll give it yer, and then take it to the place what's directed, and then (with a leer—such a leer!) you'll see what you *will* see." I thanked him, and started for Russell Square, full of wonderment. Sure enough, I *did* get a ticket, of the third person I asked. Here was fortune!—food, work, clothing, by just applying for it; and I had not known of it before; well, I *was* a fool, as the man just told me. Food, work, clothing! and with joy and boldness I knocked at the office door in Red Lion Square. "What do you want," said the opener. "Here's a ticket, sir," (showing it for fear he wouldn't believe me) "I want to see the gentlemen inside." "O, go round the corner; that's *your* way," and he slammed the door in my face. Ah! stop

[14] The "Society for the Suppression of Mendicity" had been in existence since 1818. The stated object of the Society "was to protect noblemen, gentlemen, and other persons accustomed to dispense large sums in charity, from being imposed upon by cheats and pretenders, and at the same time to provide, on behalf of the public, a police system, whose sole and special function should be the suppression of mendicancy". For a fee, recipients of begging letters could refer them to the Society for investigation. Applicants to the society were to be examined, and those found to be genuine given food, money, clothing or employment where appropriate. Those found to be imposters were to be arrested and prosecuted at the instance of the society. In 1841 the society "registered" 997 cases, "committed" a further 1,119 vagrants and provided a record 195,625 meals. The figures for 1842 were 1,233, 1,306 and 128,914. (Henry Mayhew, *London Labour and the London Poor*, London, 1861, vol. 4, pp. xxviii, 399–401.)

till I see the gentlemen, *they'll* not speak to me so, thought I, as I went round the corner, and down some dirty steps. And then such a scene presented itself to me as never can be effaced from my memory!—a hundred—fully a hundred, of the most emaciated, desolate, yet hardened, brutal-looking creatures, were congregated together in the kitchen, the majority of them munching, like so many dogs, hunks of bread and cheese. I was told to pass on, and then another hundred daguerreotype likenesses of the first hundred met my bewildered gaze, waiting to pass a wooden bar one by one. Of course I had to stay my turn; and not knowing how to be "jolly" with them—for even these neglected miserable wretches were jolly—I got finely chaffed. I dare not attempt to write their filthy remarks;—one man, however, in all that Devil's crowd, took pity on the "green one," and I began to tell him all about the food-work-and-clothing idea, which still kept wandering about my brain, though it seemed trying to find an outlet as if tired of stopping there. I shall never forget how heartily he laughed, as I related to him my affair with the board-man,—Bill Somebody, of the "Dials," whom he appeared to know very well. After informing him how long I had begged, and pretty well all my circumstances, he said to me, "I tells you what, old flick, you've been deceived,—its all lies,—they only give you a bit of bread and cheese, and you must be up to snuff to get *that*,—not one in a hundred gets more. Clothing's all my eye. And them as gets work, it's to break stones at six bob a-week—its all lies I tell you." Now by this time I scarcely knew who to believe—the gentlemen who advertised such good things, or the poor beggar who had branded them as liars. But in about an hour longer, I found out.—It was my turn to pass the barrier—I was ushered into a room by a beadle, and stood behind another bar like a criminal; and on the other side sat six gentlemen, as people call bears that are dressed well; when the following dialogue, nearly word for word, took place, between me and the chairman:—"Well, what do *you* want?" I fumbled for my *prize* ticket, and said, "Here's a ticket, sir,—a gentleman gave me in Russell Square." "Well, well, what do you want, I say?" "If you please sir, I met this morning a man carrying a board on which was stated that I could get food, work, and clothing,—but I only want work, sir." "Are you a beggar?" "Yes, sir." "How long?" "Eight days." "Only eight days,—are you sure of that?" (with a cunning infidel leer). "Yes, sir, that is all." "Are you married?" "Yes, sir." "Ah, I thought so. How many children have you got?" "One, sir." "O, I wonder you didn't say a dozen—most beggars say a dozen. How do you beg?" "I sing hymns, sir." "O, one of the pious chanters,"—with a grin at the *gentlemen*, who grinn'd too, at his brilliant wit. "Have you applied to your parish?" "No, sir." *That* did it,—that *truth*,—if I had told a lie, the wrath of his worship the Chairman might in time have been assuaged, but telling the truth proved I was not "*up to snuff*," for in a loud, angry voice he called the officer, and thus addressed him,—"Officer, you see that fellow—you'll know him again—he goes about singing hymns; he says only eight days,—is that a truth?" "O dear no," said the lying scamp, "I've known him for years!" "Ah, now, mark him well, watch for him, and directly you catch him, lock him up, and send for me. We'll have this gentleman before a magistrate, and he shall sing hymns on the treadmill."—Now its some time before I break loose, but when I do, I never stay at a half-way-house—all the way there and no stoppages,—is my motto; so I retaliated, as every honest man ought to do when he's insulted and belied by a thing that feeds on him according to law. I retaliated, I say, with equal warmth, calling him a liar (a scriptural phrase by-the-bye) point-blank, and all the *gentlemen* too; —"you advertise lies, said I, wholesale, now lock me up, and I'll show the magistrate and the world that *you* are the impostors, and obtain money under false pretences from the benevolent." Well to be sure, I expected to be collared every moment.—Yet I fired away, bang, bang, till I was more than a match for the Chairman, who at last listened staring, without saying a word, but just a grunt now and then, like a pig as he was. One of the *gentlemen* at length said—"Give him some bread and cheese, and let him go," (I was hungry enough, for not a bit of anything had I tasted since eight in the morning, and then it was late in the afternoon). Well, they gave me another *prize* (*!*) ticket, entitling me to half-a-pound of bread and a piece of cheese, and I went back into the kitchen to get it, pocketed it, and was about to sheer off, when the beadle stopped me and ordered me to eat it there. "I shall not," said I. "You must." "I won't." "Then give it back." "I won't do that either." "Then come along with me," and I was again before the immortal six. "Sir, he won't eat his bread and cheese." "O, then let him give it back." "He won't do that, sir." "You must, sir," said the Chairman to me. "I won't." "You must, I tell you, it's the rule, and you must obey it." "I don't care about your *rules*, I want to share it with those I love, who are as hungry as I am, and if you are a Devil with no natural feelings, I am not. Get out of the way, beadle," and out I rushed, like one mad, through the crowd of astonished beggars, right into the street, without one stopping me.

After I had got home, and told them of my adventures, (I had told them of my *singing propensities* a day or two before), I went downstairs to the landlord to pay him a week's rent out of the four I owed him, and the good fellow said, "Never mind, if you haven't yet got any work, I don't take any till you do, I'm sure you'll pay me—how long have you been out of work?" "Near seven months," I said, with a sigh, thinking more of the dogs I had encountered in the day than anything else. "Ah," says he, "there'll be no good done in this country till the *Charter* becomes the law of the land." "The Charter?" "Yes, I'm a Chartist—they meet to-night at Lunt's Coffee House on the Green—will you come?" "Yes." It was only a "Locality" meeting, but there were about sixty people present, and as one after another got up, oh, how I sucked in all they said! "Why should one man be a slave to another? Why should the many starve, while the few roll in luxuries? Who'll join us, and be free?" "I will," cried I, jumping up in the midst.

"I will, and be the most zealous among you—give me a card and let me enrol." And *so*, Lord John, I became a Rebel;—that is to say:—Hungry in a land of plenty, I began seriously for the first time in my life to enquire WHY, WHY—a dangerous question, Lord John, is'nt it, for a poor man to ask? lending to anarchy and confusion.[15]

Well, but it wasn't my fault, you know. When *you* are out of *a place*, you are about the first one to cry there's something wrong.—Now I was out of *a place*, and so I cried the same. Politics, my Lord, was with me just then, a bread-and-cheese-question. Let me not, however, be mistaken;—I ever loved the idea of freedom,—glorious freedom, and its inevitable consequences,—and not only for what it will fetch, but the *holy principle*;—a democrat in my Sunday School, everywhere—and whether the sun shines on my future pathway, or the clouds look black as they have ever done, neither sun nor cloud shall alter my fixed principle.

"A boy I *dreamt* of liberty;
A youth—I said, but I am free;
A man—I felt that slavery
Had bound me in her chain.
But yet the *dream*, which, when a boy,
Was wont my musings to employ,
Fast rolling years *shall not* destroy,
With all their grief and pain."

[15] It is interesting to set Bezer's personal account alongside the report made by Richard Cray to the 1839 Chartist Convention on the politicization of the Spitalfields silkweavers: "The great majority of the Weavers now are from Loyal Subjects converted to Radicals nay I may say Democrats, their extreme misery has done some good, it has taught them to think. Particularly the younger Branch of the Trade for they are more Enlightened and many of the old ones has different opinions now to what they had when they were in prosperity." (*Add. MS. 34*, 245B, f. 15.)

Benjamin Wilson
(1824-1897)

Benjamin Wilson

Benjamin Wilson's *The Struggles of an Old Chartist* was published by a local printer, John Nicholson, in October 1887. It enjoyed what the *Halifax Courier* called a "good sale" locally, but does not seem to have circulated outside the district. The *Courier* carried an extract from the account of 1848 on 5 November 1887, and early in the 1890s, Wilson wrote a series of articles for the paper on "Halifax 60 years ago and the progress it has made" which covered a wide range of social history, including living conditions, recreation, education and local superstitions. He returned to the columns in 1895 with three articles attacking the claims of the newly formed I.L.P. that they, and not the Liberals, were the true inheritors of the spirit of Chartism and Ernest Jones.[1] These were followed by a series of twelve articles entitled "Chat, on the Politics of the Century" which presented a general history of radicalism from Cato Street to the 1867 Reform Bill.[2] After the various occupations mentioned in the autobiography, Wilson finally became a gardener, and gained a considerable reputation as an expert horticulturalist, serving for many years as a judge at flower shows. As a raconteur, Wilson died with his boots on. On 21 June 1897 he was a guest speaker at the old folks treat at the United Methodist Free Church, Salterhebble, on the occasion of the Queen's Jubilee. "Towards the close he rose to propose a vote of thanks to the alderman and councillors of the ward, and told some interesting reminiscences of a tea which took place at Skircoat Green at the time of the Queen's Accession. He had just concluded a story about an old lady who on that occasion had taken as much rum punch as was good for her (a tale which caused some amusement among his hearers), when he said 'This excitement is too much for me, I shall have to sit down'."[3] He collapsed and died shortly afterwards.

Background Reading

G. R. Dalby, "The Chartist Movement in Halifax and District", *Transactions of the Halifax Antiquarian Society*, 1956; G. J. Holyoake, *The History of Co-operation in Halifax* (London, 1867); Frank Peel, *The Risings of the Luddites, Chartists and Plug Drawers*

[1] "The Independent Labour Party and Mr. Ernest Jones", 16, 23 and 30 March, 1895.
[2] The articles ran from 27 April to 3 August 1895.
[3] *Halifax Guardian*, 26 June 1897.

(3rd ed., 1895); Sidney Pollard, "Nineteenth Century Co-operation: from Community Building to Shopkeeping", in Asa Briggs and John Saville, eds., *Essays in Labour History* (London, 1960); John Saville, ed., *Ernest Jones* (London, 1952); John Vincent, *The Formation of the British Liberal Party 1857–1868* (London, 1966); J. T. Ward, *Chartism* (London, 1973).

THE STRUGGLES
OF AN
OLD CHARTIST;

What he knows, and the part he has taken in various movements.

CONTENTS

The Peterloo Massacre;
The Chartist Movement and its Leaders;
The Exciting Scenes of 1839 and '48;
How Elections and Township's Affairs were Conducted 40 years ago;
The Plug Plot Riots of 1842;
The Origin and Struggles of the Co-operative Movement in Halifax;
The Reform League's Agitation and the Hyde Park Riot;
The Marquis of Salisbury's description of the 1867 Reform Bill;
A Complete Record of the Halifax Borough and Municipal Elections
&c. &c. &c.

Price Threepence

HALIFAX
JOHN NICHOLSON, COMMERCIAL PRINTER, NORTHGATE

1887

The Struggles of an Old Chartist

by Benjamin Wilson, of Salterhebble

I was born at Skircoat Green, August 7th, 1824.[1] This village had long been noted for its Radicalism.

On August 16th, 1819, a Reform meeting was held in St. Peter's Field, Manchester, (afterwards called "Peterloo,") at which 60,000 persons were present; the magistrates ordered the cavalry to charge the people, when they dashed onward, striking a great number down with their swords and trampling under their horses' feet; 6 people were killed and 640 wounded. Meetings were held throughout the country, including one on Skircoat Moor, condemning the conduct of the Manchester magistrates. I have heard one of my uncles say that in consequence of the above massacre there was great excitement in this village, and that he, along with a number of others, went into mourning and wore grey hats with weeds around them. A great procession started from Halifax to attend a meeting near Huddersfield, marching through the streets of that town in solemn silence with their heads bare, as a token of respect for the victims of Peterloo.

The women of this village were not behind the men in their love for liberty, for I have heard my mother tell of their having regular meetings and lectures at the house of Thomas Washington, a shoemaker; she well remembered the name of Mr. Camm; and they, too, went into mourning and marched in procession, Tommy's wife carrying the cap of liberty on the top of a pole. I was not surprised at the people being so earnest in the cause of Reform when I heard my mother tell how the people had to suffer; when she was a girl she brayed sand[2] for a neighbour, getting some potatoe parings for it, which her mother boiled and they eat them.

At the passing of the first Reform Bill in 1832 there was great rejoicing and the Skircoat Green band was engaged by the Liberals. It was somewhere about this time that I first heard anything about the yellows, as the Liberals

[1] Skircoat Green was a large village of a pleasant and agreeable situation lying between the banks of the Calder and Hebble just to the south of Halifax. Its population was about a quarter of that of Halifax, rising from 3,323 in 1821 to 4,060 in 1831. It was incorporated into the borough of Halifax in 1899 and is now a suburb of the town. (John Crabtree, *A Concise History of the Parish and Vicarage of Halifax*, 1836, pp. 399–400.)

[2] Pounded up lumps of sand.

were called; they said they were the friends of the poor people, and the only reason that I had for being a yellow was that I was poor and they were my friends.

Sometime after I went to work for Mr. Wm. Denton, farmer and shopkeeper, who was very kind to me and I lived well whilst there; but many a time since then have I known what it was to be short of something to eat; I still kept talking about the yellows that they determined that I should have a new cap, with a yellow girdle round it, of which I was proud and wore it a long time. I was very fond of going to Halifax, when I could get, during the elections. I well recollect the first time that I went, but which election it was I could never tell, I was standing below the Turk's Head Inn when Mr. Michael Stocks, junior, of that day, came out from the Union Cross Inn. He pulled a yellow handkerchief out of his pocket and waved it round his head; he then said something, but what, I could not hear, the people then commenced shouting. Whilst I was standing there a procession of women came in at the bottom of the street as though they had come from Woolshops, and in a few minutes after several men on horseback decorated with yellow ribbons came from various directions, who, I have since thought, must be taking the news to different towns.

The first election for members in Halifax took place on the 12th and 13th December, 1832; the following were the candidates:

Rawden Briggs (L)	...	242	Michael Stocks (R)	...	186
Charles Wood (L)	...	235	J. Stuart-Wortley (C)	...	174

I well recollect seeing a yellow banner—with "Stocks for ever"—floating on top of his son's building at Shaw Hill. The second election took place on the 6th and 7th January, 1835; the candidates were

Charles Wood (L)	...	336
James S. Wortley (C)	...	308
Edward Protheroe (L)	...	307

Party feeling ran very high in this election, known as the "window-breaking" election. The Skircoat Green band was engaged by the Liberals, but were attacked by a number of Tories in Bull Green, who tore a banner they had with them in pieces. This news soon spread throughout the town, causing great excitement, and very soon thousands of people congregated in the streets and marched to the Tories' headquarters, breaking the windows and doing other damage; Hope Hall the residence of Mr. Christopher Rawson, many hotels and other places belonging to the Tories were visited, much damage being done. The parliament was of short duration, for King William's death on the 20th June, 1837, caused another general election, and in consequence of Mr. Protheroe being defeated by one vote only he became very popular at the coming election; a song entitled "Protheroe is the Man" was composed, and played by all the bands in the district, and nearly every boy you met whistling was almost sure to be whistling that tune; his popularity appeared to be principally amongst the working classes. As the election day drew near there was much excitement, and on the day of polling there were thousands in the town waiting for the result of the poll, which was as follows:—

Edward Protheroe (L)	...	496
Charles Wood (L)	...	487
James S. Wortley (C)	...	308

This election took place on the 23rd of July, 1837.

On the 8th of May, 1838, the People's Charter first made its appearance, and will ever take a prominent place in the history of this country. It was drawn up by six Members of Parliament (Messrs. O'Connell, Roebuck, Leader, Hindley, Crawford and Col. Thompson) and six working men (Messrs. H. Hetherington, J. Cleave, J. Watson, R. Moore, W. Lovett, and H. Vincent), and contained the following: Universal Suffrage, Vote by Ballot, Annual Parliaments, No Property qualifications, Payment of Members, and Equal Electoral Districts. On the 14th February of the year following the Chartist convention met to discuss certain programmes to be put before the country; the people were recommended to arm themselves; another question discussed but *not* adopted was what they called "the sacred month," i.e.—that the people should cease working for a month, in order to induce the government to passing the People's Charter. They also presented a petition to parliament signed by 1,283,000 persons.

Joseph Wilson, my uncle, was a small piece-maker in the village and it was about this time that I went to help him in the warehouse, and wind bobbins. My aunt was a famous politician, a Chartist, and a great admirer of Fergus O'Connor. It was whilst there that I first became acquainted with the Chartist movement.[3] The delegates to the convention broke up at Whitsuntide, and forthwith addressed meetings throughout the country. On Whit-Monday, 1839, a great meeting was held at Peep Green, which I attended along with Samuel Jackson, a neighbour; we joined the procession in Halifax, which was a very large one headed by a band of music, and marched by Godley Lane and Hipperholme, at which place the Queensbury procession joined us; on reaching the top of the hill above Bailiffe Bridge we met the Bradford procession, headed by Peter Bussey, on horseback, and wearing a green sash. On our arrival at the place of meeting some thousands of people had already assembled, and for almost an hour we witnessed the continuous

[3] Halifax had taken an active part in the anti-Poor Law agitation in 1837, and the first public meeting on the question of petitioning Parliament for reform had been held as early as January 1838. By the end of the year the local magistrates had become so alarmed at the scale of Chartist activity that a troop of dragoons was sent to the town and in April 1839 General Napier received reports that drilling and the collection of arms was going on in the Halifax area, and that copies of a book, *Defensive Instructions for the People*, were circulating in the town. (G. R. Dalby, "The Chartist Movement in Halifax and District", *Transactions of the Halifax Antiquarian Society*, 1956, pp. 94–7.)

arrival of processions from different directions, with bands playing and flags and banners flying, a great many of them far superior to any that I have seen in our late demonstrations. At the commencement of the meeting I had never seen anything to compare with it in numbers, and scarcely ever since have I seen anything to equal it. The proceedings opened with prayer by Mr. William Thornton, at the close of which Fergus O'Connor put his hands on his shoulder and said "Well done, Thornton, when we get the People's Charter I will see that you are made the Archbishop of York." Thornton I knew well, for he lived at Skircoat Green; he was a fine speaker; I had heard him lecture in the Wesleyan School in the village. He was very popular in the Chartist movement, but very soon after went to America in order, it was said, to avoid imprisonment. This was my first meeting in the Chartist movement.

Fergus O'Connor's paper "*The Northern Star*," was the recognised organ of the Chartist movement, and was doing great service on its behalf; it had a large circulation in Halifax and neighbourhood, and its total issue was reputed to be 60,000 per week.

The Chartists were becoming very numerous in this district, and throughout the country great alarm was caused by the large numbers who were arming themselves.[4] A meeting of delegates was held in Yorkshire to name the day when the people should rise; November of that year was fixed, and Peter Bussey, of Bradford, was appointed leader, John Frost, a magistrate of Newport, was chosen leader in Wales; but, when the time came, Peter Bussey had fallen sick and had gone into the country out of the way, or, being a shopkeeper, he was hiding in his warehouse amongst the sacks. Henry Vincent was arrested and imprisoned at Newport; the Chartists determined to release him, and, in a drenching storm in November, they assembled in thousands, armed with guns, pikes, &c., with Frost as their leader; and marched towards the prison; on their way they met the soldiers, a scrimmage took place in which 10 men were killed and between 40 and 50 wounded. Frost, Williams and Jones were arrested and sentenced to be hung, but afterwards reprieved and transported for life. Between 400 and 500 were imprisoned, some of whom served long periods. After twelve months imprisonment Henry Vincent was liberated, but he never afterwards took active part in the movement. He commenced lecturing and became very popular, and was one of the finest orators of his day; I have heard him several times in Halifax. Thomas Cooper, likewise, had to suffer, and whilst in prison he wrote a poem entitled "*The Purgatory of Suicides*," a work of high standing. He was born of humble parents and had to fight the battle of life through

[4] See the note signed by James Rawson and Thomas Aked and apparently written by James Rawson, giving information of alleged Chartist activities in Halifax at this time: "2 Houses taken by the Chartists of Nathan Smith that his their Meeting House the place his called the Street Queens Head they was casting Bullets from Saturday Night the Day following Joseph Spencer says he as a spike and a Gun in is possession from the information we have received had not Peter Bussey been taken badly they would of commenced the same day that Frost did." (Quoted in Dalby, op. cit., Appendix, p. 109.)

great difficulties, yet was master of several languages and a splendid public speaker.[5]

July 2nd, 1841. Edward Protheroe (L) 409. C. Wood (L) 383. Sir G. Sinclair (C) 320. Number of Voters, 899. This was the tamest election since the borough was enfranchised.

The Chartist agitation appeared to be thoroughly crushed, and the people felt great disappointment; they really had thought they were going to accomplish all they were agitating for, and some began to despair that it never would be done.[6] It was Byron, I think, who said:

> "Freedom's battle once begun,—
> "Bequeathed from bleeding sire to son,
> "Though baffled oft,—is ever won."[7]

The trade of the country had not been so bad for many years as it was in 1842, and more particularly in Lancashire, where a great number of factories were idle, thousands of people out of employment and in a wretched condition. In August of this year, nearly all the Lancashire mills were standing in consequence of the drawing of the plugs by the operatives, and it was rumoured that they were coming to Halifax to stop the mills by similar means, which greatly alarmed the local authorities who made preparations by swearing in a large number of special constables and also by bringing a great force of soldiers into the town. On August 15th the news came that the mob were marching from Bradford in thousands;[8] I made my way to Halifax

[5] See Cooper's *The Life of Thomas Cooper* (London, 1872). He was sentenced to two years' imprisonment in 1843 following his part in riots in the Potteries in 1842.

[6] Wilson gives a rather misleading impression here. Despite the set-back, Chartist activity in Halifax not only continued, but began to assume a more permanent institutional character. Following conflict with the supporters of the Anti-Corn League in 1840, the schism with the town's middle class widened still further and by early 1841 the first branch of the National Charter Association had been founded. By the end of the year there were thirteen localities in the area, and the Halifax Association had taken over a large room near the White Swan Hotel which would hold six or seven hundred people. (Dalby, op. cit., pp. 98–9.)

[7] From Byron's *The Giaour*, lines 123–5.

[8] According to Frank Peel in his *Risings of the Luddites, Chartists and Plug-Drawers* (3rd edn., 1895), the combined Bradford and Todmorden contingents amounted to a "compact mass of 25,000 men" as they approached Halifax (p. 333). Peel supports and indeed partly relies on Wilson's account, though makes no reference to the fatalities. He does, however, add his own graphic eyewitness account, which is worth adding to Wilson's: "When these stirring events were occurring I was a lad of some ten years of age, but I well remember the savage appearance of a huge crowd of men as they marched through Horton to Bradford, at the close of their day's work at Halifax. The sight was just one of those which it is impossible to forget. They came pouring down the wide road in thousands, taking up its whole breadth—a gaunt, famished-looking desperate multitude, armed with huge bludgeons, flails, pitch-forks and pikes, many without coats and hats and hundreds upon hundreds with their clothes in rags and tatters. Many of the older men looked sore and weary, but the great bulk were men in the prime of life, full of wild excitement. As they marched they thundered out to a grand old tune a stirring melody, of which this was the opening stanza:—'Men of England, ye are slaves / Though ye rule the roaring waves, / Though ye shout, From sea to sea / Britons everywhere are free' " (pp. 338–9).

as fast as possible, and met them at the top of New Bank. I was much surprised when I saw thousands of men and women marching in procession, many of whom were armed with cudgels. I then marched down New Bank with them, but we had not got far before we saw a great number of special constables, and soldiers with bayonets fixed and swords drawn coming out of the town. We met them a little above Berry's Foundry and there they stopped us; they were accompanied by some of the magistrates, one of whom read the Riot Act and declared we were not to enter the town. I was not far from the front, but seeing the impossibility of forcing our way through them, we made our way over the walls and through the fields, which were not built upon at that time, and came down Range Bank to Northgate. From North Parade to the large building now occupied as an auction room, (formerly the Temperance Hall), was one large field known as "Red Tom's field." Where the Co-operative Central Stores now stand the field wall would be about four yards high, and there, I, along with thousands, stood when the soldiers came by; the field being elevated where we stood afforded a good view of them as they passed; a great many stones were thrown at them. I then made my way to Skircoat Moor, where I had heard there was to be a large meeting held, and when I arrived I saw such a sight as I had never seen there before, the moor being literally covered with men and women, the bulk of them sat down getting something to eat which had been given them on their way. Where the Orphanage now stands were fields, and a number of men mounted the walls to speak; Mr. John Whiteley, a friend and neighbour of mine, offered up prayer on their behalf. The following day there was great excitement and business seemed to be at a standstill in the town and neighbourhood in consequence of the trial, and subsequent committal to Wakefield prison, of a number of men. They were conveyed to Elland, then the nearest railway station, in a bus, guarded by a troop of horse soldiers. Immediately on this becoming known, thousands of people gathered at Salterhebble and Elland Wood, armed with stones, ready for the return journey of the soldiers who took the precaution of coming over Exley and down the Bank to Salterhebble, where thousands were waiting, some on the roofs of houses and others on the hillside. On their arrival at the bottom of the hill, they started off at full speed amidst a shower of stones and bricks thrown at them; one or two were knocked from their horses close by the wells, one of them took shelter in a closet, and was soon surrounded by the people, who took his sword from him; he begged for his life, but died in a short time afterwards from the injuries he had received. As soon as I heard they had taken the prisoners to Elland I made my way to Salterhebble; when I got to where the toll bar then stood at Dry Clough Junction, the soldiers, along with the bus, were at the top of Salterhebble hill; I waited till they came up; Mr. Wm. Briggs, a magistrate, suffering from a broken arm and having it in a sling, was seated on the bus, which appeared to be a wreck, having all its windows smashed. I went with them towards the town, and half way between Stafford house and the top of Shaw hill we met a number of infantry coming with all speed; I was close by the officer in command of the horse soldiers when he said "that the mob were in thousands upon the hillside, and that it was of no use going further;" they then returned. The treatment the soldiers had received at Salterhebble appeared to have enraged them. On marching up Haley Hill, and a little above the public house known as the "Lower Bow Windows," a half brick was thrown from the top of one of the houses, which struck a soldier on the head; it was a young man who threw it, and he made his escape from the buildings behind, which happened to be very low, and was not seen in Halifax again for many years. The soldiers rushed into what is known as 'the Square' in search of the miscreant, they broke open the doors and windows of one house and searched it, but found no one, as the occupants were gone into the country out of the way, as many others had done; they then went to another house and broke the door open, but found no one; in the next one searched they found two little girls in the cellar, and one of the special constables with the soldiers gave them a penny each; the next they entered was a widow's and one of her sons had just gone in, he was in his shirt sleeves, being a comber and working at his own home two doors off, he had a wife and two or three small children, and seizing him they pulled him out of the house but his wife declared if they took him they would have to take her and her child she had in her arms, she went down Haley Hill with them, and just before entering North Bridge he was released. This man was more fortunate than his next door neighbour who served a long term of imprisonment; when talking this matter over a short time since he declared he was innocent. The soldiers then went up to Akroyd's shed and there fired into the mob; a man named Sloane had his boot heel shot off, several others were wounded, one of whom died whilst being conveyed to the Infirmary. The soldiers then returned into the town, and in King Street a man coming to his door to see what was the matter, was shot dead! He was a nailmaker by trade. I have heard it said there was much plundering in Halifax, but I saw none; although there might have been a baker's shop or two entered, that would be the full extent. Those who attacked the soldiers at Salterhebble were neither Lancashire people or people from a distance, but principally young men from the surrounding districts; the mills had been stopped about two days. The struggle was short but fierce.

This movement extended beyond Lancashire and Yorkshire. In Staffordshire 30,000 colliers were on strike for better wages; for miles around Wolverhampton labour was entirely suspended, whilst at Stafford 150 colliers were lodged in the jail within one week! Troops of soldiers had been marched into the town.

On March 1st, 1843, 59 chartists were tried at Lancaster before Baron Rolfe on a charge of seditious conspiracy; amongst the defendants were Fergus O'Connor, Thomas Cooper, G. J. Harney, James Leach, Dr.

McDouall, and a Halifax man named Jas. Chippendale. A number of witnesses called by the Crown said that the defendants in addressing meetings used violent language, such as upsetting the government and stopping the mills; several of the defendants defended themselves. Richard Pilling, of Ashton-under-Lyne, one of the defendants and looked upon as the father of this great movement, in his defence said "Gentlemen, I am somewhere about 43 years of age; I was asked last night if I was not 60, but if I had had as good usage as others instead of looking like a man of 60 I should look like a man of something like 36; Gentlemen, I went to Ashton myself and my two sons were then working at the mills for 12½d. a cut; our work was thirty cuts a week which makes £1. 11s. 3d., this would be 10s. 5d. each; in a little over twelve months we had to submit to three reductions in wages, bringing them down to 7s. 11d. each per week; in a short time after wages were reduced again but we turned out against it. In Ashton-under-Lyne not one pennyworth of damage was done to property, although we were out six weeks. My Lords and Gentlemen of the Jury, it was then a hard case for me to support myself and family; my second son, who was 16 years of age, had fallen into consumption last Easter and left his work; we were then reduced to 9¾d. a cut, which brought our earnings down to something like 16/. a week that is all I had to live on with nine in family,—3/. a week going out of that for rent, and a sick son lying helpless before me. I have gone home and seen that son on a sick bed and dying pillow, and having nothing to eat but potatoes and salt, with neither medical aid or any of the common necessaries of life! Yea, I recollect someone going to a gentleman's house in Ashton to ask for a bottle of wine for him, and it was said,—'Oh, he's a Chartist, he must have none!' My son died before the commencement of the strike. Mr. Rayner, of Ashton, had given notice within a day or two of that time that he would reduce wages 25 per cent., and so indignant were the feelings of the people of Ashton and the surrounding districts, that not only Chartists, but all sorts assembled. A room that would hold 1000 people was crammed to suffocation, and the whole voice of the meeting was that it was no use to get up a subscription for others, but to give up, and that was just the way the strike began." Such was the origin of this movement the people of Ashton marched out and stopped all the mills that were running for many miles round, then it spread into Yorkshire and other parts. Again he says: "I know an instance in Stockport where one master, the present Mayor of that town, Mr. Orrell, employs 600 hands, yet he will not allow one man to work within the mills. I have seen husbands carrying their children to the mill to be suckled by their mothers, and carrying their wives' breakfasts to them. I have seen this in Bradshaw's mill, where women are employed instead of men." Those were the good old days of fifty years ago. Mr. O'Connor called about fourteen witnesses, and from three of them I will make short quotations. Sir Thomas Potter, examined by Mr. O'Connor: Can you speak as to the condition of the working classes? Yes, I think I can give some account of it—I think they were in a very deplorable condition in consequence of the high price of provisions and the low rate of wages. Ald. Chappell, examined by Mr. O'Connor, Now Mr. Ald. Chappel, I understand that your works were stopped, Was there any damage done to your works? 'Not a vestige.' Was there any glass broken? 'Not a vestige.' Well, and what was the conduct of the people under the circumstances? 'Their general conduct and behaviour I must confess after being in every mob for the last fifty years in Manchester, I thought a better behaved and well-disposed mobility I never saw before.' Then a vast number of operatives were turned upon the wide world? 'Oh unquestionably, hundreds of thousands generally speaking.' Was the destitution great amongst the operative classes? 'Unquestionably they had not a sufficiency such as every Englishman would like to see his neighbour enjoy.' James Kershaw, Esq., Mayor of Manchester, examined by Mr. O'Connor: Did the hands in your employment require any great force to induce them to cease labour? 'I believe my partner, who was at the works, when he found parties coming up to insist them to desist from their labour, advised the hands to go out.' Did they go out willingly? 'I believe they did.' And no damage done whatever? 'No.' This trial lasted eight days, resulting in the acquital of the defendants.[9] The bulk of the mills in Lancashire were stopped on the 10th of August, and did not commence again till the 26th. This agitation looked very serious at one time, but was now quietly passing away. As in nature, so in agitations, after a storm there comes a calm.

The bulk of the people, particularly the working classes of Skircoat, took no part or interest in the township's business. Though they had been struggling to have a voice in national affairs they did not see the importance of local affairs, which were left in the hands of a few rich men, who took a deep interest in national affairs as well, The first vestry meeting I attended would be about the year 1843; I was the only working man present—working men scarcely ever attending those meetings then; there being about twelve gentlemen present, comprised several of the largest ratepayers in the township. I felt uncomfortable, and wished I was nicely out. Mr. Robert Wainhouse was chairman, and when he put a motion to the meeting he looked on to the table and said—"Carried unanimously, I suppose." The board of surveyors, numbering ten or twelve gentlemen, were appointed at these meetings, for the management of the highways. They always took care that the roads near their own residences were kept in good repair, although the roads in other parts were in a wretched condition; great improvements were also made on private property for which the township had to pay. I travelled the roads regularly with a horse and cart for two years, and what I say is no exaggeration of the facts. The thing became so glaring that it began to open the people's eyes, as it had certainly opened mine; to be a political

[9] O'Connor was in fact found guilty, but his conviction, together with that of several other defendants, was later overruled on technical grounds.

reformer was not all; there were other things requiring looking into besides those at London, and in this case the greatest requirement appeared to be a man with the moral courage to expose the surveyors' actions in their proper place. We had not long to wait, for a man came to the front who was equal to the occasion, Mr. James Longbottom, who spent a great amount of time and trouble in the people's cause. The agitation now begun lasted some ten or twelve years, and the struggle was as fierce as any that I have ever witnessed in the political movement. It was several years before we could make any headway; the great amount of influence that was brought to bear against us was such as I had never anticipated, for actually numbers of men were brought to the meetings with their managers, and I have seen employers stand on the benches to see how their men voted. Seeing at last that this did not answer another trick was resorted to,—'A requisition was signed to call a public meeting to take into consideration the desirability of adopting the Small Tenement Act.' If they could have carried this, landlords paying the rates of small occupiers would have deprived them of the right to attend meetings. Mr. Longbottom waited upon Mr. Thorpe and other gentlemen who had come to reside in Skircoat to attend the meeting held in the large room of the workhouse at Scarr Bottom, which was crowded; Mr. Geo Haigh and Mr. Thorpe were both proposed and seconded as the chairman, and although the former declined, they were put to the vote when Mr. Thorpe was carried by ten to one. In consequence of numbers being unable to get in, the meeting adjourned to a larger room at the Copley Arms, which was also crowded, about 300 persons being present. The Chairman called upon the requisitionists, but no one came forward, and the Chairman said he hoped the thing would never be attempted again. Skircoat at this time was thinly populated, and sent one Guardian to the Union, for which office Mr. Longbottom was nominated, and after thoroughly canvassing the township we succeeded in electing him; he rendered good service to the poor people at the Union.

On the 9th of July, 1846, Charles Wood became Chancellor of the Exchequer, and was re-elected without opposition. This was the first uncontested election which had taken place in Halifax.

The General Election was fast approaching and there was every indication of a split amongst the Liberal electors of Halifax. The Nonconformists had become a powerful party, and were entirely opposed to State-Aid for education, and were determined to have a candidate who would represent their views with regard to Church and State and other matters. Mr. Jonathan Akroyd, an intimate friend of Mr. Wood's, had been the leader of the Liberal party and represented the moderate Liberals; he was in favour of State-Aid for education, and was determined Mr. Wood should be one of the candidates. The Chartists and Radicals were also determined to have a candidate to represent their views. Mr. Protheroe, who had formerly been so popular, had not progressed with the times and withdrew from the contest. The following gentlemen were the candidates selected:—Henry Edwards, Tory;

Ernest Jones, Radical; Edward Miall, Nonconformist; Charles Wood, moderate Liberal. Meetings were held nightly, excitement was great, and party feeling ran very high. Exclusive dealing[10] became very common, and was never known to be so extensively carried out as at this election. Mr. Boddy, a grocer in Northgate and a supporter of Messrs. Jones and Miall, became very popular; I have seen his shop many times crowded with customers, and considerable numbers of people in the street opposite; he did a large amount of business for many years, and then retired. He erected the fine block of buildings in Northgate known as 'Boddy's buildings,' and it was said that he saved the bulk of money out of the profits of that agitation. James Haigh Hill, a butcher in the Shambles and known as the Chartist butcher, employed a comber named Boden, a leader of the movement and one of the best speakers in Halifax. I have seen crowds of people in front of his shop on a Saturday night and on one occasion he had a band of music there. The bulk of the publicans voted in favour of Wood and Edwards, but those who voted for Jones and Miall did a roaring business. The Queen Inn became one of the most noted and popular public houses in the town—John Bancroft was the landlord; I have seen every room in his house crowded on a Saturday night, principally with carpet weavers, and for many years it was well patronised. Several tradesmen who were supporting Wood and Edwards were annoyed by crowds of people congregating in front of their shops and hooting their customers. I was going down Crown Street when I was told that Mr. Akroyd had just dropped *dead* at a meeting in the Northgate Hotel. I made my way there and soon ascertained that it was correct. He had been chairman at a meeting of the friends and supporters of Mr. Wood, and whilst speaking on the education question was interrupted; he fell down and expired shortly afterwards. He was a staunch Free-trader and gave very largely to its funds, and was a particular friend of Mr. Cobden's. The friends of Wood and Edwards coalesced. The nomination took place in the Piece Hall in the presence of a large number of people. Wood was not a pleasant speaker to listen to, whilst Henry Edwards was a very bad speaker and cut a very sorry figure on the hustings; the principal topic in his speech was that his grandfather was a good man, and every time he was fast he repeated—My grandfather was a good man; and for some time after was known by a good many as "My grandfather." Miall was a splendid speaker, full of wit and humour, and a close reasoner. Jones had a powerful voice with a musical ring, and was a perfect master of elocution; he was the finest speaker I had ever heard, and his speech that day was copied into several continental papers. The show of hands was largely in favour of Jones and Miall, but at the poll on July 29th, 1847, it was reversed, viz.:

Henry Edwards, (C)	...	511	Edward Miall, (L)	...	349
Charles Wood, (L)	...	507	Ernest Jones, (L)	...	280

[10] The practice of boycotting and patronizing tradesmen according to their political persuasion.

There was great disappointment at the result. Fergus O'Connor had been elected at Nottingham, which was some consolation. Some time after this election Jones was presented with a gold watch and chain in the Odd Fellows' Hall. There was a tea in connection with it for which the women had made extensive preparations, and they were determined that the radical colour should be well represented on the occasion. I was at the first sitting down which was largely composed of women. Some had their caps beautifully decorated with green ribbons, others had green handkerchiefs, and some had even green dresses. I have been to many a tea party in my time, but never saw one to equal this. The tickets must all have been sold, for during the time the Hall was being cleared there was such a demand for tickets that several who had been to the tea disposed of theirs for as much as 2s. 6d., the original cost being 1s. The Hall was crowded in the evening, and when Mr. Jones rose to speak, the people cheered for several minutes.

In this year flour was very dear, reaching the price of 5s. per stone, whilst trade was also very bad. This was the time to make politicians, as the easiest way to get to an Englishman's brains is through his stomach. It was said by its enemies that Chartism was dead and buried and would never rise again, but they were doomed to disappointment. It was true there had been no meetings or processions, nor had the agitation reached the height it attained in 1839, but it was going on. Amongst combers, handloom weavers, and others politics was the chief topic. *The Northern Star* was their principal paper, and it was a common practice, particularly in villages, to meet at friends' houses to read the paper and talk over political matters. We met at a friends at Skircoat Green, but occasionally I went to a friend's house at Cinderhills, where there was sure to be a good many friends. We were only waiting for the time to come again. In 1848 it was said that the year was a year of agitations of revolutions, and thousands of men fell on the field of battle fighting for the people's cause in Europe in this struggle. The French revolution of the 24th February gave the first impulse to this movement. The first move in Halifax was a meeting held in the Odd Fellows' Hall in commemoration of the French Revolution. We had to stand in the body of the hall, which was crowded, and the resolutions put to the meeting were carried with great enthusiasm. The Chartist room was in Bull Close Lane, and became the centre of attraction. Lectures were delivered on Sunday evenings, the meetings generally being opened with patriotic hymns such as 'Men of England, ye are slaves,' 'Spread the Charter through the world,' &c. The following persons, still living, took an active part at those meetings:—Joseph Foreman, G. Webber, and C. Fielding. John Culpan was the Secretary of the Chartist Association. I sat on the Committee for several years, and know something of the services rendered by the secretary. He was looked upon as the leader amongst the workers, and as a debater and writer he had not his equal amongst our party in this town. When the agitation was at its height very few of those attending its meetings joined the Association or subscribed to its funds. We had no wealthy men amongst us; not one to give large subscriptions to the organization; we had no paid officials, all labour was done voluntarily. Meetings were held almost nightly in the town and neighbourhood; a great many being held on Skircoat Moor. It had now become a common practice to march through the streets in military order. The principal speakers at those meetings were Ben Rushton, Kit Shackleton, John Snowden, George Webber, and Isaac Clisset. Several meetings were held on Blackstone Edge and attended by people from Lancashire as well as Yorkshire. When these meetings were over, I have seen the roads crowded for nearly two miles coming down to Ripponden. A great meeting of Chartists of the West Riding was held on Good-Friday on Skircoat Moor, being one of a series held throughout the country in conformity with a recent recommendation of the National Chartist Convention held in London. It was the largest meeting held in Yorkshire during the year, and was addressed by Joseph Barker, Kit Shackleton, and others. Shackleton was considered the finest speaker in this district. A large meeting was also held on Toftshaw Moor, near Bradford, at which physical force was strongly advocated and the people were recommended to arm themselves. Matters now began to look serious. There had already been riots in Bradford and other parts. The authorities in Bradford became greatly alarmed, and issued a proclamation that processions with banners and bands of music would not be allowed to enter the town, but when the meeting was over they folded up their banners and thousands of them marched in procession towards Bradford; on our arrival on the outskirts of the town we were met by a large number of special constables, accompanied by horse and foot soldiers. I was standing with two Halifax friends in a cross street when they came up; they arrested the men who had the banner poles and made them prisoners. The horse soldiers were ordered to clear the mob, and they dashed up the street where we were standing with drawn swords slashing in all directions, causing us to run as fast as we could, they galloping after us; we climbed over a high wall into some gardens just in time to get out of their way. When we got back again into the street we found it almost empty. One man to whom we had been talking, (who was neither a Chartist or attended the meeting) received a sword wound in the shoulders. One of the friends, James Howarth, of Skircoat Green, is still living, the other was Job Jenkinson, a shoemaker, living in Caddy Field; he was born in the East Indies, his mother was a coloured woman and his father a soldier. Job was very much like an Indian too. Many years after when talking this matter over, he never liked the thought of having to run at Bradford that day, but he said "What could we do, Ben? we had no arms; and it is my firm opinion that if they could have got to us before we got over that wall it would have been a bad job for us." Now Job was no coward, and would not have run for the best soldier in the army if he had been unarmed. A great number of people met on Beacon Hill, and it was on the day of the Bradford riots that a number of men were appointed as messengers who were continually arriving with news from that town. No doubt the result at Bradford had its influence, all passing off very quietly here.

The first Municipal Election for Councillors in Halifax took place in May, 1848.[11] The late parliamentary election and the defeat of Jones and Miall left their friends in a fit state for the coming election, and it soon became evident that it was to be fought on party lines. Each side nominated the strongest candidates they could get. There was great excitement, and party feeling ran as high as if it had been a parliamentary election. Nicholl's Temperance Hotel in Broad Street was largely attended by Chartists, and we formed ourselves into a committee to do what we possibly could, more particularly in agitating the borough. Open air meetings were held in different wards, and addressed by Clisset, Straddling, and others. At the close of the poll the friends of Jones & Miall had carried all before them. Mr. Edward Akroyd, his brother Henry, and their uncle, Mr. Geo. Beaumont, were amongst the defeated candidates.[12] In the evening, a black flag was hoisted from Nicholl's Temperance Hotel.

On the 7th of June in this year Mr. Jones was advertised to address a meeting in the Odd Fellows' Hall of this town. When I got to the meeting I ascertained that Mr. Jones had been arrested in Manchester the previous evening, and all appeared confusion and doubt whether any meeting would be held, when a gentleman from Manchester mounted the platform and announced to the meeting that he had come to say a few words and explain the circumstances in connection with Mr. Jones's arrest. At the close of the meeting thousands congregated in the streets talking the matter over in groups, and it cast a gloom all over the town as Mr. Jones was very popular here. On July 10th Jones's trial took place, resulting in a sentence against Mr. Jones of two years' solitary confinement, and he was further ordered to find two sureties of £100 each, and bound in his own recognisance of £200 for three years after his release. The strongest language used by Mr. Jones and on which the charge was laid was "Only organise and you will see the green flag floating over Downing street; let that be accomplished and John Mitchell shall be brought back again to his native country, and Sir G. Grey and Lord John Russell shall be sent out to exchange places with him." He was kept in solitary confinement on the silent system, enforced with utmost rigour, for nineteen months; he was neither allowed pen, ink, or paper, but confined in a small cell 13 feet by 6 in utter solitude, varied only by a walk in a small high-walled prison yard. He obeyed all the prison regulations excepting oakum picking, observing that for the sake of public order he would seek to conform to all forms and rules, but would never lend himself to voluntary degradation; to break his firmness on this point he was again and

[11] Halifax received its Royal Charter on 25 March 1848.

[12] According to a handwritten note in Halifax Reference Library, the new council comprised 17 Radicals, 4 Chartists, 6 Whigs and 3 Tories.

again imprisoned in a dark cell and fed on bread and water; on one occasion whilst cholera was raging in London, this punishment was enforced, though Mr. Jones was suffering from dysentry at the time, and he was consigned to a dark cell from which a dying man from cholera had just been removed; their efforts, however, were in vain, as the prison authorities never succeeded in making him perform the degrading task. In the second year of his imprisonment Mr. Jones was so broken in health that he could no longer stand upright, and was found lying on the floor of his cell and only then was he taken to the hospital. He was told then that if he would petition for his release and promise to abjure politics the remainder of his sentence would be remitted, but he refused his liberty on those conditions and was again sent to his cell. During his imprisonment and before writing materials were allowed him he wrote some of his most admired poems, making pens from the quills that occasionally dropped from the wing of a passing bird in the prison yard, these he cut secretly with a razor that was brought to him twice a week to shave with; an ink bottle he contrived to make from a piece of soap he got from the washing shed, and this he filled with ink from the ink bottle when he was allowed to write his quarterly letter; paper was supplied by those quarterly letters, the fly leaves of a bible, prayer book, and any books he was allowed to read. One poem, "The New World," was composed before he had succeeded in securing ink and written almost entirely with his own blood! The poems composed in prison were "The Painter of Florence," "Baldogon Church," "The New World, or the revolt of Hindostan," and a number of smaller poems, all of which were highly praised in the reviews of the day. Mr. Jones gave up nearly all business to agitate the country for the People's Charter, and when in prison his wife and family had nothing to support them, their relatives though wealthy, were so disgusted with Mr. Jones's opinions that they would do nothing for her support. We formed ourselves into a committee at Nicholl's Temperance Hotel to raise money for her, Mr. Culpan being secretary; many an interesting tale could be told of the means adopted for that purpose in those two years.

A great many people in these districts were arming themselves with guns or pikes, and drilling on the moors. Bill Cockcroft, one of the leaders of the physical force party in Halifax, wished me to join the movement, I consented, and purchased a gun, although I knew it to be a serious thing for a chartist to have a gun or pike in his possession. I had several years practice in shooting, as the farmer for whom I worked supplied me with gun, powder, and shot for the purpose of shooting birds in summer. I saw Cockroft who gave me instructions how to proceed until wanted, which did not occur as the scheme was abandoned. It might now be said we were fools, but I answer young people now have no idea of what we had to endure. Tom Brown's Schooldays would have had no charm for me, as I had never been to a day school in my life; when very young I had to begin working, and was pulled out of bed between 4 and 5 o'clock in the morning in summer time to go with a donkey 1½ miles away, and then take part in milking a number of cows; and in the evening had again to go with milk and it would be 8 o'clock before I had done. I went to a card shop afterwards and there had to set 1500 card teeth for a ½d. From 1842 to 1848 I should not average 9/- per week wages; outdoor labour was bad to get then and wages were very low. I have been a woollen weaver, a comber, a navvy on the railway, and a barer in the delph[13] that I claim to know some little of the state of the working classes. I well remember only a few years ago having some talk with a friend who told me he was moulding bullets in the cellar in 1848; he had a wife and five children dependent upon him, but was unable to get work, trade being so bad. Since then, however, under the blessings of free trade and by dint of perseverance he has succeeded in saving a considerable sum, and is now living retired from business. Many a time in winter have I known what it was to be short of the commonest of food, and thousands in this parish were in the same condition. A great many tales of sorrow could be told, but enough has been said to shew that those were times to make men desperate, for life then was not so valuable as now. Many persons were arrested and imprisoned, and several had narrow escapes of being caught with arms in their possession, whilst many who had arms were getting rid of them as fast as possible. The Chartists were called ugly names, the swinish multitude unwashed and levellers. I never knew levelling advocated amongst the Chartists, neither in public or private, for they did not believe in it, nor have I known a case of plunder in the town, though thousands have marched through its streets to meetings in various places. What they wanted was a voice in making the laws they were called upon to obey; they believed that taxation without representation was tyranny, and ought to be resisted; they took a leading part in agitating in favour of the ten hours question, the repeal of the taxes on knowledge, education, co-operation, civil and religious liberty and the land question, for they were the true pioneers in all the great movements of their time. Fergus O'Connor tried to grapple with the land question. He formed a company on the small farm system and purchased several large estates and a great many thousands became members, including several of my friends, and although trade was bad, they cheerfully made great sacrifices to raise the money.[14] Fergus had a great many difficulties to contend against, for he had nearly all the press in the country against him, whilst a great many got on to the land who had no knowledge of it, and what with the opposition outside and the dissatisfaction within, the company was thrown into Chancery. Two or three from Halifax went on to the land, but the scheme was before its time; yet I believe the day is not far distant when it will be successfully carried out.

[13] A "barer in the delph" was a semi-skilled quarryman whose task was to dig out and wheel away the "baring" which overlay the stone in the quarries. There were large quarries at Elland, Southowram and Northowram at this time.

[14] The Halifax Chartists subscribed £193 2*s.* 2*d.* in the first year of the scheme.

Lord Morpeth being called to the Upper House caused a vacancy in the representation of the West Riding, and the nomination took place at Wakefield in December. The Chartists of the West Riding decided to nominate Samuel Kidd; he was acknowledged to be the ablest lecturer on the labour question amongst the Chartist leaders. He was not going to the poll, as he would not have stood the slightest chance of being returned, but intended to use the occasion for bringing his principles before the public. It was requested that each town should take a person qualified to vote with them, and meet at the Black Boy Inn in Wakefield, on the morning of the nomination day. We took Mr. Joseph Hanson, landlord of the Crispin Inn in this town. We met in the large room of the Black Boy to select a mover and seconder of Mr. Kidd, resulting in Mr. Isaac Ironside, of Sheffield, and Mr. Richard Brook, Huddersfield, being appointed respectively. The Dewsbury brass band was engaged by the chartists of that town to play them to Wakefield, and in front of the Black Boy was a large crowd waiting to join them; they brought a very large procession with them, which we joined, and then marched through the streets to the hustings, and the people in front opened out for us so that we got in a good position; there were a great many thousands of people present. Mr. Beckett Dennison (C) was nominated, and when he arose to address the people he was met with yells and not a word could be heard, but he addressed the reporters who were close to him. Sir Culling Eardley-Eardley (L) was nominated, but owing to illness was not present being represented by John Bright, M.P., and when he arose to address the people he was very well received, excepting from the Tories on the hustings. Mr. Samuel Kidd (Chartist) was nominated, and when he rose to address the people he was met with tremendous cheering and was well listened to throughout. In show of hands Mr. Dennison had a poor muster, Sir Culling a very good one, and for Mr. Kidd a large forest of hands were held up, but he withdrew from the contest which resulted in Mr. Beckett Dennison's return.

Mr. Fergus O'Connor was announced to lecture at Batley the same evening and a few of us made at once to that town; on our arrival there was a large crowd waiting, and on the doors being opened I got such a squeezing that I have not yet forgotten it, having one of my coat laps almost torn off. The room was uncomfortably crowded, and on the speaker commencing it was so hot that he stripped his coat and rolled up his shirt sleeves; he quite electrified the audience, and kept them till a late hour. We met other friends who had come direct from Halifax, and we all walked back over Hartshead moor; I arrived at Skircoat Green in the small hours of morning. Fergus O'Connor was a well-built strong powerful man, 6 feet in height, with large broad shoulders. He was the founder and leader of the Chartist movement, and no man was better adapted for the purpose, he being a giant in intellect as well as in frame.

It was at the latter end of this year that a few of us met in the Chartist room to talk over the matter of Co-operation, and we decided to placard the town for a meeting to be held in that place, but when the night came the meeting was only thinly attended. We formed ourselves into a committee, of whom I only remember Mr. Joseph Foreman and Mr. J. D. Taylor, manager of the Permanent Building Society, besides myself, still living. We had several meetings in the above place, but thinking it might be looked upon as a party movement we removed to the Odd Fellows' Hall. We issued a number of coloured bills announcing the night when the committee met to enrol members. Its name was "The Halifax Co-operative Trading Society," and the first night of entrance was on the 15th Jany., 1849. I entered on the first night, the number of my card being 18. Each committee-man had to canvas for members in his own locality, consequently I canvassed Skircoat Green but with poor success. We proposed to pay no bonus but to add it to stock, so that it would become more powerful and give us more capital. Mr. J. D. Taylor who had acted as secretary from the commencement left us, as the scheme did not meet his approval. Our expenses at the Odd Fellows' Hall were too large, inducing us to remove to a temperance hotel at the back of the Sportsman Inn. Mr. George Buckley, who had been a shopkeeper and who we knew to be a friend of the working classes, gave us his advice with regard to purchasing groceries. We bought 2 or 3 cwt. of soap and sugar, made up into 1lb. and 2lbs, and sold them out to ourselves, but we began to see that our scheme was not patronised as it ought to have been, so we had to abandon it and lose nearly all we had put in, which was not much; according to my card, which I have preserved, we only existed about five months, yet whatever we took in hand seemed doomed to disappointment. We had every confidence, however, in our principles, and thoroughly believed that the time would come when they would have a better chance of success.

My mind for some time had been occupied with the temperance question. I thought if working men could have been induced to invest in the co-operative movement what they were spending in intoxicating drinks it would have greatly improved their condition. I had heard of a politician in Leeds, a moulder by trade, who used to visit public-houses to discuss politics, and one night whilst speaking on Lord John Russell, who, he said, was unfit to govern the country, was interrupted by his wife entering and suggesting that he should take his money home to her and his starving children, make his own home as comfortable as he possibly could, and then find fault with Lord John Russell. It was about Midsummer, 1849, that I resolved not to taste of any intoxicating drink or smoke tobacco as long as I lived. I undertook this as an example for others.

A great many having left the Chartist Association, the expenses of the room were found to be too heavy for the number remaining, so that we removed and continued the association at Nicholl's Temperance Hotel in Broad street. Our aim was to carry on the agitation by engaging such men as Kidd, Fynland, Gammage, and others to lecture in the town, but it appeared to be to no purpose for very few came to hear them. I well recollect our engaging the Old Assembly Rooms for a lecture on the labour question by Mr. Kidd, but, in addition to the committee, there were very few persons present; the rent of the room, the printing and posting of the bills, together with the travelling expenses and small remuneration of the lecturer had all to be paid by us, and this kind of business had to be done for one thing or another for a good many years, yet no part I have taken since I became acquainted with the movement gave me so much pleasure as at this time for the memory of those men will ever be kept dear to me.

The time for Mr. Jones's release (July 9th, 1850) was fast drawing nigh; during his imprisonment we had forwarded subscriptions regular to his wife, and for seventeen weeks prior to his release we had doubled our subscriptions. We formed ourselves into a demonstration committee as Halifax was the first place he intended to visit. We engaged the West Hill Park for the purpose it being the best adapted place in the town. We provided an open carriage, with four grey horses, and a band of music and marched to Sowerby Bridge in procession to meet him, as he was to get off at that station. Thousands of people congregated in King Cross Lane to watch him enter the town. The admission to the meeting in West Hill Park was 6d. each, and it proved a magnificent success. We presented Mr. Jones with a purse containing thirty-eight guineas (I think that was the amount speaking from memory). At the close of the meeting as Cockroft, myself, and a few others were standing talking, Mr. J. U. Walker, editor and proprietor of the *Halifax Guardian*, came and wished us not to put too much upon him, and reminding us that he had only just come out of prison and was weak, but as clever as ever. Every room of Nicholl's Temperance Hotel was crowded in the evening, and several of the middle class came to see him. I recollect Mr. Joseph Leyland, carver and sculptor, and another gentleman coming to invite Mr. Jones to meet a few gentlemen at one of the hotels in the town, but he declined their invitation. The following day Mr. Jones and Mr. Harney were entertained at dinner in Nicholl's large room when about thirty of us sat down and spent a jovial evening together.

At the end of the Hungarian struggle[15] a number of those who had been fighting for their independence made their escape to England in order to escape death or imprisonment, some of whom came to Nicholl's Temperance Hotel in this town. They were known by the name of 'The Refugees.' We formed ourselves into a committee to adopt the best means of raising support for them, and it was agreed that I and another should wait upon Mr. Henry Martin to ask his opinion on the subject. He was a printer, his place being in the Upper George Yard, and a man of large experience; he advised us to see Judge Stansfeld as the likeliest man in the town to give us help in this

[15] The defeat of Kossuth and his republicans by the Austrians under General Haynau in 1849.

cause, for, he said, he has a son in London who took a deep interest in their welfare and who has given several lectures on their behalf. This advice we acted upon, with very fair success. The refugees were an intelligent class of men, and a few of us spent a great deal of time in their company, particularly on Sundays. Mr. Adam Foster, a solicitor in the town, took deep interest in their cause; he could speak their language and I have seen him conversing with them many times. There is one still left in the town, who is in business, and appears to have done very well.

Fergus O'Connor had been broken down in health for some time, and the *Northern Star* had passed from his hands. It being said that he was very poor a great many meetings were called for the purpose of raising subscriptions on his behalf. A district delegate meeting for the above object was held on Sunday, April 4th, 1852 in the Chartist Room, back of Nicholl's Temperance Hotel, Halifax. On the same day a West Riding delegate meeting was held at Balmforth's Coffee House, Queenshead, for the purpose of carrying out a resolution of the West Riding delegates—that an appeal be issued from the committee to the Chartists of the West Riding calling on them to assist in this object. I, along with Harrison Holt, represented Halifax. The following address was adopted:—"Brother Chartists, We deem it our duty to appeal to you on the present occasion on behalf of that suffering and ruined patriot, Mr. Fergus O'Connor, who, according to the statement put forth by his nephew, Mr. Roger O'Connor, is now in a state of destitution; such has ever been the lot of those who have marched in the vanguard of progress; but seeing that his talents, his time, and his means have been used by the people as public property, we deem it to be the duty of the people to use its utmost endeavours to assist in relieving him from want and placing him in comfortable circumstances during the remainder of his life. He may, and no doubt has had his faults,—who amongst us is without? but it must be admitted he has been the means of arousing the people to a sense of their social and political degradation, and awakening in them a feeling of liberty which will never be quenched. We consider, therefore, that in responding to this appeal the people will only be paying a small instalment towards a large debt of public gratitude, and we earnestly request that all parties who intend assisting us in this work will get out collecting books with speed and energy which the importance of the case demands. All monies must be sent to Mr. John Moore, of Bowling, near Bradford, and all correspondence addressed to Mr. Christopher Shackleton, Queenshead, near Halifax. *Signed by the members present,*—Thomas Wilcock, Richard Gill, Thomas Cameron, Harrison Holt, and Benjamin Wilson. C. Shackleton, West Riding Secretary.

On the 18th of this month we had a District meeting for the above object at Mixenden Stones attended by several delegates from various associations in the district, including our old friend Mr. Snowden, whom I had not seen many times during the last two or three years, as he lived in the country and took no part in the organization of the town, but was a member of either the Ovenden or Mixenden association, I cannot say which; now that Ernest Jones and other Chartist leaders were agitating the country, it appeared he was prepared to take some part again, and more particularly to raise funds for our old leader.

The organization of the Chartist movement in the country had been neglected for some time in consequence of the broken health of Fergus O'Connor, and the *Northern Star* passing out of his hands; and also a great number of Chartist leaders being imprisoned. We had an executive at the head of the movement who were not considered genuine chartists. Ernest Jones and his friends arranged the calling of a conference in Manchester to be held on the 17th of May, 1852, to take into consideration the re-organization of the movement. It was not very well attended, as many towns had broken up their organizations. A few important towns were represented, and a number of letters of encouragement were received. Mr. Cockroft represented Halifax. A scheme of organization was arranged, and Messrs. Gammage, Fynland, and Ernest Jones were appointed an Executive Committee. The Chartists of Halifax wrote to the West Riding Secretary to call a meeting to consider the new organization, resulting in a meeting being held at Mitchell's Temperance Hotel, Bradford, on Sunday, the 19th June, 1852. William Cockroft and Isaac Clisset were the delegates from Halifax, and several of us arranged to go with them, meeting them at the station,—friends were admitted but not allowed to take part in the business; when the train came into the Halifax Station the first man to get out, to our surprise, was Ernest Jones; he consented to go with us to Bradford, and got into the carriage whilst one of the friends got him a ticket. We had seen ten or twelve persons enter the train who were going to the meeting, and from their movements we expected opposition. At the meeting Mr. Brook, Leeds, was called to the chair; the first business was for the delegates to hand in their credentials; two delegates represented the labour and health party, other two from a beerhouse called Thorn Tree Inn; there were about ten of them we knew very well did not represent any genuine Chartist association, but had gone to swamp the meeting of legally appointed delegates. Mr. Cockroft objected to their sitting, knowing, he said, that they represented no association. They were entirely opposed to the new organization, but scarcely a word could be heard as it was one of the stormiest meetings I ever saw, and lasted several hours. Mr. Shackleton and Mr. Geo. White, of Bradford, two of the opposition leaders, withdrew, and our friends went into business at once and adopted the new organization. The question was—Who was to be the leader? They were for G. J. Harney, our friends were for Ernest Jones. In a short time Mr. Jones became the recognised leader of the Chartist movement, and many who had been very strongly opposed to him became his friends. I have often thought that if the leaders of our movement could have worked a little more harmoniously together at times, we might have been more powerful. It is not the only movement that has suffered from this very cause, for those who have read the debates in the House of Commons during the last 40 years know very well that it has had its Horsmans, R. Lowe, who Mr. Bright described as forming the Cave of Addullam to defeat a Liberal Government when it brought in a Reform Bill, and further compared them to a Scotch terrier, unable to discern the head from the tail; then there was Mr. Roebuck, dog tear-'em, and Mr. Goschen of the present day, men who do not believe in stooping to conquer. Mr. Culpan resigned the secretaryship of the Chartist association and Mr. Thomas Wood succeeded him.

It had been arranged for some time that Mr. Jones should bring out a weekly newspaper and the Chartists of the country had been appealed to raise money for that purpose, as a certain sum was wanted before the paper could be brought out. The Chartists of this town did their duty well in contributing £8., whilst some towns did not raise as many shillings to the fund, the total amount not being one tenth part what it ought to have been; but it was decided to bring out the paper at once.[16] I wrote Mr. Jones a letter asking him to keep personal quarrels out of the paper as they did no good. I received the following reply:—

London, May 22nd, 1852.

Mr. B. Wilson,—

"I thank you for your kind letter which press of business has alone prevented me from answering sooner.

"You may rest assured that as one of the objects of the paper is to lift the movement out of the grovelling depths of personal contention and ambition, so not one syllable of personality shall intrude itself into its columns."

Yours fraternally, Ernest Jones.

The price of the paper was threepence, of which the government got one-third, as every paper bore a penny stamp. There was also a heavy duty on paper, making it a very difficult matter to establish a newspaper without a large capital. Our money was soon done, and as the circulation did not come up to our expectations we had to subscribe weekly towards its funds. We sent from this town upwards of £30. in the first three months, which would be nearly one-fourth of what the country sent; the price of the paper was advanced to 4d. at the end of the first fifteen weeks.

Another general election was near at hand; the shadows had already been seen of the coming events. Sir Charles Wood had a quick eye and a sharp nose, and could see further than a great many men. Frank Crossley was to be his colleague. We again selected Ernest Jones as our candidate, not liking Sir Charles for the treatment Mr. Jones had received during his imprisonment from the government of which he was a prominent member. He had often been asked to look into this matter but took no notice of it, and we

[16] The first issue of the *People's Paper* appeared on 8 May 1852.

believed it was because of Jones giving him such a thrashing in the Piece Hall at the preceding election. Lord Dudley Stewart brought Mr. Jones's case before Parliament, and compared the different treatment accorded to Fergus O'Connor and Mr. Cobbet under similar circumstances. W. J. Fox, Sir D'Lacy Evans, George Thompson, Colonel Thompson, (the father of the Corn Law agitation), and a number of others spoke against the government, condemning them for the manner Mr. Jones had been treated. Mr. Jones addressed several meetings; one of the largest was held at the back of the Northgate-End Chapel; the next being held in the Odd Fellows' Hall, with Mr. B. Rushton as chairman, when a resolution in favour of Jones was moved by Mr. Clisset, seconded by Mr. Snowden, and carried unanimously. There were a great many people present at the nomination,—the candidates being Frank Crossley, Henry Edwards, Ernest Jones, and Sir Chas. Wood. Mr. Jones in his speech did not forget his old friend Sir Charles. I had a very good view from the hustings, and on the show of hands being taken Wood had very few. Edwards & Crossley appeared to be very equal, and for Jones there was one forest of hands, he having a great majority over the others. The Mayor, Mr. Saml. Waterhouse, asked for a second show for Edwards and Crossley, and then declared Jones and Edwards to be duly elected. I knew that Jones would poll very few votes, for Mr. Jones, myself, and a friend spent eight or nine days canvassing. We met at night in the Chartist Room, when twenty or thirty volunteered to do duty for the night. Bottling voters was then a common practice. It was done by getting voters 'who liked something to drink' in the public houses and making them drunk; or those who were wavering would be sent away until the election was over. Public houses were kept open all night if they had company in, and it was there where the mischief was done. We marched out at 11 o'clock, and whilst in Northgate some of our friends came to tell us that the opposite party had 'bottled' one of our voters at the Bridge Tavern, and we went there and were rushing in when some one was pulling me from behind on which I turned round; it was a policeman named Edward Schofield, and he marched me off for the Town Hall; I made no resistance, but when we had got a short distance we met Mr. Supt. Pearson, who said "Hallo Ben!" and wanted to know what I had been doing; I told him on which I was liberated. This was the only occasion that I was under the immediate care of a policeman. When it came daylight I made my way home to Skircoat Green to have a few hours' rest for the coming day. In the morning I was at Mr. Jones's Committee Room. There was very little for us to do as we had only obtained about forty promises, and they did not require looking after. Working men were of very little use in canvassing, as this was often done by some of the leading gentlemen in the town; small tradesmen were canvassed by their largest customers, and in many instances great pressure was brought to bear upon them. At four o'clock when the poll closed several of us along with Mr. Jones had a walk on the hillside above Shibden; the day was clear, and the view magnificent, Mr. Jones remarked that it was one of the best he had seen. The result of the poll, July 7th, 1852, was as follows:—

Sir Charles Wood (L) ...	596	Mr. Henry Edwards (C) ...	521
Mr. Frank Crossley (L) ...	573	Mr. Ernest Jones (R) ...	37

Of the thirty-seven who voted for Mr. Jones on this occasion only three that I am aware of are still living—Harrison Holt, Geo. Buckley and James Priestley. With the exception of the returning officer's charges, our expenses for this election were very small as every man had to give his services; some of us gave as much as a fortnight, in addition to subscribing towards the expenses.

Sir Charles Wood's acceptance of office caused another election. Mr. Jones had returned to London, it having been decided not to contest this election. Many hard words were spoken against Mr. Jones and the Chartists in consequence of this decision, and it was said they had been bribed by the Tories in order that Edwards might have a better chance of success. Some of the very men who were talking so loud had in 1847 voted with the Tories to keep Jones and Miall out. The Saturday night previous to the nomination a committee of Jones' friends sat at Nicholl's hotel for several hours discussing as to whether he should stand or not. I knew Mr. Jones' feelings with regard to this election, as myself and Joseph Binns were with him for several hours during the time the committee were discussing the matter, and he spoke very strongly in favour of standing as he was very anxious to get into parliament. It was late when we left him, but he wished us to see him in the morning and he would tell us how he had gone on with them. I went, but he had returned to London as the decision of the committee was against him standing.

It was said that Mr. Jones and other Chartist lecturers were making plenty of money out of us, but there was not a worse paid lot of men in the country than they were. All places were not so good as Halifax, and 10/- would be something like an average of what they would get, out of which they had their expenses to pay. Many were the trials and hardships they had to undergo when on their lecturing tours. Mr. Robinson, of Wilsden, one of the ablest speakers in Yorkshire, when on one of his lecturing tours obtained work in Durham and cancelled his engagements because he and his family were starving. He wrote to say,—"He piped, but the people would not dance." Mr. Harney when lecturing in this district stayed at the "Labour and Health," and sent for Mr. Burns, a tailor, to mend his trousers whilst he remained in bed. Mr. Kydd, another lecturer, had to sit in a shoemaker's shop in this town whilst his shoes were repaired. On one of Mr. Jones' visits he stayed at Mr. Nicholl's and the person who had the boots to clean noticed that his boots were worn out and shewed them Mr. Nicholl, who went across the street to Peter Taylor's and bought him a pair of new ones. On another occasion we had to buy him a new shirt and front before he could appear at the meeting.

Wood and Edwards were nominated, and it was decided by Mr. Jones' friends who had votes to be neutral at this election, and to meet at Nicholl's on the polling day and remain there till the close of the poll. A good many of them met in the large room upstairs, and two of us were appointed to guard the bottom of the staircase and prevent any canvasser or stranger going up. Mr. Robt. Stansfield, of Sowerby, father of Col. Stansfield, and Mr. Kirk came and wanted to see the voters but were told that no one was allowed to go up. I was standing on the second step from the bottom and Mr. Stansfeld looked at me and said "I have seen the day when I would have brought thee down." When they saw they could not get up they went away, and these were the only canvassers who troubled us that day. The following was the result of the poll—(January 4th, 1853):—

Sir C. Wood (L) ... 580 Mr. H. Edwards (C) ... 524

There were 104 who did not vote. I have looked carefully through the poll book of that date and only find one Chartist who voted for Edwards,—Joseph Hanson, the landlord of the Crispin Inn; several of them voted for Wood, but the majority of them stood neutral.

Soon after the commencement of the People's Paper, a committee of inspection was appointed at the suggestion of Mr. Jones to audit the accounts of the paper regularly. The paper had been in existence twelve months and the price increased to fivepence, which had caused the circulation to fall, and necessitated an appeal to the country for funds. A meeting was held at Nicholl's to consider the best means of raising money for the paper. We formed a committee with Mr. Joseph Binns as secretary. It was resolved that £100 should be raised for the paper, and Mr. Harrison Holt of this town should be appointed treasurer and Mr. Thomas Wood, secretary. It was also agreed that an appeal should be issued through the People's Paper asking the Chartists of the country to assist in the undertaking, and to send their money to Mr. Holt, which would be acknowledged in the paper; and it was also agreed that we should subscribe £12 to the £100 fund, in addition to weekly subscriptions we had sent to keep the paper going. Delegates were appointed to visit several places in the district to ask them to subscribe to the fund. I went to Cinderhills, and met a few friends there who promised to do all they could. Mr. Wm. Ramsden was always ready to put his hand into his pocket, and he took this matter in hand and sent a subscription to the treasurer. I went to Elland next and saw Mr. Geo. Beaumont, who was always a staunch friend of the Chartist movement, who also forwarded a subscription from his friends. I met a few friends at the house of Mr. John Hey, Ripponden, but they had already taken the matter in hand, for Mr. Samuel Moores was taking a very active part at this time. At the end of two months we had succeeded in accomplishing our object.

The death of Benjamin Rushton occurred on the 19th June, 1853, at his residence at Friendly, in Ovenden, in his 68th year. He was highly respected by the Chartists of Yorkshire and Lancashire, and was looked upon in this town and neighbourhood as the "grand old man," he had been a reformer before such as myself were born, and a leader amongst the Chartists since its commencement. He had been the chairman of some of the greatest demonstrations of his time; was a good speaker, although using rather broad language, but never failed to make an impression upon an audience. He died poor, as many other reformers have done, and it was decided by the Chartists of Halifax that his funeral expenses should be borne by them, and his funeral to take place on Sunday, June 26th, and be a public one. It was arranged that six of the oldest Chartists should bear him to the grave, and twelve of the younger be conductors, with wands crape-tipped. We met at Nicholl's Hotel, and marched from there, with Ernest Jones and Mr. Gammage; to the Northgate Hotel fields, which had been engaged purposely, and mounted the platform. Mr. Jones wished the people to join in the procession. The field at an early hour presented a dense mass of human beings, through which it was almost impossible to force a way; we had not much difficulty in forming the procession, as all appeared willing to obey the orders given here. It was led by Ernest Jones and R. Gammage, after them came the public walking six abreast; the hearse, a modern one, was drawn by two horses. At the entrance of the village the Odd-fellows were waiting at their lodge to the number of 140, and walked in advance. On approaching the house of the deceased patriot they opened out in double line. The sight was magnificent, and whilst waiting the notes of a band of music were heard, and soon came in sight the Bradford procession, led by Chartist veterans, including our old friend, Joseph Alderson. The coffin—a double one, covered with black cloth, and very elegant—was borne from the house at twelve o'clock.

"Chartists weep, and let your grief be true,
A nobler patriot country never knew."

The coffin was carried by six veteran Chartists, and the splendid pall by six Odd-fellows. The return to Halifax was then commenced, the distance from the Cemetery being about two miles, and from one end of the route to the other the people lined the streets, particularly in the heart of the town, where the processionists had scarcely room to walk, whilst at the Cemetery the gates were closed after the corpse had entered to prevent the crush of the people. The wish of the departed patriot was that no paid priest should officiate at his funeral. Mr. Gammage spoke at the grave side, and after him a member of the Odd-fellows said a few words, and then Mr. Ernest Jones delivered a long address of which a few lines will not be out of place. "We meet to-day at a burial and a birth—the burial of a noble patriot, the resurrection of a glorious principle. The foundation stones of liberty are the graves of the just; the lives of the departed are the landmarks of the living; the memories of the past are the beacons of the future. We meet to honour a departed brother; then who is the man we honour? There rests a working man, there rests a producer, &c." Mr. Robert Sutcliffe then spoke over the grave and said—"He was one of the oldest friends of the deceased patriot, and they had mutually agreed that whichever of two lived longest should attend the funeral of the other and pronounce a eulogy over his remains." The funeral ceremony was here closed. A meeting took place in the West Hill Park to petition Parliament in favour of the People's Charter; a large audience assembled, and Mr. Harrison Holt occupied the chair, the meeting being addressed by Mr. Mitchell, Stanningley; Mr. G. White, Bradford, (who had been a Chartist prisoner); Mr. R. Gammage; Mr. Alderson, Bradford; Mr. Isaac Clissett; Mr. Ernest Jones; Mr. John Snowden; and Mr. North, of Low Moor. It was decided that Mr. Frank Crossley, M.P., be requested to support the motion. Some idea of the immense number of people in Halifax on this occasion may be gathered from the fact that five extra trains were engaged in conveying people from Bradford alone, in addition to the procession from that town. One of the local papers, I believe it was the *Guardian*, gave the numbers marching in the procession from 6,000 to 10,000, and it took an hour and a half to pass through the town. I will not give any numbers myself, but I will say that I saw more people in Halifax that day than I had ever seen before or since, and the public funerals that I have seen in this town have been a mere nothing in comparison to this.

The Chartists took a large room of the Co-operative Society at Cow Green and removed from Nicholl's. During the ensuing winter several lectures were delivered by Snowden, Stradlin, and others. Mr. Adam Beaumont was appointed secretary. They remained here about twelve months, and then removed back to Nicholl's. 1855.—The large room of the Odd Fellows' Hall was the only large room in the town where public lectures could be delivered, and the want of another room was much felt. The Chartists had long talked the matter over, and in April of this year a meeting was held at Nicholl's to discuss the question of building a lecture hall; the meeting passed a resolution in favour of building such a place, and a deputation was appointed to wait upon Mr. John Crossley to ask him if he would sell a piece of land in the Swan Coppice (the site of the White Swan Hotel) but his answer was not favourable and the matter dropped.

Several West Riding delegate meetings were held during this summer, and at a meeting held in May *Co-operation* was advocated and the Chartists were recommended to join that movement. Two meetings were held in this district—one in the large field near the Northgate Hotel in June, presided over by Mr. Snowden, and addressed by Messrs. White and Robinson; the other on Skircoat Moor in August with Mr. Clissett as chairman, the speakers being Messrs. Paterson, of Ripponden, Snowden, Robinson, and Stradlin; this was the largest meeting which had been held in this district for some time.

Fergus O'Connor died September 6th, 1855. He had been in Dr. Tuke's

Asylum where Mr. Jones's visited him in March, 1853, on which occasion he was up in one of the large rooms playing with Dr. Tuke's little boys; on seeing Mr. Jones he broke out with saying

"The lion of freedom has come from his den,
We'll rally around him again and again."

This song was composed by Thomas Cooper on O'Connor whilst he was in York Prison, and was to be sung on his release. Mr. Jones conversed with him for a time on various subjects but he rambled in his talking. Mr. Jones said it was a very nice place, and that he was well cared for, also having full liberty to walk out in the grounds but his reason was fast leaving him that he could not live more than two years which proved to be the case. Mr. Sweet, a Nottingham friend of Mr. O'Connor's, visited him, and in their conversation about his election for that town he remarked "How I thrashed those Nottingham lambs!" referring to the roughs of Nottingham who were hired to break up meetings and who attended one of O'Connor's for that purpose, but O'Connor and his friends cleared them away; twelve of them summoned Mr. O'Connor for ill-treatment, but the case was dismissed, the magistrates saying O'Connor must have been a powerful man to give twelve men a good thrashing. He was removed from the asylum by his sister, but only lived eleven days after; an inquest was held, and several witnesses stated that his sister had done all that it was possible for him; the verdict of the jury was death from natural causes. The foreman of the jury said he would give £1. as he died very poor. Dr. Tuke said he would bear all the funeral expenses, but the Chartists of London took the matter in hand and paid the expenses. The funeral was a public one, and was attended by great numbers. They raised a small monument to him. All honour to Nottingham, for it is the only place in England (with the exception of the small one in London) where a monument was raised to that great man. In the summer of 1883 I went on a day trip to have a look over this beautiful town; and also at the monument, which is situate in the park; it is a good likeness of him, in a standing position, about eight feet high. From 1838 to 1848 O'Connor was the most popular man in England amongst the working classes; the bulk of old radicals still living got their political opinions from him and the *Northern Star*. Before entering the Chartist movement he had sold his estates in Ireland for £7,000.

"He's gone! 'tis said, be still false tongue,
He's with us yet in what he's done;
Confessing ages shall have flown
E'er such another patriot is known."

The above lines were written by Mr. Jones on hearing of a poet's death, but I have altered them somewhat to suit the present case.

Sir Charles Wood on becoming First Lord of the Admiralty was re-elected without opposition,—March 3rd, 1855.

The election held March 28th, 1857, resulted as follows:—

Frank Crossley (L) ... 830 Sir Charles Wood (L) ... 714
Henry Edwards (C) ... 651

I was in the Committee Room at the Old Cock Hotel when the last return came in; Sir Charles Wood congratulated Mr. Crossley on his being at the head of the poll.

If someone had said to me when John Frost was transported for life for the riots in 1839 that I should meet and shake hand with him, I should have come to the conclusion that it would have to be in Van-Dieman's Land. The Chartists never forgot him, but did all they possibly could by agitations and by petitions to Parliament to obtain his freedom. Seventeen years elapsed before his free pardon was granted, and in 1857 he came to Halifax to give us a lecture after which a few friends spent several hours with him in talking over old times. He had been Mayor of Newport, and also a magistrate, but sacrificed the prospects of a comfortable life for the people's cause. He died a few years ago at the age of 90, having lived to see the extension of household suffrage to the boroughs.

The question of modifying their demands to meet the views of the middle classes had been discussed for sometime amongst the Chartists; Mr. Jones suggested that manhood suffrage and vote by ballot should be the future programme, and a conference held to consider the question. At a meeting of the Chartist association held at Stephenson's (late Nicholl's) Temperance Hotel, Dec. 13th, 1857, we decided to send a delegate to the conference to support Mr. Jones's suggestion. Mr. Binns, Mr. J. Thompson, and myself were appointed to wait upon the household and the ballot association of this town asking them also to send a delegate to the conference; it met in London, Feb. 8th, 1858, upwards of 40 delegates being present, with Ald. Livsey, of Rochdale, as chairman. Mr. Snowden represented Halifax district. Mr. Jones's suggestion, with a slight alteration by G. J. Holyoake, was adopted. Invitations to the middle classes had been sent for the third day, when upwards of 100 delegates and friends were present. Mr. S. Morley and several other gentlemen addressed the conference, but, after a short discussion, the proposed union failed—manhood suffrage being too extreme a measure for Mr. Morley and his friends. It was decided to agitate the country in favour of manhood suffrage and the ballot. Before the close of the conference the veteran Robert Owen, then in his 88th year, delivered an address in support of the people's charter, and was greeted with tremendous applause. He was the greatest social reformer of his time and Founder of the present Co-operative Movement; the improvements he carried out in New Lanark will long be remembered by those who have read that account. 40 years ago I have heard men say such men as Owen were not fit to live, whilst by others he was looked upon as a wild dreamer; but Mr. Jones has said in one of his poems on such a man as he was:—

"Men counted him a dreamer! Dreams
Are but the light of clearer skies
Too dazzling for our naked eyes,
And when we catch their flashing beams
We turn aside and call them dreams.
Oh! trust me every thought that yet
In greatness rose and sorrow set,
That time to ripening glory nurst,
Was called an idle dream at first."

He died in the month of September following.

The agitation for the People's Charter had been in existence for nearly twenty years, but had at length come to an end. The name is still dear to the few old Chartists living, and I have often wondered how it was that the history of this movement has not been written. I heard some time ago that G. J. Harney, who went to America many years ago, had come over to this country and was seeking information for that purpose. I know no man better qualified to write the history of the Chartist movement than him.[17] Our future programme was to be manhood suffrage and the ballot, in which we had the support of Cobden, Bright, Fox, and a few other leading men.

In June the people's paper ceased after an existence of six years, carried on at a great loss; if all places had been like Halifax it would have made profits quite sufficient to pay all expenses of the Chartist executive, it having a great circulation in the town and district, and although it had cost a great amount of time and money its services to the people's cause were of such a character as to make us satisfied with our effort. No sooner had the paper left Mr. Jones's hands than he was charged by Mr. Reynolds with pilfering the money sent to support the paper, compelling Mr. Jones to bring an action for libel against him; it was tried before Lord Chief Justice Cockburn and a special jury, in the Queen's Bench, on the 9th of July, 1859. The *Saturday Review*, a paper entirely opposed to Mr. Jones politically, had an article on the trial from which I quote the following:—"The course he took exposed him to the abuse of Mr. Reynolds, who accused him in so many words of pilfering the funds sent to support the paper and appropriating them to his own use. No charge was ever more triumphantly refuted, and the proper application of the money received from subscribers was shown to have been guaranteed by weekly audits. Mr. Reynolds was obliged, through his counsel, to withdraw the charge and make an humble apology, as the Lord Chief Justice declared there was not a stain on the reputation of Mr. Jones; he had sacrificed everything—time, fortune, and prospects—in order that he may

[17] Harney retired permanently to England in 1888 and collected a good deal of material for a projected history which for a number of reasons, including increasing ill-health, he never managed to write. Like a number of other old Chartists, Wilson seems unaware of Gammage's *History*.

preach the gospel of Chartism; he even renounced a very considerable fortune which he might have had if he would have paid the chief price of holding his tongue. His uncle, who was possessed of an income of £2,000 a year, put it to him whether he would become heir to his wealth and abandon his political life, or renounce the money and retain his position as a Chartist leader; nobly and honourably Mr. Jones choose the latter course, and the uncle left his fortune to his gardener. We are proud of this history of our English democrat,—the unselfishness, the patience, the steadiness with which Mr. Jones has met temptations, disappointment, and obloquy. It is something that there should be a few persons in a nation who look at politics seriously."

1860.—Co-operation in Halifax after some years' struggle for an existence had at last gained the confidence of a great many, and was now beginning to move. Flour was issued from the Halifax Flour Society, May 1st, 1848; we had been members and had purchased flour from the commencement. I attended the half-yearly meetings for a long time, at which the following persons took a leading part:—Esau Hanson, John Shackleton, Eli Dyson, Abram Illingworth, and James Ellis; the Board of Directors were principally small tradesmen, with Thomas Booth as secretary. The elections for president were very keenly contested. Esau Hanson and Henry Bates were appointed to examine the books and members' cards in 1849; when I went for my card Mr. Bates told me they had found a great many serious mistakes, having found more money on the members' cards than in the books, and he accounted for this in having no proper system, and having too many receiving members' subscriptions. In forming the rules a great mistake was made in giving equal bonus to all members whether they purchased or not. I was in the agent's shop at Skircoat Green between 30 and 40 years ago when a member's wife came for their bonus,—it was given in flour, and this half-year I think it was a ¼-pack; she said co-operation was a good thing and that the society had done well this half-year. I knew her well, and suspected she was not a purchaser, upon which the agent said she never entered his shop only when she came for the bonus; it took several years to alter this. The productive principle of co-operation has been tried in Halifax by the Cotton Co. I was a shareholder in it, and although it was a failure I believe the day not far distant when it will succeed.

The Halifax Industrial Society commenced 1850, then at Cow Green.[18]

[18] After the initial failure, the "Halifax Men's Co-operative and Provident Society" was launched in 1850. It began in a cottage in Back Foundry Street and later in the year moved to Cow Green. Progress during the first ten years was slow, and in 1855 the Society suffered a severe setback when it lost £81 through a dishonest treasurer, John Dennis. The event caused a minor panic and the board was one night stormed by some of the 316 members. (G. J. Holyoake, *The History of Co-operation in Halifax*, 1867, pp. 15–16.) In October 1851 the Society wrote to John Bezer at the *Christian Socialist* asking for four dozen copies of the journal and the journal published the Society's half-yearly accounts on 21 June 1851 and 20 December 1851, which together showed an annual turnover of £2,175.

The society at that time caused dissatisfaction by purchasing flour from private millers and an agitation was started in favour of purchasing from the flour societies. Mr. Job Whiteley took a leading part in this agitation, and meetings were held at many of the branches to discuss this question. Mr. Whiteley, myself, and several others attended a meeting at Greetland in winter,—the night being so dark that many took lanterns with them; both sides were well represented, and we had a good debate on the subject. This agitation lasted a long time, ending in a resolution being passed by the members "that in future all flour be purchased from the Halifax and Sowerby Bridge Flour Societies." In 1860 the society began to grow rapidly; at the close of 1859 the number of members was 414, and the receipts £6,260.; at the close of 1860 the number of members were 1,374, and the receipts £16,875. The first portion of the Central Stores were commenced in this year, comprising the grocers' and woollen drapers' shops. I became a director in 1862. Mr. John Shaw was president, but was soon after succeeded by Mr. Job Whiteley. The question of building another block at the Central Stores was brought before the directors, and, after a long discussion it was decided to complete the block comprising the present linen drapers shop, boot and shoe shop, and two above the archway and all the arcade; this would cover about three times as much ground as the first block, and the contract alone was the largest undertaking the society ever undertook. It had been decided when the shops were built to commence the butchering, boot and shoe, woollen drapery and tailoring businesses, and this was looked upon as the most difficult part of the undertaking as those businesses had not been tried with the exception of a few boots and shoes sold at Cow Green and the Central. All those points had been discussed previous to the Board deciding to build. A large number of tenders were sent in, and included the principal builders in the town; Mr. Richard Horsfall, the architect, was present when they were opened and said that we had a capital selection to choose from and at low prices. Mr. Whiteley, the president, said this was a very important subject, and one that should not be decided in haste, and he would suggest that the board should not come to decision that night, having come to the conclusion that it would not be wise to build all the lot at once but only build up to the archway, which would be equal to the first block, for if the members should come rushing to withdraw their money it would place the board in a very difficult position. After Mr. Whiteley sat down I got up and said this subject has been before the board for a long time and the members have not raised the slightest opposition but on the contrary were favourable to building at once, and whatever the president might say I for one was determined that we should let the works to-night. After a short discussion that course was adopted, and Mr. Jonathan Charnock's tender for mason's and joiner's work was accepted. Before the works were completed wages advanced and material in the building trade became dearer, so that we saved money by the course adopted.[19] It is rather singular that in 1842 a great many people were throwing stones at the soldiers from the very ground where this Society has erected the magnificent building, and which stand as an evidence of what the people can do when united and have confidence in each other. The election system at that time was unsatisfactory to the branches, the directors being voted for in one block; we had voting papers similar to those used in election for Guardians. There were not many branches, but they contended they had not a fair chance of electing directors, so that it was decided three should be elected from the Central, the remainder being divided amongst the branches. The first election under the new system took place on July 26, 1863, but as the change did not answer the purpose intended, we returned to the old system. Considerable grumbling by members at not being supplied with the particular flour asked for led the Board to adopt a suggestion by Mr. Job Hesselden and myself, viz., to have the name Halifax or Sowerby Bridge, with the quality and price printed in front of each bin. This eventually gave satisfaction both to customers and shopmen, although the latter were opposed to it at first. The shopmen's check system was introduced and proved to be one of the most important improvements yet made; by this system we knew how many customers were served and the amount of money he had drawn each day, and he was held responsible for that amount; some of them did not like it; Mr. Geo. Spencer, the waiter in the flour shop, said it was impossible to do without making mistakes, and it was very hard of the Board to make them responsible. We told him he could if he would give it a fair trial. A short time after I had some talk with him again, he said he was very sorry for what he had said before, being now satisfied that it could be done; it made them more particular in giving change and paying attention to the customers, and was the best system the Board had ever adopted. Mr. Job Whiteley was the author of this system, as well as many others which were beneficial. At the first half-yearly meeting after I got on the board, a member proposed that a sum of money be granted to the directors for their services, which was carried unanimously; this took us by surprise, as we had never expected it. This was the first grant to the directors to my knowledge, and has been advanced several times since. The directors took part in stocktaking, which took about a day at the branches, and were allowed 5s. each; this being nearly all the remuneration they received, as although time was broken for the society's business no charge was made. The president, Mr. Job Whiteley, retired from the board, and Mr. J. Greenwood was elected in his place. At this time High Sunderland Farm was to let, and as we were commencing the butchering business it was thought to be just the place for the erection of a slaughterhouse of our own. The President, Mr. David Wadsworth and myself were appointed as a deputation to meet Mr. Walker, the owner, and Mr. R. Horsfall, the

[19] The eventual cost of erecting and stocking the building was £15,000.

architect, at High Sunderland; we looked over the land and buildings and took it on a 14 years' lease. I was placed on the butchering and farming committee; I lived at the top of Range Bank and could go to the farm in about ten minutes; in summer I spent an evening or two in each week up there. We built a slaughterhouse, and made a large tank for the refuse, which formed good tillage for the farm. A short time after we took possession, Mr. Ernest Jones was staying in Halifax and several of us invited him to go with us to look at the co-operative farm. When he saw the building at High Sunderland he was surprised, having no idea there was such a building in the neighbourhood; we spent some time examining the building, inside and out, and Mr. Jones translated several inscriptions, one over the western door to the garden being "Never may he who violates justice seek to enter this gate." Mr. Jones said it was a pity such a building should have been so neglected and allowed to get out of repair, if it had been his and he had money he would have it thoroughly repaired and reside there, and the hillside at the back he would plant with Scotch firs; it was a beautiful day and we had a good view of the surrounding country, but if Mr. Jones had seen it as I have on a winter's day when the smoke out of the town was driving over it, I think he would have altered his idea as regards planting Scotch fir. I have seen when a boy Scotch fir growing on Beacon hill side, but they have disappeared many years ago. When the second block of the Central Stores were opened, we had a Great Tea Party in the Odd Fellows' Hall, followed by a crowded meeting in the Mechanics' Hall; Mr. Abel Haywood, of Manchester, was chairman, and the principal speakers were Mr. Lloyd Jones and Mr. G. J. Holyoake[20]—two gentlemen who have most ably advocated the co-operative movement during the last 40 years; Mr. Holyoake took a prominent part in the agitation for the repeal of the taxes on knowledge, and had to undergo a term of imprisonment along with Hy. Hetherington, Richard Carlysle,[21] and a number of others taking part in that cause. All the new buildings had been occupied and well stocked for some time; the Boot and Shoe, Woollen Drapery and Tailoring, Dining and Coffee Rooms, Millinery and Dressmaking businesses had done very well, but the Butchering business was very difficult to manage, and only small profits realised; the committee brought the matter before the board and an arrangement was made with Mr. Samuel Wright, cattle dealer, to supply us with first-class cattle, after which the department succeeded much better.

[20] As if to demonstrate that in Halifax at least the co-operators had not lost sight of the long-term goals for which they had been striving as Chartists, they asked the Italian revolutionary Mazzini to be the principal speaker at the opening on New Year's Day 1865. Mazzini's reply, declining the invitation on the grounds of ill-health but praising the co-operative idea "as the beginning of an immense revolution which will do more for the brotherhood of man to man than all the eighteen centuries of Civilisation have done . . ." was read out to the gathering. (Holyoake, op. cit., p. 9; see also pp. 7–8 for a detailed description of the magnificent new building.)

[21] i.e. Richard Carlile (1790–1843), the leading publisher and distributor of infidel literature (see Watson, above).

We had been extending our operations in other districts, having opened seven or eight branches, and at some of those we had built very large stores with a number of cottages adjoining. We had an injunction filed in Chancery against us in connection with our property at Skircoat Green, and on account of the great influence opposed to us we were expected to lose, but we won the trial, and the building was finished without one stone being altered. The directors were divided into sub.-committees, and placed over the departments, and brought their reports to each board meeting which were held twice and occasionally three times a week. They purchased all the principal goods in connection with the grocery department, and a great many travellers came before the board; I have known five or six seeking orders for butter alone in one night; this caused the board to sit till a late hour; business commenced at 8 o'clock, and if over by 11 was considered early, but we often sat into morning; Mr. Joseph Bairstow, the secretary, was very attentive to his duties. Many men, many minds,—but of Mr. Leonard Storey, the society's cashier, I have never heard a member say a dis-respectful word, as he is looked upon as the right man in the right place. Having removed to Salterhebble in 1866, I did not seek re-election on the expiration of my term of office. I never liked the late hours to which the board sat, and would have preferred an extra meeting each week so that we might have got home at a reasonable hour.[22] We took part of a room from the Halifax Cotton Co., purchased a quantity of looms, and tried our hand at manufacturing, but it did not answer and after three or four years experience had to be given up. I had seen some progress whilst I had been a director for in 1862 the number of members was 3,210, capital £17,959. 13s. 9½d., receipts £74,995, profits £5,646. 16s. 5½d.; in 1866 the number of members 6,000, capital £60,636, receipts £168,222, profits £13,749. 13s. 4d. What a change since 1849! If, at the last meeting when we broke up our co-operative society in that year, some one had said that in less than twenty years there would be a co-operative society in Halifax with 6,000 members, a capital of £60,000, and having a turnover of £3,000 per week, there was not one that would have credited it.[23]

Mr. F. Crossley accepted the invitation to contest the West Riding along with Sir John W. Ramsden at the coming election. Mr. James Stansfeld, son of Judge Stansfeld, was selected to contest the borough as Sir Charles Wood's colleague; it was expected Mr. Stansfeld would be treated as a gentleman by his opponents, he being no stranger and his father highly-respected; but that was not the case, for he received similar treatment to that accorded Mr. Bradlaugh at Northampton,—being called an infidel, an

[22] Despite the inconvenience, Wilson managed to attend 56 of a possible 58 Board meetings during the last year of his term of office.

[23] The Society continued to expand throughout the remainder of Wilson's lifetime. By 1904 it possessed 34 branches, a membership of 10,691, a workforce of 330, a share capital of £121,875 and an annual turnover of £312,911, and was able to declare a dividend of 2*s*. 9*d*. in the £. (G. J. Holyoake, *The History of Co-operation*, vol. II, London, 1906, p. 626.)

atheist, and one who did not believe in the bible. I was present at the White Swan Hotel when Mr. Stansfeld answered these charges made against him, although the chairman, Mr. John Whitworth, objected to any candidate being questioned as to his religious opinions. It was said Mr. Samuel Waterhouse had been asked to contest the borough by the conservatives, but refused. Sir Charles Wood and Mr. Stansfeld were returned unopposed April 29th, 1859. Our Chartist friend Mr. Joseph Foreman worked hard for Mr. Stansfeld, as there were some of the Liberal party favourable to the candidature of Mr. Remington Mills. Sir Charles Wood, having accepted office as President of the Board of Control for India, was returned without opposition on the 28th June, 1859.

The Chartists and Radicals of this town, still agitating for manhood suffrage and the ballot, met at Stephenson's Temperance Hotel. The organisation of the Radical movement in the country was at the lowest ebb that it had been for some time, for the people appeared to have lost all confidence in agitating for political reform. Our old friend, Mr. John Snowden, left the radical party and joined the middle class movement.

Our member, Mr. Stansfeld, had made his mark in the House of Commons; he was offered and accepted a seat at the Board of Admiralty, and was returned unopposed April 28th, 1863.

The Reform League was formed by Ernest Jones, Edmond Beale, and a number of other leading Radicals. Edmond Beale, (president), J. A. Nicholay, (treasurer), and George Howell, (secretary). Its principles were manhood suffrage and the ballot, and had become very popular and branches were formed in all parts of the country. We formed a branch in Halifax with Mr. G. Webber as secretary; each member had to subscribe 1/- per year to the general fund in London for carrying on the agitation, for which he received a member's card. A number of gentlemen lectured the country on behalf of the League, Mr. Beale came and lectured in Halifax; he was a good speaker.

Another general election was drawing near, and it was rumoured that Mr. Edward Akroyd was going to contest Halifax and play the same game as he had done before by dividing the Liberal party and opposing a personal friend of his father's; this he had done at the Huddersfield election of 1857, where, by a combination of whigs and tories, he defeated Richard Cobden; on the nomination day a number of workmen from Messrs. Akroyd's works at Halifax and Copley had a day's pay given them to go put up their hands for Mr. Akroyd, but one of those who went told me when he had heard Mr. Cobden speak he decided not to hold up his hand for Mr. Akroyd. The result of the poll,

Mr. Akroyd ... ... 823 Mr. Cobden 590

This was looked upon by Mr. Akroyd's friends in this town as a great triumph, for they arranged to meet him at the outside of the borough on his return; a great many wore blue ribbons in their coats; the horses were unyoked and a number of working men seized his carriage and pulled it up Haley Hill. I said "Britons never shall be slaves," a remark which roused the ire of a few of his enthusiastic supporters. In a little over two years I witnessed the same gentleman returning from Huddersfield as the defeated candidate; and on this occasion "Cheer, boys, cheer," was the strain with which they endeavoured to keep up their spirits, but it came from a very low key.

Mr. Akroyd determined to contest Halifax, saying that Sir Chas. Wood ought to be made a peer for his past services. The treatment Sir Charles received enlisted the sympathy of the bulk of the Chartists in Halifax, and a committee was formed on his behalf, but he declined to stand again. He was nominated for Ripon, for which city he was returned. Mr. Stansfeld and Mr. Akroyd were returned unopposed for Halifax on the 11th July, 1865. It was said that we had turned our backs upon Mr. Ernest Jones and supported one of his greatest enemies, but we were disgusted with Mr. Akroyd's conduct towards Mr. Cobden at Huddersfield, whilst we looked upon Sir Chas. Wood as a consistent politician, and though we had been against him owing to the treatment Mr. Jones had received whilst in prison we were not prepared through personal revenge to oppose him and support a far worse man. Mr. Jones visited Halifax a short time after, and our conduct in supporting Sir Charles Wood was brought before him in our presence. Mr. Jones spoke in very strong language against Mr. Akroyd for his actions towards Mr. Cobden, saying that if any of his friends had supported Sir Charles Wood they had done quite right, and had he been here he should have done the same.

On the death of Lord Palmerston, Lord John Russell became the Prime Minister with Mr. Gladstone as Chancellor of the Exchequer. The Liberals had a majority of 60 in the House of Commons, and on the 12th of April, 1866, Mr. Gladstone moved the second reading of the Reform Bill. Earl Grosvenor (the present Duke of Westminster) moved, and Lord Stanley (the present Earl of Derby) seconded, an amendment. The debate lasted twelve nights, the second reading being carried—ayes 318, noes 313; Mr. Lowe, Mr. Horsman, and a number of other liberals voted with the conservatives. This bill would have enfranchised 400,000, and it was asserted by the conservative leaders, including Mr. Disraeli, that it would revolutionise the country. In committee, an amendment by Lord Dunkeld was carried by 315 votes to 304 against the government, and as a consequence on June 26th the ministers resigned. On the 23rd of July a new ministry was formed; Lord Derby being Prime Minister, and Mr. Disraeli, Chancellor of the Exchequer. No sooner had they got into power than they prohibited public meetings being held in Hyde Park. The Reform League had advertised a meeting to be held in the park, but the government made large preparations to prevent it taking place. Mr. Edmund Beale and Col. Dixon marched at the head of a large procession to the Marble Arch entrance, but the police were there in great numbers and refused to let them go in. Col. Dixon, as a Deputy Lieutenant of the County, demanded admission, but the police drove them back. Edmund Beale and other leaders returned to Trafalgar square and there held a large meeting; resolutions were passed condemning the government for prohibiting public meetings. The bulk of the people remained in the neighbourhood of the park, and eventually made a rush and tore down the rails, thus entering amidst great enthusiasm. A desperate struggle ensued between the police and the people, and a great many were wounded; the military had to be called out before peace was restored. The Hyde Park riot occurred on the 23rd of July, and on the 25th a deputation from the Reform League waited upon the Home Secretary, Mr. Walpole, with regard to the prohibition of public meetings; he informed them that if they went in a peaceable and orderly manner they should not be interfered with; Mr. Walpole was deeply affected, and it is said that he shed tears. Parliament was prorogued on the 10th of August, and the agitation commenced by the Reform League was carried on with great success until Parliament met in the spring. A West Riding demonstration was held on Woodhouse Moor, near Leeds, to which a good many went from Halifax; a number of us engaged a bus and four horses with which we joined the procession in Leeds and had a good view of the people as we passed through the streets to the meeting. It was one of the largest meetings ever held in Yorkshire, and the principal speakers were W. E. Forster, M.P., Ernest Jones, and Ald. Carter. At night we attended another large meeting in the Leeds Town Hall at which Mr. Bright and Mr. Jones were the speakers. Several of us also went to the demonstration at Manchester; it was a great success, though not to be compared with the Leeds meeting. The evening meeting in the Free Trade Hall was magnificent, and the largest indoor gathering I had ever seen; the speakers were John Bright, M.P., T. B. Potter, M.P., George Wilson, chairman of the Anti-Corn Law League, Sir Wilfred Lawson, Ernest Jones, and that grand old veteran reformer, Elijah Dixon, who had been taken in a stage coach from Lancashire to London in chains and there imprisoned about the time of the Peterloo massacre. Parliament assembled on the 5th February, 1867, and the government had decided to bring in a Reform Bill. Mr. Disraeli stated that they proposed to proceed by way of resolutions, but this did not suit the Liberals and a meeting attended by 298 members was held the day following. Mr. Gladstone and Mr. Bright spoke in strong language against proceeding by vague resolutions, and it was agreed to move an amendment. Mr. Disraeli the same evening announced that the government had abandoned the idea of proceeding by resolutions, but would bring in a bill on the earliest possible day. When introduced, the bill contained:—Franchise in Boroughs to be £6 rateable value; in Counties £20; the Franchise also to be extended to any person having £50 in the funds or £30 in a savings bank for a year; payment of £20 direct taxes; a university degree; and also to clergymen and ministers of religion generally, members of the learned professions, and certificated school masters. Gen. Peel, Earl Carnarvon, and Lord Cranborne resigned office in consequence of the introduction of the bill. Lord Cranborne said it was no part of a Conservative government to bring in a reform bill, maintaining that if the party accepted it they would be committing political suicide; then again when the bill was read a third time he made his final protest, expressing his astonishment at hearing the bill described as a Conservative triumph, and demanded that its real parentage should be established as it had been modyfied and amended at the dictation of Mr. Gladstone,—who demanded the lodgers' franchise, the abolishment of distinctions between compounders and non-compounders, a provision to prevent traffic in votes, the omission of the taxing franchise, the omission of dual votes, the enlargement of the redistribution of seats by fifty per cent, the reduction of the county franchise, the omission of voting papers, and the omission of the educational and savings bank franchise, all of which had been conceded; if the adoption of the principles of John Bright could be described as a triumph, then indeed, the Conservative party in the whole history of its previous annals had won no triumph so signal as this. I desire to protest in the most earnest language I am capable of using against the political morality on which the manœuvres of this year have been based; if you borrow your political ethics from the ethics of the political adventurer, you may depend upon it the whole of your representative institutions will crumble beneath your feet." The Lord Cranborne who used this strong language against the reform bill and its authors is the present Marquis of Salisbury. Mr. Disraeli dubbed him the great master of gibes and flouts. The bill was brought into the House of Lords by the Earl of Derby and read a third time on the 6th of August. Earl Derby described the measure as "a leap in the dark." The bill when brought forward by Mr. Disraeli would have enfranchised 418,500 people; but when passed upwards of 1,000,000 received the franchise, credit for which is due to the Liberal party, who carried on the agitation and made the bill what it is.

The Halifax Liberal Registration Association, (composed of a number of gentlemen who paid an annual subscription, and had their office formerly in Wade street with Mr. Stead as agent), had for many years the principal management in the selection of the Liberal candidates, and the question now discussed was—Would they consult the new electors in the future selection of candidates? It appeared they did not consider it their duty to do so, as they brought out Mr. Stansfeld and Mr. Akroyd,—a decision which gave very much dissatisfaction. A meeting of the Radical party was held and a committee appointed to select a candidate to be submitted to a public meeting for approval. One Sunday evening a hansom stopped at the Central Co-operative Stores, Northgate, from which a gentleman alighted and entered the dining room; meeting several men he asked if any members of the radical party were about? they answered they were members; he said he wished to have a little conversation with them and produced a letter from Ernest Jones recommending him as a candidate; they had a long conversation with him, and he gave them to understand that if selected, he would contest the borough; this gentleman was Sir John Simon, the present member for Dewsbury. Mr. Edwd. Owen Greening was the selected candidate, with Mr. S. T. Midgley as chairman of his election committee. We had very few of the middle class on our side, and the conservatives deciding not to bring a candidate forward, voted almost to a man for Messrs. Stansfeld & Akroyd. A great many meetings were held on both sides, Mr. Greening addressing out-door meetings, and Messrs. Stansfeld & Akroyd in-door meetings, several being held in the Mechanics' Hall, when amendments in favor of Mr. Greening were carried on nearly every occasion. On Stansfeld and Akroyd addressing the electors at Salterhebble they were accorded a good hearing, although the bulk of the meeting was against them; I put several questions to them on certain reforms, to which Mr. Stansfeld's answer was Yes! and Mr. Akroyd's No! The only vote put to the meeting was one of thanks to the chairman. A large crowd assembled in support of Messrs. Stansfeld & Akroyd in the large room at the back of the Talbot Hotel when many windows were broken and much damage done. There had been no election since 1847 where the excitement was so great as at this election. Every night hundreds were in the streets, and in the public houses and temperance hotels discussing the election. One of the principal places was the Co-operative Coffee rooms in Northgate; I had here a regular set-to with Mr. Snowden, and though we got rather hot in the debate, it never interfered with our friendship. About two years before his death, when paying one of his visits to Salterhebble, he asked me if I recollected the debate we had on Greening's election, for, he said, I had cut him up more than any other man ever had done; I asked what with; and it was by repeating Burns' celebrated lines:—

> "Oh, wad some power the giftie gie us,
> To see oursels as others see us,
> It wad frae monie a blunder free us,
> And foolish notion."

The nomination was held in the Piece Hall, and a great many people were present. The show of hands went largely in Mr. Greening's favour, upon which Mr. Akroyd demanded a poll. We were better organised in Skircoat at this election than any other I have ever taken part in. A good number of us marched from Salterhebble to the polling booth at King Cross, having volunteered our services for the day. My duty was outside the booth, to see that our men voted as they came. When the first return for Skircoat was issued we were ahead, but on the returns from all the wards arriving we were a long way behind, and it soon became evident we were fighting a losing battle. It was thought by some that when the working men came to vote at the dinner hour we should come to the front, but that was not so, for at two o'clock the returns showed us still further behind. We had a desparate struggle in Skircoat for the majority; at half-past three the voting was nearly exhausted. I went into our committee room and read a list of names of those who had promised us but had not voted, I said do let us have those men here at once; the answer was the men had been seen two or three times, but said it was no use breaking time as Mr. Greening was so far behind. One of the workers said he had been running about since seven o'clock that morning until his shoes were like sponges and his trousers wet almost to the knees, for the streets had been very sloppy all day. When the last return came in we went very carefully over the list of those who had voted and we had a majority of 3, although the other side claimed a majority of 8, in Skircoat. I and a friend went down to the Co-operative Dining rooms to get our tea, and in Northgate, opposite the Temperance Hall, there was several hundred young men behaving so roughly that we came to the conclusion that they were in for a row. We had not been long in the dining rooms before some one came in and said Mr. Akroyd had been somewhat roughly handled, and that it was dangerous in Northgate. Number of voters, Nov. 17th, 1868, 9000. The result of the poll:

Stansfeld, 5278. Akroyd, 5141. Greening, 2802.

A large majority of voters at Salterhebble had voted for Mr. Greening and were greatly disappointed with the result, for they expected him being returned. On the polling day several conservatives of this district came running into the village and shouting and throwing their caps into the air, but I have never heard of them repeating it as I believe they have never given a vote on the winning side in a parliamentary election since. We had to subscribe weekly towards Mr. Greening's expenses. Ernest Jones, Edmund Beale, Col. Dixon and Geo. Howell were candidates at this election, but like Mr. Greening, defeated.

The Halifax Liberal Electoral Association was formed by the supporters of Mr. Greening to look after the registration and the organisation of the radical interest in the borough. Mr. S. T. Midgley was elected president, and the executive was composed of two delegates from each ward. I was elected to represent the lower division of Skircoat.

The melancholy news of the death of Ernest Jones came to me as a shock, for I had been reading a speech in the daily paper delivered by him in Chorlton Town Hall on Wednesday, Jan. 20th, 1869, and he died on the 26th. The funeral was a public one, and took place on the Saturday following. I never saw such a sight as was presented by the streets of Manchester that day. *The Examiner and Times* had a long report of the funeral, the following being taken from it:—"The streets for the entire line of route, about three miles in length, was crowded with onlookers, the assemblage for the whole distance being almost without a break, and at one period the principal thoroughfare of the city at its most spacious part, near the Royal Infirmary, was rendered impassable by the congregation of so many thousands of spectators. The occasion excited more public attention than any similar event that has happened in recent times. The mutes who headed the array were four of the reformers who were present at the affair of Peterloo. The coffin bearers were old Chartists who were associated with Mr. Jones in the agitation of 1848,—Mr. Benjamin Whitley, Mr. John Bowes, Mr. James Cunliffe and Mr. Thomas Topping. The pall bearers were Mr. Edward Hooson, Mr. Jacob Bright, M.P., Mr. Benj. Armitage, Mr. Elijah Dixon, Mr. Abel Heywood, Mr. T. B. Potter, M.P., Sir Elkanah Armitage, Chairman of the Executive Committee of the United Liberal Party, Mr. Francis Taylor, Chairman of the Office Committee, Mr. James Crossley, Mr. H. M. Steinthal, Mr. Henry Rawson, and Mr. C. H. Bazley. At the outset the procession was nearly a mile in length, and before it had reached the Assize Courts it had swelled so greatly that it occupied nearly forty minutes in passing this point. The number of friends who preceeded the hearse walked in about 130 files of six deep, making a solid mass of from 800 to 1000 men, but as the funeral proceeded their number increased in every street that was traversed. A long train of private carriages and cabs, 60 in number, containing mourners and deputations followed the hearse, and those again were followed by a long array of friends on foot. The Halifax Branch of the Reform League was represented by Messrs. G. Webber, B. Wilson, J. Hesselden, and J. Mitchell. Mr. Jones had many friends in Halifax, he having contested the borough in the Radical interest in July, 1847, and in July, 1852; he was also invited to become a candidate for the representation of the borough at the late election. As already indicated the crowds in the streets were immense, and though the afternoon was stormy and occasional heavy showers of rain fell, the crowd never slackened during the three hours that so many would have to wait before the procession arrived at the points which they had selected for viewing it." Mr. Jones died very poor, and his wife being left unprovided for, a committee was formed in Manchester to raise a fund on her behalf. In response to their appeal to Mr. Jones' friends throughout the country we formed a committee in Halifax and three of us waited upon Mr. J. D. Hutchinson to ask him to be chairman, and in consenting he remarked that Mr. Jones had died in harness. I got between £13 and £14 in my book; I should not have more than forty names in it, and they were nearly all working men. In 1849, 30/- would have taken more collecting than this did. When I took my book in I thought it would be the best, but Mr. John Snowden was head and shoulders above me in that respect, and altogether we did exceedingly well in Halifax.

The Halifax Liberal Electoral Association had got well organised and there was a strong feeling in favour of the two associations being amalgamated. Mr. J. D. Hutchinson took the question up and after a short agitation the two societies were dissolved and a Liberal association formed in which, for the first time, all shades of opinion in the Liberal party of Halifax joined.

At the late election the Liberals were returned by a large majority, and the government formed (Mr. Gladstone being Premier) was looked upon as the most Radical that we had ever had in this country. They soon set to work, for they Disestablished the Irish Church, gave us the Ballot, and carried the Education Act.

School accommodation in Siddal and Salterhebble was very bad, and we felt the want of a good school very much. The question of building one at Siddal came before the School Board, but was strongly opposed by the Sectarian party on the Board. No sooner had the building of a board school at Siddal been mentioned than the Messrs. Holdsworth decided to build a school on Siddal side, and Mr. W. I. Holdsworth purchased ground at Salterhebble to build an infant school there. With these obstacles our prospects looked very gloomy, but we persevered with our agitation until we succeeded. There was more opposition to the building of this school than all the other board schools in Halifax put together, for nearly all the conservatives in the district had been against it, and when opened many of them sent their children to other schools rather than send them there.

By the votes he had given in Parliament Mr. Akroyd had made himself very unpopular to a great many who had voted for him at the late election, and it was out of the question his being selected as one of the candidates of the Liberal party at the coming election. At a meeting of the members of the Liberal association, Mr. Stansfeld was selected as one of the candidates, and a deputation was appointed to wait upon Mr. John Crossley to ask him to become a candidate along with Mr. Stansfeld. We met him at Manor Heath, and spent a long time with him talking matters over; he was very free and jolly, and said he would think the matter over and reply in a day or two; he said he never considered himself equal to either of his brothers as a business man. He accepted the invitation. The Conservatives brought out Mr. McCrea as their candidate. This was the first election under the Ballot Act which had taken place in the borough, and was a great improvement of the old system as it did away with much excitement. The election took place on Feb. 3rd, 1874; the number of voters being 11,286. The result was declared at the Town Hall as follows:

Crossley, 5563. Stansfeld, 5473. McCrea, 3927.

The same night we were anxiously waiting to hear the result of the poll; the Liberal Club was crowded and a large crowd was outside when the messenger arrived with the news that the Liberals had been returned by a majority of 1,500 it was received with loud cheers; the women were as enthusiastic as the men. On the following morning three of us agreed to give all the children a treat; I went to Halifax and purchased a box of oranges, and though it was noon before I got back it did not require the bellman to go round to inform them for at night several hundred children were present; many had come from Siddal side, but every one was supplied with an orange. At the late election the Conservatives were returned by a majority, and Mr. Disraeli became Prime Minister.

When I removed back to Skircoat I began to take an interest in the township's business and attended the vestry meetings, although held in the afternoon when very few working men could be present. I found a great change, many of those who had taken a leading part being dead. Mr. John Wainhouse was now taking an active interest at the meetings and was very popular amongst the ratepayers. For some time the meetings had passed off quietly, but on the commencement of the agitation against the vicar's rate a resolution was moved and seconded condemning it which caused the stormiest meeting I had seen for a long time.[24] Mr. Wainhouse was chairman, and spoke at great length against the resolution until he wearied the meeting and was asked to put the motion to the vote; he still went on talking; I told him if he did not put the resolution we should put some one else in the chair, but after a while he put it when it was carried by three to one. Then came the dispute about stopping the water supply at Cockett Wells. Mr. Wainhouse made certain charges against Sir H. Edwards with regard to those wells which created a great amount of ill-feeling. A public meeting of the ratepayers of the township to take this question into consideration was held at the Copley Arms Inn, at which a large number were present; it was moved that Mr. Wainhouse be the chairman but he declined, and moved that I should take it which was carried. Mr. Wainhouse opened the question, and a long and exciting debate followed in which Mr. Walter Storey, Mr. H. M. Smith, Mr. Jo Shoesmith, and others took part; the meeting was adjourned when a resolution was carried condemning the taking away of the water supply. The water has not been restored to my knowledge, but Mr. Wainhouse erected those beautiful wells at the top of Washer Lane and supplied them with water at his own expense. There was something about Mr. Wainhouse that I greatly admired; he had none of the stiffness of that class which Sir Francis Crossley said was too proud to tell who their grandfather was; if he met a man in his working clothes he would stop and talk with him if he knew him, without being fidgety to get away. On one occasion when I went to see him at his house one of the servants asked my name, and on returning invited me into Mr. Wainhouse's room, but, as he was dining, I said I would withdraw until he was at liberty; he, however, invited me to dine with him,—I told him I had only just had dinner, on which he said I must have a glass with him, but being a teetotaler I declined. I had gone to ask him to sign a requisition to the Alderman of Skircoat Ward to call a meeting. I had got a good many signatures, including

[24] See also Dunning, p. 143–4. There was a long and bitter struggle against the Vicar's rate in Halifax, led first by the Halifax Working Men's Association and then by the Anti-Vicar's Rate Union.

Wm. Irvine Holdsworth, Edwd. Crossley, and several other large ratepayers, but he thought the Councillors of the Ward ought to have been included, and declined to sign on account of that omission.

The retirement of Mr. John Crossley, as one of the members for the borough, came upon the town with surprise, and much sympathy was felt for him on account of the cause which had compelled him to take this step. What he, along with his two brothers Mr. Joseph and Sir Francis, has done for the town will long be remembered.

Mr. J. D. Hutchinson was selected as the Liberal candidate. He was very popular and the party was well organised. The Conservatives selected Mr. Gamble as their candidate, and the election took place on the 20th Feb., 1877. The number of voters was 11,740.

Hutchinson, 5,750. Gamble, 3,624.

On the 24th June, 1879, the Halifax Liberal Club's trip was to Hawarden Castle, the seat of Mr. Gladstone, and the committee decided to present an address to Mr. Gladstone. He could not be present, but arranged that his son, the Rev. Stephen Gladstone, should accept it on his behalf. It was beautifully got up, and the presentation was made by Ald. Longbottom in one of the rooms at the Castle to which the committee and a few friends were invited; we were shewn round the library, and Mr. Gladstone's son told us how many thousand volumes it contained, but I have forgot the number; he remarked that his father could go straight to any volume he required. This had been a wet and cold season, and when we left Halifax in the morning it was raining very fast, but at Hawarden we had a beautifully warm summer's day, which was a treat to us and added greatly to our enjoyment. Being Chairman of the Trip Committee I received the following letter from Mr. Gladstone:—

June 27th, 1879.

Sir,—"I thank you and those on whose behalf you act for the very kind address, and I hope that you were allowed by the weather to enjoy the expedition which it required some spirit in this uncertain season to undertake.

Yours faithfully,
W. E. Gladstone."

Both parties were making great preparations throughout the country for the coming general election, and there was every indication that the struggle would be a severe one. At the election in 1874, a good many liberals, including Mr. Baines at Leeds, lost their seats by too many candidates. Mr. Gladstone's Mid-Lothian speeches had put new life into the Liberal party. Mr. Stansfeld and Mr. Hutchinson were the Liberal candidates and Mr. Barber the Conservative, but the main question at this election was what will be the majority of the Liberal candidates. March 31st, 1880. No. of voters, 11,728.

Stansfeld, 6,392. Hutchinson, 6,364. Barber, 3,452.

A personal matter concerning myself which I consider it my duty to mention occurred at this election. A friend told me he had heard it said that "I was making a good thing out of politics, as gentlemen connected with the Liberal party had given me plenty of money." This was something new to me, but in a short time after my name was freely mentioned in a certain quarter by two or three persons who came to the conclusion I had made plenty of money out of politics; those men were Liberals. At the parliamentary election last July, a neighbour of mine came to vote, and outside the polling booth in the presence of a number of people told me I had £20 per day for my services; this man was a Conservative, but I must say that another Conservative went to him and asked him to be quiet and afterwards came to me and wished me to take no notice of him. I have never received any money or money's worth, neither in gifts or presents in any shape or form, for any services I have ever rendered, or for any expenses it incurred upon me, in connection with any parliamentary election I have ever taken part in, or any political movement in which I have been interested, except a little refreshment as a worker at parliamentary elections when it was lawful. I have received payment on three occasions in municipal elections; the first of which was the keenest and closest municipal election that ever took place in Halifax, as several times during the day on the state of the poll being issued the candidates were equal, and at the finish our candidate was returned by a majority of one! I was there when the poll opened and never left my post or had anything to eat or drink until it closed, when I went home to tea, and for my services received 2s. 6d. On the second occasion I was asked to canvass a district I knew well as no one in that ward would undertake it; I got a friend to assist me and we also took charge of it on the polling day and were supplied with men and conveyances; we went to a public house to our dinner, and what was got there during the day in connection with us was paid for by my friend and me, amounting altogether to about 12/. A few days afterwards 5/- was forwarded to me for my day's services, but I told the bearer I accepted it towards my expenses out of pocket, and not in any sense as payment for my services. On the last occasion I and a friend took charge of a municipal election and made all the necessary arrangements; I devoted all my time to it for a week at some inconvenience and to the detriment of my business, and received the sum of 30/., out of which I had to pay for my dinners and teas, being unable to go home. All the men are still living who paid me the money, and should they see what I have said I think they will look upon it as a very fair statement of what took place. I regret having to introduce this matter, but from what was said I feel fully justified in mentioning it.

Mr. Thomas Shaw was looked upon as a coming man for parliamentary honours, and on Mr. Hutchinson's resignation he was selected as the Liberal candidate and elected without opposition August 19th, 1882. The deaths of J. D. Hutchinson, Dr. Mellor and John Snowden were severely felt by the Liberal party, they being looked upon as the ablest advocates of our cause in the town; it is to such men as those we owe our thanks for many reforms we have got.

In March, 1885, I mentioned to Mr. John Culpan and Mr. Joseph Foreman that I should like us to have a meeting of the few old Chartists still living as soon as the reform bill was passed, and it was agreed that I should make all the necessary arrangements. I had a number of circulars printed as follows:—

"SALTERHEBBLE, JUNE 29th, 1885.

"DEAR SIR,—You are cordially invited to meet a few old Chartist friends to take Tea and spend a Social Evening together at Maude's Temperance Hotel, Broad St., Halifax, on Tuesday Evening next, July 7th, to commemorate the passing of the Reform Bill. Tea on the Tables at Half-past Six. Hoping you will be able to make it convenient to be present."

Yours truly, B. WILSON."

The following account is taken from the *Halifax Courier*.—"Unique Gathering of Old Politicians.—Twenty-two members of the old Chartist Association of this town met at Maude's Temperance Hotel to spend a Social Evening in celebration of the incorporation in the law of the land of the principal portion of the Charter. The chair was occupied by Mr. John Culpan, who was secretary when Mr. Ernest Jones was a candidate for Halifax in 1847, and also all the time Mr. Jones was in prison for advocating measures which have now a place on the statute book. An excellent repast having been served, the chairman delivered an address of unusual interest; he reviewed the progress of the people from 1844 to 1885, and related remarkable incidents of each epoch of social advancement and political triumph; his very suitable observations were listened to with evident pleasure, and on their conclusion the old veterans shook the chairman cordially by the hand. Mr. Joseph Foreman then moved—"That the best thanks of this meeting be given to Mr. Gladstone and his government for passing into law those principles which we have endeavoured during a long life to enjoy." He congratulated the assemblage on their fortune in living to see the realization of those things for which a comparatively weak and despised class they struggled forty years ago; formerly persecuted and taunted as revolutionists and levellers, they were now freely acknowledged as law-abiding citizens not that they had changed their attitude but because the opinions for which they suffered now prevailed. The motion was seconded by Mr. Geo. Webber, one of the Chartist speakers of '48 and who gave some reminiscences of the old days. The resolution passed with manifestations of enthusiasm. Mr. B. Wilson moved, and Mr. Shackleton seconded, a vote of thanks to the two Liberal members who have given Mr. Gladstone and his government continuous support. This was also cordially adopted, the company rising to their feet. The ages of those present averaged upwards of 65 years, and varied from 62 to 76. At the time of the Chartist agitation they were all poor working men earning low wages, not the least interesting part of the speeches therefore was their account of the hardships the working classes had to endure within living memory, enabling younger politicians to make a useful and instructive contrast. Their humble origin nevertheless, the majority of those attending the meeting have become men of business and in some cases employers of labour, and a few by economy, industry, and temperance have secured a competency for their old age. Public exultation may be paraded once in a while when it is considered that merely because of their early efforts to improve the condition of their fellows, they were denounced as the unwashed scum and the like. Tuesday's proceedings was diversified by songs and recitations, and the party enjoyed themselves till a late hour."

November, 1885. Number of voters, 12,289. This was one of the coldest and wettest election days that ever I took part in.

Shaw, 6,269. Stansfeld, 6,053. Morris, 3,988.

Mr. Stansfeld having accepted the office of President of the Local Government Board was returned unopposed April 3rd, 1886.

General election, July 5th, 1886. Number of voters, 12,289.

Shaw, 5,427. Stansfeld, 5,381. Morris, 3,612.

Index